Cause, Principle, and Unity

Five Dialogues by

GIORDANO BRUNO

Cause, Principle, and Unity

Translated with an Introduction, by

JACK LINDSAY

GREENWOOD PRESS, PUBLISHERS
WESTPORT, CONNECTICUT

Library of Congress Cataloging in Publication Data

Bruno, Giordano, 1548-1600.
    Cause, principle, and unity.

    Translation of De la causa, principio e uno.
    Reprint of the ed. published by Daimon Press,
Castle Hedingham, Essex, in series: Background books.
    Bibliography: p.
    1. Metaphysics--Early works to 1800. I. Title.
[B783.D43E6 1976]   110   76-28448
ISBN 0-8371-9040-1

© *1962 by Jack Lindsay*

This edition first published in 1962 by The Daimon Press Ltd.,
Castle Hedingham, Essex

Reprinted with the permission of Jack Lindsay

Reprinted in 1976 by Greenwood Press,
a division of Williamhouse-Regency Inc.

Library of Congress Catalog Card Number 76-28448

ISBN 0-8371-9040-1

Printed in the United States of America

Contents

Introduction

Cause, Principle, and Unity

Notes and Appendices

To Mulk Raj Anand

The world is there and then is here
the fire without is deep within
and near is far and far is near
and the stars in my hand spin
and in the stars I am spinning:
love has cast out fear—

Bruno is that moment when
we find the hidden heart of things
in the colliding lives of men
as in the aspiring lark that sings
small in the light's tall tree
with gyring wings:

when the large joy we recklessly spend
finds securely its home and finds
at last the casual destined friend
the shaping hands inside the mind
present past and future one
in struggle with no end

J. L.

INTRODUCTION

I. Giordano Bruno

FELIPE BRUNO was born in the ancient town of Nola, near Naples, in 1548. His father, Gioan Bruno, was a soldier serving the Spanish lords of Naples; his mother, Fraulissa Savolini, suggests in her name the German mercenaries settled in the region. Gioan, far from wealthy, seems to have had some minor claim to gentility and to have been friendly with the poet Tansillo, who was of local stock and paid passing visits to Nola. (Bruno mentions Tansillo in his play, makes him a speaker in *Transports,* and amiably cites his verses.)

Bruno always retained strong memories of 'the golden fields of Nola.' He called himself the Nolan, and his system the Nolan Philosophy. As a child he saw spirits on the hills of beech and laurel; and Nolan images keep intruding in his work: his father's garden and its produce, Franzino's melon-plot, the cuckoos, the bugs in Costatino's bed, the burnt smell when Vesta, Albertio's wife, used curling-tongs, and the way she shook her head afterwards. Once his father took him from vine-clad Cicala to Vesuvius, which from the distance had looked forbiddingly bare; there the boy found everything luxuriant, while Cicala was far and dim. 'I became aware for the first time that sight could deceive.' He began asking, 'What are the grounds of certitude?'

When about eleven, he was taken to Naples to study 'humane letters, logic, and dialectic': Latin literature (with perhaps some Greek), philosophy, and the modes of reasoning and expounding. He also had private lessons in logic from an Augustinian monk, Fra Teofilo, whom he seems gratefully to commemorate by calling his main speaker in the *Supper* and the *Cause* by that name. He read Peter of Ravenna's *Fœnix* on mnemonics, a subject of much vogue, and used the method of visual association to strengthen his memory.

In Naples, beggared and badly governed, the only opening lay in the Church, which owned two-thirds of the property. The most

3

powerful Order was that of Dominic, possessing inquisitorial powers and making intellectual submission its first demand. At the age of fifteen Felipe entered it. He was renamed Giordano; and, passing through the various stages, became in 1572 a priest. He was then twenty-four. Having dedicated to Pope Pius V a satirical allegory, *Noah's Ark*, he was called to Rome 'in a coach to set forth his Artificial Memory. He recited the Psalm *Fundamenta* in Hebrew.' In his lost satire he used the folk-method of animals representing vices and follies, who struggle for the poop (the faculty of reason); the ass wins.

For some time he had been chafing against the system of the Dogs of the Lord. 'The authority of directors, barring worthier and higher matters to which he was naturally impelled, puts his mind in fetters,' he wrote in *Transports*, 'so that, from being free in manhood, he becomes a slave under most vile and subtle hypocrisy.' And he told his judges in Venice that he 'began to doubt the doctrine of Three distinct persons in the Trinity from the age of eighteen.' While still a novice, he got into trouble through giving away saints' images and retaining only a crucifix, and for telling another novice it would be better to read the *Lives of the Holy Fathers* than the *Seven Joys of the Madonna* in verse. In 1576 he unwarily showed too much learning in an argument about the Arian heresy. Hearing that proceedings were to be taken, he left for Rome. His wandering life had begun.

At Rome, 'I learned that, after I left Naples, certain works of St Chrysostom and St Jerome containing the forbidden annotations of Erasmus, which I had secretly used and thrown into a privy when I came away to prevent their being found, were discovered.'[1] He discarded his monkish garb and moved to Genoa, then to Noli, where he taught for four or five months. After a short stay at the port Savona, he reached Turin; but, despite the enlightened duke, he found no livelihood there.

After visiting Venice and Padua, he heard at Milan of Sir Philip Sidney, who had been travelling in Italy. Passing over the snows of Mt Cenis, he meant to try Lyon; but a frosty reception at

---

[1] Mocenigo at Venice accused him of having thrown an informer, or a man he considered such, into the Tiber; Cotin at Paris recorded in his diary that Bruno had fled as much through a murder committed by his brother as through fear of the Inquisition. Nothing of these matters was raised at his trial. See *Il Sommario del Processo di G. B.* (1942), for the statement, 'From a child I began to be hostile to the Catholic faith,' 61.

the Dominican house of Chambéry sent him to Geneva, which was ruled by the Calvinists. He entered his name at the academy, read the works of the Reformers, and was soon involved in disputes which brought about his arrest for a 'libel.'

In 1578 he went through an intellectual crisis.[1] He had been nourishing, it seems, an atomistic materialism, drawn largely no doubt from Lucretius—a copy of whose poem he carried about with him. Now he saw the way to express the active existence of spirit and the stability of forms in nature without surrendering his belief in the primacy of matter. Probably his extension of the Copernican outlook to the whole universe came about at the same time and was inseparable from his sense of a philosophic break-through into entirely new dimensions. His dispute at Geneva was very likely his first outright attack on Aristotelianism and the scholastics, in which he found that the Reformers could be as bigoted as the Catholics.[2]

From Geneva he went to Lyon for a month, then on to Toulouse where he lived by teaching philosophy and 'the Sphere' (astronomy). He had given up communion with the Roman Church and never entered into communion with any of the Reformed Churches; he mocked consistently at the fuss that men made about 'mysteries of Ceres and Bacchus' (bread and wine). At Toulouse he gained a chair at the university, but seems to have aroused opposition. In late 1581 he moved on to Paris. He had composed a large work on mnemonics, parts of which seem to survive in two of his books. The importance of mnemonics lay in the fact that, stimulated by the ideas of Raymond Lull, he hoped thus to work out systems showing how the structure of thought corresponded with the structure of nature.

At Geneva he had signed as Philippus; at Paris he re-became Giordano. A brilliant lecturer and teacher, he spoke on Aquinas

[1] According to *Gli Eroici* (*Op. Ital.*, 508–10) about 1573 he had abandoned Aristotelian abstractions, with their rationalising and idealising basis in both ethics and physics, and had arrived at the materialist concept of ceaseless becoming (generation and corruption). The discoveries of 1578 would then represent the solution of the problems thus raised.

[2] Melanchthon fought the idea of a plurality of worlds as impious, since the Saviour could not have died and been resurrected an indefinite number of times (*Initia Doctrinae physicae, Corp. Ref.*, xiii, 220ff). There could only be one world, he insisted. He used Aristotle and the Holy Father together to prove that the earth was at rest. The argument and the texts are exactly the same as those invoked by the Inquisition to refute Galileo, declaring the thesis of the earth's movement *falsa in philosophia et formaliter haeretica.*

and was called to court to discuss his mnemonics, which was the main theme of the three Latin works published in 1582. The same year saw his bawdy and vigorous comedy *Il Candelaio* (*The Chandler*: symbolically *The Light-bearer*) where he depicts the world of cheats and cheated against which he marshals his powers. In *De Umbris* he raises the problems of the structure of the universe that were to haunt him till the end. He already sees the world of ideas as the transformation of reality 'in a field of intelligible entities internally animated by the dialectic, which allows one to be linked with the other and which gives the mind the capacity of grasping this all that coincides with the infinite physical universe' (Badaloni).

In 1583 he left for England, with a letter from King Henri to his ambassador there, Michel de Castelnau.[1] He set up a class at Oxford, but found the place 'the widow of true knowledge as far as philosophy and mathematics are concerned.' In 1574 one Barebones had been ejected for daring to attack the Aristotelian system, and the statutes laid down that any master or doctor diverging one jot from Aristotle's teachings should be fined five shillings for each offence. Bruno decided that the dons 'knew far more about beer than about Greek.' However, he gained some friends whom he respected: Matthew, Dean of Christchurch; and Culpepper, Warden of New; Alberico Gentile, an Italian, professor of Civil Law; a young Welshman Gwinne, who later helped Florio in translating Montaigne; Alexander Dicson or Dickson, who imitated Bruno's mnemonics in *The Shadow of Reason* and whom Bruno held 'dear as his own eyes.' Dicson appears as a leading speaker in *Cause*.

Soon Bruno was in trouble. He took part in disputations before a visiting Polish prince.

Learn how they replied to his argument and how on that great occasion a wretched doctor got stuck, like a chicken in stubble, fifteen times in the fifteen syllogisms he propounded as Coryphaeus of the University. Hear how vulgar and violent the pig was, and how patient and forbearing the other, who showed his Neapolitan breeding and rearing under a kindly sky. Ask how they put a stop to his public lectures, both on the Immortality of the Soul and on the Quintuple Sphere.

Forced out of Oxford, he was stranded in London. Castelnau came to the rescue and gave him a home, though himself suffering

[1] Frances Yates, in *The French Academies of the 16th century*, 1947, traces the connections of Bruno and these bodies, and suggests that, after some political activities in Paris, he was sent on a secret political mission to London. See criticism: Badaloni, 248.

through the irregular payment of his salary. Sixty-three years old, he had been one of the first men north of the Alps to become a professional diplomat: not without learning, he translated Ramus's book on the Gauls, and in the memoirs written for his sons he shows his scrupulous and balanced mind. The embassy, Beaumont House, stood in Butchers Row, a narrow lane running into the Strand near St Clement Danes: a timber-framed house with projecting upper storeys, barge-boarded gables, and fleur-de-lis and coronets decorating the front.

Bruno stayed there more than two years, often going with Castelnau to court. In both *The Supper* and *Cause* he praises Elizabeth. And he was friendly with Fulke Greville and Sidney, though his relations with Greville grew strained—perhaps because he set *The Supper* at Greville's place and the work's strictures on English ways had caused much offence. Sidney seems to have remained a patron, and Bruno dedicated to him both *The Expulsion* and *Transports*.

He began by publishing in London another mnemonic work on an ambitious scale, in Latin. But then he turned to the Italian which he had tried out in his comedy. The result was the six books of lively dialogues, in which he let himself go with sudden ease and vivacity, confidently exploring the new world of thought he had been building up in his mind: *The Ash-Wednesday Supper; On Cause, Principle, and Unity; On the Infinite Universe and Worlds; The Expulsion of the Triumphant Beast; The Cabala of the Pegasean Steed; Heroic Transports*. The imprints named Venice or Paris as the place of printing; but the books were all done by J. Charlewood of London.

In these works he sets out his vision of the infinite universe and his theory of being. From the outset he is aware of the new space in which his thought lives, and the new tasks to which it calls men. In the second dialogue of *The Supper* he writes:

O difficulties to be endured, cries the coward, the featherhead, the shuttlecock, the faint-heart. . . . The task is not impossible, though hard. The craven must stand aside. Ordinary easy tasks are for the commonplace and the herd. Rare heroic and divine men overcome the difficulties of the way and force an immortal palm from necessity. You may fail to reach your goal. Run the race all the same. Put forth your strength in so high an affair. Strive on till your last breath. . . .
The Nolan has given freedom to the human spirit and made its knowledge free. It was suffocating in the close air of a narrow prison-house, whence, but only through chinks, it gazed at the far-off stars.

Its wings were clipped, so that it was unable to cleave the veiling cloud and reach the reality beyond.

But the reality-beyond is always for him also the reality here-and-now, the reality-within; and especially in *Cause* he attempts to show how the breakdown of the old rigid cosmological systems implies a concept of unitary process. More, he feels that the great liberation of which he is the prophet involves a new concept of man himself, of the individual and of society. In *The Expulsion* and its appendage *The Cabala*, he defines the way in which the new unitary outlook is to transform men. 'Jove stands for each one of us.' The existing system based on greed, ignorance, falsity, and hypocrisy is to be ended. And he makes a passionate call for a life of dedicated action.

Let the virtues and studies that are useful or indispensable to the general good be encouraged, pushed to the van, safeguarded. Let those who contribute to progress be honoured and rewarded, and let those who do no work, and the misers enslaved to property, be despised and held as beings of no value whatever.

He wants 'the day when man would walk like a new Adam in a world of new creation.'

England may claim to have helped in bringing forth these six works. In London Bruno seems to have found an atmosphere that helped him to the free expression of his ideas and encouraged his use of the vernacular.[1]

But after two years he returned to Paris with Castelnau. For a year he found 'boarding and lodging with the gentlemen I knew there, the greater part of the time at my own expense.' He now wrote again in Latin, continuing his polemic against Aristotle in *A Relation to the Imagery of the Physics* and *120 Theses*; he also took up the cause of F. Mordente who had invented a new form of compass. Then, after some tumults among the students against his teachings, he left for Germany. At Mainz he could find no opening; at Marburg (July 1586) he was refused the right to teach and quarrelled with the rector; but at the liberal university of Wittenberg in Saxony (where the jurist Gentile was lecturing) he settled down. He published more Latin books on mnemonics and against Aristotle, as well as writing mnemonic works which have come down in manuscript. In his farewell address of 8 March 1588 he praised

[1] See Aquilecchia, Intro. to his edition of *Cena* and his essay in *Cultura Neolatina*, 1953, xiii, fasc. 2–3, 165–89.

such Germans as Albert the Great, Paracelsus, and the patron of Copernicus; said of Nicholas of Cusa that he'd have equalled Pythagoras if his genius had not been stifled under priestly garments; and called Luther 'the mighty hero who resisted the voracious monster half-fox, half-lion; the vicar of the princes of hell. . . .' But though he thus admired the destructive side of the Reformation, he had no liking for its creeds which tended to elevate faith at the expense of good works.

Turning to the Catholic university of Prague, he published books again on mnemonics and against Aristotle. He still hoped to find a basis for reconciling his vision of liberation with the humane elements in the religions of the day, especially in Catholicism. In a dedication to the emperor he states that he looks forward to 'a religion of love which shall be no cause for controversy and above dispute, being the desire of the soul and required by the reasonable covenants of the nation and of society.' He protests against sectarian conflicts and intolerances; above all he abhors those who 'enforce their own prejudices with fire and sword.' He saw how 'authority usually binds and deceives in countless ways,' and announced the need for freedom of thought, regardless of all consequences.

It is sheer prejudice to settle a matter with small consideration; it is an evil deed to follow obsequiously the lead of another man; corrupt, slavish and traitorous to the dignity of free men to consent and surrender; wholly stupid to believe because of wont and usage; and imbecile to assent to the opinion of the mob.... We wish this law to be vigorously observed, that reason is as true as it is necessary, and the authority of no men, howsoever true and excellent persons they may be, is admissible as an argument....

Thus do we go forth to the most delightful splendour of light, understand nature (which is crying aloud to be heard) and follow wisdom (which we hold supreme above all) with singleness of spirit and an honest heart.

Given 300 dollars by the emperor, he went on to Helmstedt in Brunswick, where in 1576 a university had been opened and where he matriculated on 13 January 1589. He gave an oration on the death of its Protestant duke, in which he again made harsh remarks about the Papacy, saying that, though now a free man, he 'had suffered from the hungry tooth of the Roman wolf'; worse, he sets papal tyranny among the allegorical constellations as 'the Gorgon's head, nourishing snakes for hair and infecting the world with the rank venom of ignorance and vice.' He wrote several works which have come down in manuscript: two on magic, others on the cosmos, on Lullian medicine, and on mathematical magic. Then, excommunicated, he went to Frankfurt. The burgomaster on 2 July 1590 refused to let him lodge in the house of the printer Wechel; but the latter found him lodgings at a Carmelite monastery, where the prior noted that 'he was a man of fine intellect and erudition, a universal man, but he did not believe him to possess a trace of religion; adding that he professed to know more than the Apostles and could, if he wished, make the whole world of one religion.' Between staying at Frankfurt and making a visit to Zurich, he published his three important Latin poems, *On the Triple Minimum, On the Monad,* and *On the Immense,* which make the main addition to the positions set out in the London dialogues. In them he attempts to work out the atomic basis of his concept of matter and being and to define his dialectic of unitary process as composed of significant opposites. He also wrote an unfinished work *De Vinculis in Genere,* seeking to reduce all emotions to a basic opposition of love and hate, which form a unity; and published yet one more mnemonic book. (A *List of Metaphysical Terms,* which he now compiled, was published in 1595.)

A certain Giovanni Mocenigo wrote asking him to come to Venice; he wanted to learn from him his mnemonic or Lullian art. Bruno decided to go. He did not anticipate any conflict with the Roman Church, and he still held to his belief that some accommodation could be found between his ideas of free inquiry and the positions of dogma. He hungered for a catholic body which could accept his ideas, or at least tolerate them. By basing himself on the Republic of Venice he hoped to carry into Italy the liberating ideas which he had managed to propagate, despite difficulties, in France, England, and Germany; he was particularly encouraged by the success of Henri of Navarre in gaining the French throne and felt that the new era of the national secular states which he foresaw was going to make possible a rapid expansion of his ideas among the groups directing those states. (There was thus a mixture of acute historical insight with much utopian over-simplification in his hopes.)

Yet at the same time he was preparing himself for some terrible ordeal. A tragic element in him longed for the test which would confront him and his doctrines with the one great power of his world: the one power which, if converted, could bring before all men the world-view on which he felt freedom and rationality depended. In *De Monade* he had written:

> Whatever cruel fate awaits me yet,
> far back in my boyhood the struggle began,
> and, God my witness, I follow the truth unvanquished,
> and death itself can't bring me the smallest terror
> and I do not shrink at the powers of any man....
>
> I have fought. It is much....
> In Fate's hand, Victory lies. Then let that be,
> however. it will; whoever proves the victor,
> future times will not deny I owned no dread
> of death, was beaten in constancy by none,
> and preferred a spirited death to a craven life.

He went to live at Venice or at its university town of Padua, some twenty miles off. In March 1592 he was residing with Mocenigo, who had been an assessor at sessions of the Inquisition. Mocenigo reported his arrival to that body. 'I am compelled by my conscience and the order of my confessor.' He may have lured Bruno to Venice to betray him; he may have now acted through disappointment at Bruno's magical powers. On May 23rd Bruno was arrested. He seemed at first quite confident. The Inquisition had little control inside the Republic, which had refused it entry; but this time it won. At the secret sessions, where the patriarch and three state-assessors sat, all witnesses or officials were muzzled with a sacred oath; the prisoner was allowed no advocate and bore the onus of proving his innocence; he had no means of communicating with the outer world, did not know who were the accusers or witnesses, and had no opportunity of cross-examining; the prosecuting ecclesiastics were the judges. Bruno did his best to answer truthfully but con-ciliatingly; he still hoped to win over the Pope.

But on 23 February 1593 he was handed over to the prison of the Inquisition at Rome, where he was kept for seven years. We may assume that he was tortured. Campanella was tortured twelve times, the last time for forty hours. During torture a notary took down the words of the anguished man; if the latter remained silent, torture was reapplied. Early in 1599 Bruno was examined by the Congregation, who included the learned Jesuit Bellarmin (who denounced the Copernican theory and persecuted Sarpi and Galileo). In April a visitation of the prison was made. On December 21st Bruno was brought before the Congregation of nine cardinals, six coadjutors, and a notary. On January 20th the Pope presided. Bruno is said to have refused to abjure, asserting that he was misunderstood. On February 8th he was delivered to the secular arm for burning.

Schopp, a recent convert, witnessed the passing of sentence. Bruno was forced down on his knees, unfrocked, and handed over. 'When all these things were done,' says Schopp, a fiercely hostile witness, 'he said not a word except in a menacing way, "Perhaps your fear in passing judgment on me is greater than mine in receiving it." ' On the 17th he was burned alive in the Field of Flowers, with a gag on his tongue. Schopp records that when the crucifix was offered to him, 'he turned his face aside in disdain.' His ashes were scattered to the winds. On 7 August 1603 all his writings were placed on the Index.[1]

2. Medieval Philosophy

BRUNO may be defined as the last great medieval philosopher and the first great modern one. He faces both ways and in the problems he tackles he sums up the whole of medieval philosophy. To understand his work we must, then, have some idea of

[1] A search was made for documents bearing on his case during the short-lived Roman Republic of 1849; but time allowed only for a checking of the Vatican secret documents from February 1600 to November 1598. For long Catholic apologists called Schopp's account a forgery and said that Bruno was burned in effigy; and it was denied that any documents existed in the archives of the Brotherhood of Pity of St John the Beheaded, who accompanied heretics to the stake; examination was refused. (Example of the apologies: T. Desdouits, *La légende tragique de J. B., comment elle a été formée, son origine suspecte, son invraisemblance*, 1885.) But when Crispi was in power he wanted to inquire into the Brotherhood's finances; they thought that he was after information about Bruno and to avoid inconvenient investigations informed the Royal Commissioner of the entry in their registers. They were found indeed to have registers of the burning of twenty-five other persons in the 16th century, some cases aggravated by atrocious cruelty (A. Pognisi, *G. B. e l'archivio di S. G. Decillato*, 1891). Schopp's original letter was found at Breslau and published by B. G. Struve in his *Acta litteraria*, 1709, v, 67–74. Schopp gloated over Bruno's martyrdom in a book published in 1611. A. Mercati, in *Studii e testi*, no. 101, 1940, published a new Vatican document (*sommario del processo di G. B.*) probably written in the spring of 1597.

what that philosophy attempted and achieved. Its elements may be roughly summarised as consisting of the Bible and Early Fathers, the classical Greek thinkers, especially Plato and Aristotle, the Neoplatonics of the 3rd–4th centuries A.D., and the Arab and Jewish philosophers of the 10th–12th centuries—together with a slight amount of Greek and Arabian science. In the following comments no attempt is made to expound adequately the ideas of the various thinkers who are mentioned; the aim is to bring out certain leading lines of thought which were still influential in the 16th century and which determined the angle from which Bruno approached his problems and made his formulations.

Greek thought had posited the problems of flux and stability. Plato saw ultimate reality in absolute ideas or forms, but was little concerned how his timeless system came into existence. To this abstract vision however he added a concrete concern for the processes of knowledge; and by his dialectical methods of defining those processes he brought the abstractions down to earth. Aristotle devised the discipline of Metaphysics as a study of being and its properties; he divided being into matter, a pure nothingness, which he calls potentiality, and form, which actualises matter. The universe thus shows a ceaseless realisation of matter into the actuality of its form. Four causes bring this about: material, concerned with the stuff to be realised; formal, concerned with the form into which it has to be realised; efficient, concerned with the agent by which it can be realised; and final, concerned with the end to which it strives. Final and formal causes thus control the process and merge into a single cause. Behind the efficient stands God the prime mover who started things off, the unmoved mover who remains totally outside the processes he has precipitated. The Neoplatonists, especially Plotinus and Proclus, strove to weld Plato's hierarchy of forms into a more cohesive and unified structure: a linked progression of being from the lowest level in the human soul to the supreme one.

The first great synthesis for the Christian West came from Augustine. From his early influences of Scepticism, Manicheism, and Neoplatonism, he took into his Christian system a total distrust of the senses with a consequent total reliance on faith and illumination, a stress on dualism, and the idea of immaterial truth residing in forms or ideas derived from God. (The tradition of Christian materialism found in Tertullian was discarded.) Augustine's ideas held sway, together with a smattering of Aristotle and Neo-platonism, till the 12th century, when Arab and Jewish thought began to impact with systems seeking to combine Plato and Aristotle (often mixed up with the Neoplatonists). The Christians, with their personal God, brought in a scheme of history embracing all things in its pattern of fall, redemption, and last-judgment; and deepened the gap between the One and the Many, at the same time making the need for a bridge ever more urgent. With the reinflux of ancient thought from the 12th century on, thinkers felt that they must somehow establish a harmony of faith and reason, theology and philosophy.

Through the writings of Boethius, who died *c.* 525 A.D., the question of the relation of matter and form, and of universals and particulars, had early come in. The first important stirring of new ideas appeared with John the Scot (Irish) in the 9th century. John knew Greek and was influenced by Byzantine thinkers who had reoriented Neoplatonist schemes in a Christian direction: pseudo-Denys the Areopagite and Maximus the Confessor. Then with the town-growth and the big economic advances of the 12th century came the Arabian influences and a more direct knowledge of the ancients. Scholasticism was born. The 11th century had already seen a growing stress on dialectic, which was resisted by the orthodox. The posing of a *quaestio* became a basic feature of medieval philosophy, with *pro* and *contra*, from the 12th to the 15th century.

The dangers of dialectic showed up quickly. Berengar used its arguments to deny Transubstantiation; and his doctrines, with those of John the Scot, were condemned in 1050. From now on a complex struggle was waged, with many sharp oppositions as well as compromises, into which we can enter only briefly. Already in the 11th century Peter Damian, in the effort to counter dialectic, claimed God's will as above all laws and unrestricted even by impossibility. The gap between reason and faith grew wider; and scholasticism set out to close it, coming to an apex with Thomas Aquinas (who had taught at Bruno's Neapolitan monastery). With Roscelin and Abelaerd the dispute on universals reached its height, Abelaerd arguing that universals, genera and species, were not things but were categories of logic which corresponded to what existed in things and expressed status: the general idea being abstracted from a number of individuals.

In the 12th century the growth of Platonism brought about the first examination of the relation between the existence of the world and that of God. Thierry of Chartres appealed to the Pythagorean theory of numbers in an effort to show that unity alone was stable and immutable, while William of Conches took up the atomic theory, which had been introduced into the West by Constantine Africanus and Adelard of Bath. Elements of pantheism in the school of Chartres burst out in Amaury of Bène and David of Dinant, who were both condemned in 1210 and in 1215. The tendency in such thinkers was to cut God off from any active relation to men and so to eliminate the whole Christian system. David, whom Bruno looked on as a forerunner, followed John the Scot in dividing nature into three: matter, thought, God; but then went further in reducing the three to one. The ultimate effect was to identify God and matter.

The conflict in philosophy grew deeper. On the one hand were the efforts to systematise faith and apply the principles of the dialectic to dogma; on the other hand the Augustinian tradition, which centred everything on illumination was strengthened, as for example, in St Bernard the Cistercian. A similar conflict had been going on inside the Moslem world since the 9th century, where Aristotle, often Neoplatonised, had been used to support faith. With Alkindi the distinction of potency and act appeared; Alfarabi more fully fused Plato and Aristotle; Avicenna worked out a Neoplatonism largely controlled by Aristotelian concepts, and by transferring God's Necessity to his universe he made everything follow inexorable laws. He saw matter as eternal and bodies as composed of form and matter, with form the constitutive element; he also saw a single active intellect at work in all men, enabling them to understand one another. Averroes in Spain sought to delimit the areas of faith and reason, and held necessity to be inherent in being; by handing necessity and possibility over to the mode of being he was able to discard the Neoplatonist hierarchies of separate Intelligences, on which Avicenna relied, and go back to the idea of a prime unmoved mover, who, as pure act, held the necessary ideas of the potential beings of the sublunar sphere.[1]

[1] Averroes objected that Avicenna broke the unity of being by introducing it from without, and defined the active intellect's function as the transfer of potency into act, not as the creation of forms. Avicebron broke from Avicenna in considering that all being resulted from God's will, taken as an emanation rather than an attribute.

Further contributions were made by Jewish thinkers, especially Ibn Gabirol (known to the medieval world as Avicebrol or Avicebron, and thought an Arab) and Maimonides. Avicebron divided all things into God, God's will, and Being (composed of matter and form). His matter-and-form, or hylomorphic being, embraced all beings corporeal or incorporeal, with only God left outside; it constituted a universal essence. Otherwise he used the graded Neoplatonist hierarchies inside being, and held matter to be the cause of individuation, with form as the agent actualising matter.

The Arabian-Jewish impact had the effect of providing both the pressure for an extended metaphysic and the terms in which the struggle to develop that metaphysic could be fought out.[1] It produced a set of challenges to the traditional Catholic ideas. The idea of the Unmoved Mover tended to push God out of the universe, and against it Aquinas built up his system. The idea of a universal active intellect tended to deny the individuality and therefore the immortality of soul. The idea of God's necessity tended to stimulate determinism, with the ultimate supplanting of theology by science; hence the condemnation of Averroism in 1217. Arabian influences fed the pantheism of men like Amaury and David.

The 13th century was the high point of medieval philosophy; for thinkers, aware of all the unsettling ideas, made a supreme effort to synthesise and rationalise, reconciling the difficulties inside a deepened concept of God. But this philosophising of theology in due time made possible the emergence of philosophy without theology: a movement that reached its climax with Bruno. At first the orthodox struggled to ban Aristotle; but even the effort to refute him led to enriched study of his works, of which at last correct translations were made available. The advent of the universities provided the stage for the arguments, with the friars intensifying the debate: Dominicans tending towards Aristotle, Franciscans towards Augustine.

Oxford held to a platonic bias and became more successful in science than the Aristotelian schools. Mathematics were stressed,

[1] It brought about the use of metaphysical categories to distinguish God's existence from the existence of all other beings or things. Other distinctions included that between essence and existence; between necessary and possible being—with Aristotle's theory of abstraction as a means of tracing God's existence. The notion of hylomorphic unity had a powerful dissident effect which provides the main line leading from medieval thought into Bruno.

and the general method was at once deductive and *a priori*. What is called the light-metaphysic was a natural accompaniment of the idea of illumination. Thus, Grosseteste argued that God created the universe from a single point of light, which expanded and diffused, engendering spheres and dimensions. The emphasis was on corporeality and on individual essence; and the light-metaphysic led to the study of light itself as well as of optics. Thomas of York discussed matter under three heads: corruptible, spiritual, universal. The Augustinians tended to an idea of hylomorphic unity in matter, since they rejected the Aristotelian scheme of pure matter as pure potency lying ready for the act of pure form.

Albert the Great was important in using direct observation of natural phenomena; he cut theology and philosophy apart, basing himself on a Neoplatonised Aristotle, and substituted God for the Arabian separated-intellect. He held that 'form is the universal being, not matter,' and thus opened the way to Aristotelian influences among the Dominicans. Thomas Aquinas strengthened this trend. Separating faith and reason, he made the senses the source of human knowledge; and on this basis, using Aristotelian categories, he tried to reunite faith and reason, and to prove the existence of God. Using the matter-form opposition, he sought to found all intelligibility and rationality on being. On the other hand, Siger of Brabant and others clung to the Averroist tradition, leading to two condemnations of Siger's work, in 1270 and 1277. These condemnations were the last all-out attack on the Arabian influx. Meanwhile, Augustinians, holding to an Avicebron kind of matter-form unity, resisted Thomism.

Raymond Lull, a Spaniard, attacked Averroism and elaborated a mechanism for relating concepts to one another so as to reach the truth; his aim was a 'general science for all the sciences.' His work much influenced Bruno, whose mnemonic systems look forward both to such works as Leibniz' *Dissertation on the Art of Combination* and to a full dialectical notion of the unity of spiritual and natural process. Richard of Middleton (who died *c.* 1307) was an English Augustinian holding to hylomorphism; he considered the universe capable of contraction or expansion—though this position came from the reaction against the idea of eternal necessity and did not spring from any brilliant scientific intuition.

We may summarise then that Aristotelianism led to inquiry into the metaphysical principles of being, though it also stimulated the study of zoology, medicine, and the like—while Augustinianism led to the study of mathematics, light, and optics. Roger Bacon, with his wide range over optics, astronomy, alchemy, and physics, was a Franciscan, a pupil of Grosseteste, who held to the two sources of knowledge, inner illumination and empirical investigation.

With the 14th century came a deepening of scepticism. The sceptics stressed the split between faith and reason in order to assign each position a different universe and to gain freedom for reason on its own ground. The orthodox helped them; for, in order to strengthen the claims of faith, they cut it totally away from reason. Empiricism was thus highly developed in thinkers like William of Ockham, who mocked at Aristotle's assumption that there cannot be a regression to infinity, and as a result insisted a body moved not through inner impulsion but from outer impetus, and that it fell, not through a separate principle moving it to realise its nature, but through the attraction of the earth's mass; there was no assurance that the world was infinite or eternal or possessed of a governing unity, or that there were not several worlds.[1] Ockhamite arguments discredited the need of grace, excluded theology from its own domain, and produced a fluid situation where good and evil were not necessarily exclusive. The only adequate reply, as in Bradwardine, was to exclude everything but God. The medieval synthesis had broken down.

3. Nicholas of Cusa

THE great thinker who linked the medieval positions with those of the Renascence was Nicholas of Cusa, son of a boat-owner of Cues on the Moselle, born in 1401, who became bishop and cardinal. He was educated in the Platonic tradition by the Brothers of the Common Life at Deventer, and went on to Padua, the one Italian university with no effective religious tests for professors or students and hence a centre of bold intellectual activity.

[1] See Appendix I on *impetus*.

He knew Greek, and advocated the widest tolerance, though at the Council of Bâle in 1436, forced to choose between support of the Papacy and outright revolt, he acquiesced. He tells us that the clue to his system flashed on him during a voyage to Constantinople round the turn of 1437-8; he felt that he had discovered how to reconcile unity with a world based on contradictions and contraries. He built on the Neoplatonism of the pseudo-Denys, John the Scot, Eckhardt. God and the world are one; the finite is implicit in the infinite, the infinite explicit in the finite. (Bruno takes over these terms and views development as a process of unfolding and enfolding: implication, explication, complication, contraction.[1]) One and infinity, and multiplicity and finity, press upon one another; every possibility must exist; God is necessary for the world and the world for God (though the necessities here are not of the same order).

Thus, rest and motion imply one another. Motion is implicit in rest, rest explicit in motion: with rest prior and containing the whole possibility of motion—therefore containing also the whole actuality, since potency and act are one in the eternal unity. Rest is the eternal possibility of the actuality, and the eternal actuality of the possibility, of temporal motion. And so on. The universe is the evolution of limited possibility into limited actuality, which becomes manifold in the process. So multiplicity arises out of unity. Unity is not a number, but is the principle of number as the minimum and the end of number as the maximum. All that can be truly said of God is the one and same truth of his immutable nature, since his being, will and act are one.

Nicholas continually used mathematical and geometrical terms to express the relation of the One and the world, and was especially fond of playing about with the absolute minimum and absolute

---

[1] Everything, in its perfection, is included in the absolute maximum, and the infinite unity is the aggregate of all, the *complicatio*. Identity is the complication of difference, and likeness is that of unlikeness. Things are the evolution or *explicatio* of God, as the finite multiple differentiates expression of what is grounded in him, though in him the finite is infinitude, the multiple is unity, and the difference is identity. (Cf. Eckhardt: Pfeiffer, *Meister Eckhardt*, 222.) The nature of the finite universe comes about through *contractio*. From the absolute One issues a second unity, the universe, and from this a third unity, that of the genera (constituted by the species, which are constituted by the individuals): Duex, *Der deut. Card. N. von Cusa*, ii, 322. Note, however, that Bruno's *complexion* is simply the Aristotelian term for the combination of qualities supposed to determine the nature of a body.

maximum, which coincide. All contraries thus coincide in God. The idea of the unity-of-opposites Nicholas considered the core of his system: an idea partly derived from the mystic Eckhardt. (Anti-rationalists could afford to stress the basis of existence in contradictions, since they wanted to destroy the claims of reason conceived in terms of the Aristotelian logic which Aquinas had employed.) Sense-impressions, Nicholas held, were united in the activity of thought. He posited a world-soul as intermediary between God and his universe, which is infinite and triune. Nature is animate and articulated; everything is a more or less imperfect mirror of the universe in its own place, and preserves itself in relation to and in community with other things. In conscious experience there is an indivisible continuity; in things, an indivisible minimum. The centre of things is everywhere, and the circumference nowhere. The earth is therefore not the world-centre, and the sphere of the fixed stars is not the circumference. Thus Nicholas throws overboard, on general grounds, the whole Aristotelian geocentric scheme. There is no quintessence, distinct from the four elements, to make the material structure of the stars different from that of the earth; the earth itself is a star, and the same laws of matter and motion apply throughout the universe. 'Perhaps the inhabitants of other stars are nobler than ourselves.'

Thus Nicholas foreshadowed Copernicus and Bruno, declaring that the earth like all things was in motion. He was much interested in scientific matters, wrote on the calendar, and was the first man in the West who used weighing for the discovery of natural laws. In *On Static Experiments* in his *Wisdom of a Simple Man* he described experiments on the floating properties of pieces of wood of different sizes and shapes. He noted that the earth in a pot where seeds were growing diminished in weight.[1]

The unresolved problems left by Nicholas are indicated by his ambiguous use of terms. The *complicatio-explicatio* relationship can express both the descent from the one to the particular and the ascent of the particular to the one. Absolute actuality is in God alone; concrete actuality is only in individual existence. Thus things grow more actual according as they approach the one, and also according as they are separated out. 'His doctrine amounts to this:

[1] See Lynn Thorndyke, *History of Magic and Experimental Science*, iv, 75f; he was in part anticipated by Blasius of Parma.

the more abstract, *simplex*, united, the more actual; and also the more concrete, *complex*, separate, the more actual.'[1]

4. Bruno's Renascence Forerunners

BRUNO was deeply read in medieval philosophy, knew Aquinas well, and did his best to get first-hand knowledge of the ancient thinkers. He knew the Epicureans largely through his beloved Lucretius, accepted the atomism of Democritus (though seeking to purge it of mechanism), and was much affected by Arab thinkers such as Averroes and Avicebron. In reading Aristotle and other authors he picked up ideas about the pre-Socratics, which strongly influenced him. And Lull, we have noted, suggested to him that it was possible to isolate and define the stages and inter-relations of mental activity in the same way as those of nature— one system reflecting the other. Nicholas of Cusa gave him the broad lines on which he felt that he could demolish Aristotelianism while carrying on the tradition of hylomorphism.

But it was Copernicus who enabled him to bring the Cusan system down to earth and deepen its scientific content. The Aristotelian scheme, as worked out by the astronomer Ptolemy, had suited the medieval world with its need of a geocentric universe. What Copernicus did in 1543 was to put the sun at the motionless centre instead of the earth and to put the earth into one of the rotating planetary spheres; the stars remained fixed in the eighth sphere. (His theory was introduced into England by Thomas Digges in *A Perfit Description of the Caelestiall Orbes* in 1576, though there are references to it as early as Robert Recorde's *Castle of Knowledge*, 1556.) Bruno by applying the general theory of Nicholas eliminated the motionless centre and the fixed eighth sphere surrounding the world. He had found a scientific and concrete point for the Cusan's ideas.

[1] T. H. Betts, *Nicholas of Cusa*, 1932, 135; Charbonnel, *Pensée Italienne au xvie s.*, 466f.

Among his Renascence predecessors it is worth while to glance at Porzio, Fracastoro, and Telesio. Simone Porzio, pupil of Pomponazzi, denied immortality, and saw matter, not as 'something invented by the mind, but the origin and eternal cause of all things' in his *De rerum naturalium principiis*. The totality of matter could not be generated or broken down as the parts could be.

Change involves the conflict of opposites: 'necessary also is a contrary form, *forma opposita*, or something that includes the contrary, *oppositum*.' Only in this sense does he admit the Aristotelian privation of matter, its need of form. He looked, like Bruno, to Pythagoras and Anaxagoras, and attacked Aristotle for declaring that nature acted through a final cause. He identified matter and infinity, and appealed to the ancients who held 'all things come about through the necessity of matter.'

Fracastoro may have been one of Copernicus' masters during the latter's stay at Padua in 1501–6. In his *De Sympathia et Antipathia Rerum* (1546) he pointed to the unitary nature of matter, which is configured in determinate action and reaction, and ruled by sympathy and antipathy, attraction and repulsion; that is, by a principle of opposites. He considered however that 'all things do not act on all things, but only certain things on certain things' (in specific interactions). Bruno gave the name of Fracastoro to one of the speakers in *On the Infinite Worlds*.

Bernardino Telesio (1509–88) was born at Cosenza and founded the Cosentina Academy at Naples. He stressed observation, with the motto, 'Not by reason, but by sense,' though he admitted that the mind co-operated with the senses. An anti-Aristotelian, for the relation of matter to form he substituted the relation of matter to force; and he reduced the forces to two—one of dilation (heat) and one of contraction (cold). Under the movements brought about by these forces (which are in fact one: cold being considered as the negation of heat), matter goes through various changes but does not increase or diminish, and remains everywhere uniform. He attributed consciousness to matter, since he could not understand how it could appear in animals unless primary matter already owned it. However he did not take over the Copernican system and held that God endowed each thing or being with its own way of behaving, a way which harmonised with the ways of other things or beings. The soul was material, situated in the cerebral cavities. In activity, which had for its end self-preservation, the soul felt pleasure. But no one could live in isolation; and for reciprocal action to yield its best, a sort of sympathetic cohesion was needed—social virtues that were expressed in humanity. Wisdom, suggesting the best means of self-preservation, was the necessary general condition of the good life; *sublimitas* was a yet higher state, resuming all the virtues in their most perfect form. (Telesio then added a second or immaterial soul, which combined with the material one when the body had achieved its full development.[1])

Such thinkers show the general climate of advanced thought in which Bruno matured. Telesio in *Cause* he calls 'the most judicious.' In the same work he pours scorn on men like Ramus and Patrizzi who attacked Aristotle only on the logical side and were unconcerned with his physics. For Bruno, with his unitary outlook, it was impossible to separate the logical positions of a thinker from his world-outlook. He brings this point out strongly in *Cause* through the character Poliinio whose Aristotelian views on matter are linked with his attitude to women. Bruno is saying that the medieval notion of passive deprived matter was also the ecclesiastical notion of depraved sensual woman. He thus identifies the Aristotelian system with a life-denying morality.[2]

We may note too how Bruno is in the line of the *libertin* composers of Paradoxes. Thus Ortensio Landi in his *Paradossi* states 'that woman is of greater excellency and dignity than man' (25) and 'that Aristotle was not only ignorant but the most obnoxious (*malvagio*) man of that time.'

[1] Other thinkers worth adding are Cardan with his stress on physical inquiry, who saw nature as space, matter, and intelligence (one with the world-soul); the alchemist Paracelsus who held all creatures to be emanations of the world-soul and believed in a subtle sympathy or correspondence of heaven and earth; P. A. Manzoli (Palingenius), a Ferrarese poet, whom Bruno cannot have known well as he takes him for a German, and who held the universe to be infinite—he had a process brought against him at Rome; Louis le Roy, Platonist at Paris (died 1577), who set out the thesis that 'everywhere contraries balance one another,' and said that 'it seemed to Plato the world was nourished by the consumption and decay of itself producing always new creatures from the old,' and who stressed the relativity of 'upper' and 'lower' positions: *Douze Livres de la Vicissitude*, 1576. (D. Singer suggests the notion of coincidence-of-contraries was not unconnected with a tolerant attitude to warring religions, *G.B.* 23; Le Roy published an appeal for concord in 1570.)

[2] See B. Farrington, *Greek Science*, 1949, i, 146, for the correlation of Aristotle's concept of matter with his views on slavery.

2+

5. Cause, Principle, and Unity

We are now in a position to consider what Bruno set out to achieve in his work in general and in the dialogues on Cause, Principle, and Unity in particular. Here he most systematically braces himself to demolish the Aristotelian positions once for all, in all their ramifications; and that, as we have seen, means for him the breaking-down of a whole way of life and its substitution by another. *The Expulsion of the Triumphant Beast* which soon follows gives the full social programme which is to supplant the social and moral systems linked with Aristotelian logic and geocentric mechanism. But though he wants to bring about a totally new attitude to reality, he is constrained to use the only available tools and terms. Much of his difficulty comes from this fact. He is employing terms based on division to express unity, terms based on abstract logic to express a new sense of dialectical conflict and resolution.

We may omit the First Dialogue here, since that is a personal apologia. The Second begins by stating that all things have both immediate and first causes and principles. But how is one to define the terms, which are often used loosely? Cause is what produces an effect without being lost or confounded in it; principle is what comes together internally in the formation of a being and remains in its effect. In specific cases, cause and principle can be thus separated, but in the last resort they are one in the first cause.

But for the moment he is not concerned with first causes. He turns to nature and asks what is principle and what is cause there. He takes up the prevailing distinctions drawn from Aristotle, of efficient, formal, and final causes. The efficient cause, he says, is the Universal Intellect, which for Aristotle is external to the world. Bruno, setting out to get rid of all transcendental positions, sees the Intellect as the formative and organising force which operates from the depths of nature and is unthinkable apart from nature. The formal cause is the totality of the ideas or forms of this Intel-

24

lect, according to which beings are formed; it is that in nature which
evolves definite and specific structure. The final cause, the aim, he
defines as the universe's perfection: that is, the fullest possible
actualisation of all the possible determinations of matter.

Now he turns to principle. It is the World-soul. Again he sets
himself to break down transcendental hierarchies. Thus, Plotinus
made the Intellect distinct and transcendental with regard to the
Soul; Bruno makes the latter simply the main function of formative
energy. Universal Intellect and World-soul become in effect terms
that can be used in place of one another. The World-soul is then
the principle of nature, the inner force, which persists (provides a
constant and stable element) and which links together (through the
underlying unity of matter). Bruno follows this idea logically out,
insisting that all nature is to some extent organically alive.

The indestructible element (matter) and the stable element
discards the Aristotelian concept of form and matter as separable
from matter, appears as the creative and yet constant force persisting through all changes of things and beings. Bruno attacks and
discards the Aristotelian concept of form and matter as separable
things which form an external combination. The material form is
seen as no inert and passive thing, but as identical with the form
which organises all things.

Reality is thus defined as a unitary process in which matter is
both content and form. The essence of matter is the dynamic form
that produces the infinite universe of species and individuals.

The Third Dialogue goes on to deal with the Intellect-Cause
and Soul-Principle, which are substantially identical. But the direction of the argument is towards showing the key-significance of
matter as the constitutive principle of reality. Logically, for the
purpose of analysis and exposition, Bruno says, we may separate
matter and cause-principle, but in fact they are one. Matter and
soul or spirit are different aspects of a unitary substance.

Here are the stages of his argument. He deals with the atomists
or mechanists who reduce reality to the movements and inter-
lockings of atoms. For a while, he says, he accepted this position,
taking form in its Aristotelian sense and seeing it only as an accident of matter. But on further reflection he decided that form could
not be thus disposed of. In such terms we cannot explain the actual
stability of forms in nature or the way in which they arise. Form

must be a reality even if we cannot detach it abstractly or transcendentally from matter. The problem then is to deepen one's understanding of matter.

He begins afresh with a comparison borrowed from Plato, Aristotle, and Plotinus: that of nature with art. In nature the relation of a thing or being to matter is the same as the relation of an artist to his material—save that whereas the materials of art vary, matter is one. (Both matter and material are *materia* in Italian.) Matter he then identifies with the absolute; it is what subsists under all change.

We cannot call it corporeal, since it includes both spirit and body, and in its absolute sense it has no determination. It is indestructible. Only compounds or composite bodies come and go, cohere, and break up, not matter itself in its pure nature. What the Aristotelians call substance is in fact only the accidents of matter.

What is matter? He considers it as a potency of being and as the universal subject or substratum from which all things and beings arise and into which they return. Matter as potency represents the total possibility of the universe's development. The universe, as we know it, shows a ceaseless struggle to realise the full possibility of the existence of things. In matter as the absolute (as true substance) the contradictions of potency and act, of possibility and actuality, are overcome, and there alone. Bruno thus sees reality as involving two levels: matter or substance in its absolute sense, where, since potency and act are one, the universe is perfected; and matter or substance in the relative sense, where every object or being partakes of the essence of the whole (holds the passive potency and so is one with Act, with the World Intellect-Soul), yet can express or reflect only an imperfect or specific aspect, so that potency and act are never in fact identical.

In the movement of the argument, the opposition of form and matter is further broken down, and the meaning of unitary process is deepened.

In the Fourth Dialogue, Bruno goes on to examine matter as the universal substratum or subject, and to identify it with the substance of incorporeal things (*e.g.* Intellect-Soul) as well of corporeal. His steps are as follows.

He begins with the Neoplatonists. Plotinus recognised that the multiplicity of intelligible species presupposed a uniting element, an intelligible matter; the unity of the mind presupposes the unity of matter, with which it is one. But is it to degrade higher things by linking them thus with matter? Bruno distinguishes, with Plotinus, two matters, intelligible and sensible: the first containing all beings in a uniting and intensive sense, the other containing them in their separate specific aspects, extensively. But having made the distinction, he declares that all such abstractions are useful only for analysis; they break down when we drive them past a certain point, and we are forced once more to admit the unitary nature of matter in which the uniting and the separating aspects, the intensive and the extensive, coincide. For matter is no more 'corporeal' in bodies than in minds—that is, pure matter includes both corporeality and incorporeality, and cannot be reduced to either. It follows, Bruno says, that Arabian thinkers like Avicebron were right in positing a universal matter which exists in both a corporeal and an incorporeal form.

Next, he argues that Form (the World Intellect-Soul) produces the accidental (actual) forms, and is itself a single dynamic process beyond them all. It is the same with matter, which contains and begets all the figurations in the sense-world, and is also a single stream beyond them as well as in them. Form and matter are thus eternal aspects of the single substance. (He glances at David of Dinant's notion of matter as divine.) Reality is the unitary process.

Finally he attempts further to demonstrate that reality is a single process, which is nothing else than matter.

In the Fifth Dialogue he lets himself go in a rhetorical and lyrical exaltation of the unitary principle, asserting that all aspects and contradictions are merged and resolved in it: part and whole, century and instant, point and body, centre and circumference, maximum and minimum. Universal being is everywhere, sustaining, resolving, harmonising the conflicts and contradictions which inhere at every point of time and space in the actual universe and our experience of it. But near the end of his exposition, he expands the concept of the unity-of-opposites and insists on its essential nature for the understanding of reality. 'It is profound magic to know how to draw out the contrary after having found the point of union.' That is, it is essential both for understanding reality and for entering into it with a view to grasping and controlling process.

6. Some Comments

EVEN the rough summary given above will serve to bring out how powerfully Bruno grapples with the whole inheritance of medieval and ancient thought, and how thoroughly he transforms it. In a sense he views the medieval tradition, and the ancient world of thought behind it, through the perspective of Nicholas of Cusa, from whom he draws so many terms and arguments. But equally strong is the scientific attitude reaching back through Arabian thinkers like Averroes to Democritus and the pre-Socratics. We see at a glance how he completes certain anti-Aristotelian or anti-metaphysical trends which go back to Abelaerd's bringing of the controversy about universals down to earth, his refusing to accept concepts or logical distinctions as things. The whole medieval or idealist method of inventing principles and causes to escape from a scientific investigation of phenomena is halted; and there is no longer any excuse for putting abstractions in the way of that investigation. Further, Bruno gives a new force to the concrete elements in the pantheism of David of Dinant and other rebels, and in the hylomorphic tradition of Avicebron.

The great force in his thought lies in the way in which he steadily breaks down the concepts and terms through which a bifurcation of reality into spirit and body, form and matter, has been brought about; and in which he shows that they hold necessary clues to reality only if they are seen in a fuller view which consistently moves towards a unitary concept of process. In the end he has identified this unitary process with matter, and has banished all transcendental and other-worldly ideas. There is only the one universe, the one nature, the one life. God has become a term for exalting the unitary process with its inner creativeness, which requires no prime mover, no transcendental or external force. Everything is included in this unitary process, always has been, and always will be.

The profound originality and significance of his system can

28

hardly be exaggerated. In one sense it resumes the unitary outlook of the early Greek philosophers; but what was naive in them has become a fully worked-out philosophy, enriched by the subtleties and complexities of analysis which the post-Heracleitan development has brought about, yet getting rid of the dualities and dichotomies, the hypostases and reifications of process, which had been the price paid for analytic depth. To a considerable extent correctly, Bruno sees Plato as the last Greek thinker who has preserved an underlying Ionian unitary outlook, even though he perverted that outlook with his theory of Ideas or Forms, seeking to explain the stability and inner coherence of material existences. He seeks to repeat this role of Plato in a reversed form: going back to the unitary conception without sacrificing the gains made by the theory of Ideas. He reads both Plato and Plotinus materialistically, and uses their ideas in this revalued shape to explain the constancy of forms (which however for him are still an aspect of the Democritean universe of atoms, a part of matter and materially conditioned).

The key to the understanding of Bruno, then, lies in his dialectic, in his polemic against Aristotle as the dominant idealist thinker of his world, and in his conclusion that reality consists of a unitary flow of matter, within which change and movement, generation and dissolution, occur, and which consists in essence of united opposites. To call him an eclectic is to admit that one has simply missed his consistent purpose. To call him a pantheist is to abstract one aspect of his unitary position, while ignoring the real content of that position; it is to ignore all that is most characteristic of his thinking, all that infuses his polemics with power and passion, all that builds his specific historical role and makes him different from other thinkers.

I have called him a consistent thinker, since all his work is directed to the solution of certain definite problems. But that does not mean that he is without flaws, weaknesses, and confusions. The criterion we must take in defining his flaws must derive from all that is most concrete in his dialectic, since there lies the dynamic core of the man. By that criterion we find that he carries on the contradictions analysed above in the thought of Nicholas of Cusa, and indeed worsens them to the extent that his dialectic is fuller and more concrete than that of Nicholas. These contradictions all centre around the concept of absolute substance or matter.

Bruno opposes his absolute substance or being (as something

in which potency and act are one, in which all is perfected) to the actual universe with its endless imperfections, in which nothing is all that it can be in the full range of its temporal or dimensional possibilities. That is, a child cannot simultaneously be a man; even less can it be absolute matter. Here then Bruno commits the sin that he has protested against in other philosophers. He sacrifices the dynamic complexity of existence on the altar of an abstraction.

He sees all process as involving a unity-of-opposites; but he then opposes to process itself a concept or state of perfected potency-act, of absolute unity, in which all contradictions are automatically resolved and balanced. There is no possible point of contact between this immobile completed and symmetrical totality and the eternally changing unsymmetrical world of process. We have seen how in his destructive analysis of all previous philosophies Bruno works out a materialist dialectic which includes the achievements of ancient materialism but refuses to accept its mechanist method or conclusions. We have seen how he takes over the complex metaphysical development that reaches from Pythagoras, Plato, and Aristotle, on through the Neoplatonists and the Arabs into medieval scholasticism; but consistently up-ends that development, in order to bring out the material truths which had been abstracted or hypostasised.

We have seen how he thus achieves a materialism which, while insisting on the atomic basis of matter, proceeds to consider the nature of wholes and of structural organisation. But the legacy of the denied idealisms remains in the conviction that some sort of absolute must be defined and that an immobile symmetry is essentially superior to a dynamic asymmetry. In positing a universe of unceasing change and movement through conflict and contradiction, he feels the need to set over against it an unchanging universe. True, he wrests this unchanging universe from the theologians and makes it logically this-worldly. But the cleavage remains. He has introduced a dualism at the heart of his cherished unity, by pressing the claims of unity too far. His universal and identical matter or substance is an abstraction, a ghost, a logical invention.[1]

How is he able to convince himself that he has not undermined his notion of unitary process or matter? By his application of the ancient system of correspondences. Every existence insofar as it

[1] Horowitz makes this criticism at length, but undervalues the positive aspect of Bruno's very varied thought.

includes substance reflects the wholeness of the universe, though in its specific nature it denies that wholeness. Bruno feels that he has thus tied up universal substance and specific being, but in fact he has indulged in the sort of abstract play with terms which he rejects in other thinkers. The full logic of his method insists that he should consider unity to be as relative as the contradictions it overcomes; the only absolute can be the law of development which embraces unity and contradictions alike.

If he had made the final step in the rejection of metaphysics, which is demanded by the whole powerful direction of his thought, he would have had to bring down into process the various aspects or qualities he attributes to his absolute. As he cannot do that, he is left in fact with two kinds of resolution: that of the dialectical unity-of-opposites in the actual world, the world of flux and change, and that of a total conclusion and absorption of all opposites in absolute substance. The latter is merely the metaphysical and dead reflection of the former. And this dead reflection stands in the way of the full understanding of the unity-of-opposites in the actual world. Since all finite things and processes are seen as in the last resort indifferently one thing, there can be only one real quality, which resides in infinity, in the absolute. Therefore all change is purely quantitative. Only combinations and recombinations of given factors or elements are possible. Thus, by his idealist abstraction of matter, Bruno ends by flattening process as much as if he had held to an atomistic mechanism. He has done the very thing he wanted to escape. He cannot proceed to make the necessary distinctions between things, processes, concepts, and categories.[1]

He tends to see the forms or stabilities, which are one aspect of matter, as derived from some sort of imposed or preordained order and kept in being by his absolute substance in which potency is one with act. The absolute concordance of things he is forced to assume is in fact non-existent; and the endless concatenation of

---

[1] The modern concept of *development* was impossible till the growth of chemistry proper and of biology. Before that the word means: unfolding. unwrapping, and is applied to unfurling a standard. In the 18th century it comes to mean, first, 'bringing out a latent quality or force,' *e.g.* Pope (*Dunciad*), 'Then take him to devellop, if you can, And hew the block off, and get out the Man.' The notion of latency grows. Warburton, 1750, 'to instruct us in the history of the human mind, and to assist in developing its faculties;' Reynolds, 1790, 'to develope the latent excellencies' of art. The crucial point for the idea of the emergence-of-the-new comes through Lamarck and Lavoisier.

2*

things which his dialectic implies is swallowed up in the abstract system of reflections and harmonies. He has stressed—one of his great achievements—the inner nature of organisation and growth; but he fails to take full advantage of this notion and to develop it in terms of his principle of the unity-of-opposites. Instead he has to rely in the last resort on a basis of universal harmony; to defend his position he would have to fall back on a pre-established harmony of mind and body. Despite his insistence on unitary process, he is left with the need to appeal to the Universal Intellect as a directive force through which nature produces in an orderly and rational way and the mind forms rational ideas corresponding to the objective universe. This weak side leads on to Leibniz, whether or not that philosopher had read his poem on the Monad, as his unitary aspect leads on to Spinoza.[1]

These criticisms are logically correct; yet in the last resort they give an inadequate idea of Bruno's thought and its direction. The deepest effect of his work is to deny the way of abstraction and to link ideas with their objective basis. His dialectic 'consists in seeing universals no longer moved in the field of abstraction, as entities of pure reason, but as set instead in the becoming-itself of reality. . . . The active intellect does not reveal a world of ideas placed over against the real world, but the real world itself insofar as it is seen, beyond its separate and changeable individuality, in the universality of all that is reflected even in the single particular' (Badaloni). Bruno attributes to matter an ideal matter which contains the formal aspects of things and links them in the final coincidence of one and all. The eternal changing of matter gives birth to relations that are not accidental but derive from the inner order of matter. Within nature, matter is the source of ideas; it embraces both the intellect and the soul, which represents the inner vitality of things. Bruno transforms his initial Averroist positions by adding the materialist concept of infinity, formulated at first in atomistic terms, then linked with a thesis of the constant inner elements persisting despite change. As we follow out the development of his thought, we witness the tremendous effort that has to be made in discarding the ingrained idealist attitudes of philosophy and in

[1] The argument that Leibniz did not draw on Bruno because their systems are unlike, falls to the ground; Leibniz's thought could be defined as elaborated abstraction of one of Bruno's weaker sides: see Charbonnel, 546. For a significant reference by Leibniz to Bruno see his *Opera Omnia*, 1708, iii, 146f: he is noting Bruno as anticipating Descartes on vortices.

swinging the whole body of ordered thinking in a materialist direction without losing what has been valuable in the distinctions and constructions of tradition. I have stressed the debt that a work like *Cause* owes to Nicholas of Cusa; but we miss its whole point unless we see it also as one long polemic against Nicholas, a steady reversal of the latter's positions: finding in matter the resolutions which Nicholas found in God, and driving all providentiality out of the universe. Bruno finds the point of union in matter, Nicholas in God.

7. Bruno and Science

IT is necessary to make the above criticisms. But we must recognise that the vital element in Bruno's thought already provides the basis for them. The following passage from *On the Infinite Universe* shows how he wanted to embody his principle of the unity-of-opposites in actual process, and also how he realised that his philosophy turned the prevailing idealisms upside-down.

Fracastoro. On this diversity and opposition depend order, symmetry, complexion, peace, concord, composition and life. So that the worlds are composed of contraries, of which some, such as earth and water, live and grow by help of their contraries, such as the fiery suns. This I think was the meaning of the sage who declared that God creates harmony out of sublime contraries; and of that other who believed this whole universe to owe existence to the strife of the concordant and the love of the opposed.

Burchio. In this way you would put the world upside-down.

Frac. Would you consider a man to do ill, if he upset a world which was already upside-down?

Burch. Would you then render vain all efforts, study and labours on such works as *De Physico auditu* and *De caelo et mondo* wherein so many great commentators, paraphrasers, glossers, compilers, epitomisers, scholiasts, translators, questioners and logicians have puzzled their brains? On which profound doctors, subtle, golden, exalted, inexpugnable, irrefragable, angelic, seraphic, cherubic and divine, have established their foundation?

Frac. Add the stonebreakers, the rocksplitters, hornfooted high-kickers [asses]. Add also the deep seers, Palladian knowalls, the Olympians, the firmamenticians, celestial empirics, loud thunderers.

Burch. Should we cast them all out at your suggestion into a cess-pool? The world will indeed be ruled well if the speculations of so many and such worthy philosophers are to be cast aside and despised.

Frac. It would not be right to deprive the asses of their fodder and want them to adopt our own tastes. Talent and intellect vary no less than temperaments and stomachs.

Burch. You maintain that Plato is an ignorant fellow, Aristotle an ass, and their followers insensate, stupid, and fanatical?

Frac. My son, I do not say these are foals and those asses, these little monkeys and those great baboons, as you would have me do. As I told you from the first, I regard them as earth's heroes. But I do not wish to believe them without cause, nor to accept those propositions whose antitheses (as you would have understood if you were not both blind and deaf) are so compellingly true.

Burch. Who then shall judge?

Frac. Every well-regulated mind and alert judgment.[1]

We may note how here as elsewhere Bruno appeals from the expert to the common man who can use his mind. This democratic atti-tude follows necessarily from his rejection of authority.

He expounds the same positions in *The Expulsion*, showing that he wants his dialectic to be applied to every aspect of life:

The beginning, middle, and end of the birth, growth, and perfection of whatever we behold is from contraries, by contraries, and to contraries; and wherever contrariety is, there is action and reaction, there is motion, diversity, multitude, and order, there are degrees, succession and vicissitude. (I, i)

He is there dealing with morality.

We must also note that his whole theory of Magic is concerned with the problem of change and transformation, and the function of opposites in bringing about a new unity. He uses the term magic to cover the scientific effort to grapple with the unknown, *e.g.* with such matters as action and reaction at a distance.

Magic is in substance the possibility that we can acquire of foreseeing and of controlling the passages that come about from one species to another in the becoming of beings. That is why it is defined as a know-ledge of the comprehensive behaviour of things, through which, given

[1] Based on D. Singer's version, 323–5. The sages: Nicholas of Cusa (though pseudo-Denys says the same), and Heraclitus (see Aristotle, *Nicom. Ethics*, viii, 2, 1155b, 5f). For turning-upside-down: Badaloni, 242: 'The *Spaccio* up-ends the terms of traditional humanism; the *Degli Eroici* up-ends Platonism. . . .'

the particular case, it can be seen in the light of the normal behaviour of nature. Nature appears as a vast ocean. Its inner energy begets life as the waters of the sea take various shapes under the force that constrains them; the difference lies in the fact that movement of things can be controlled and foreseen by man.[1]

That was why Bruno used the term magic for the grasping of the point where united opposites meet.

He stressed the need for observation and experiment. 'Why turn to vain fancies when there is experience itself to teach us.' Before Bacon he declared, 'By induction we are made rich in spirit,' and added, 'If the road of investigation is open, to attain the truth it is only necessary to hold fast to nature.' 'He who impedes nature is impious and insane.'

Amid many confused suggestions, he often intuits important lines of inquiry. He points to the expansive force of steam. He dreams of a triangular instrument for determining degrees of latitude. In mathematics he states that we must assume a physical unit which is not to be appreciated by sense any more than is a true sphere.[2] He argues that there are no perfect geometrical forms in nature, since there is a ceaseless exodus and influx of the particles in every material body. He comes near Galileo's law that in rotary motion the direction of the axis remains parallel to itself. Before Galileo and Newton had confirmed the idea, he held that the earth is not the heaviest thing in nature where worlds move securely through space (by their own intrinsic energy, he thought). In 1584 he held the sun to be a solid metallic body, but in *De Immenso* he conceived of its light and heat as produced by chemical changes in the liquid parts of its body; the incessant inner commotion due to these chemical changes caused the sun's rotation, and the

---

[1] Badaloni, 109; cf. Corsano, 281–3 who however, tries to link Bruno's magic with the emotions shared by those who have a religious faith in common. Bruno's magic is concerned with objective causes; it is concerned with the link between the world-soul and the individuals. The link, *vincolo*, is an element of action. Magic is that by which reason grasps, in the changing world of time, the constancy of its appearances: cf. *Degli Eroici* where *magia* is the supreme wisdom whereby the thinker gains consciousness of the changing course of things and so can direct action with prevision. 'The magical science is the transposition on the practical plane of the Brunonian vision of the objective behaviour of reality,' Badaloni, 174; see 251f for the theory of incantation and its political relations.

[2] His mathematics are often derided, but little work has been done on them. The one exception is Xenia Atanassievitch's *La Doctrine Metaphysique et Géometrique de Bruno*, 1923, which is very respectful; she analyses his *Triple Minimum* and his position as a founder of discrete geometry.

scintillation of the stars was due to rapidity of rotation, whereas the effect was not observed in planets which merely reflected light. All planetary life in any sidereal system is derived from the light and heat of its central sun. There is no absolute lightness or weight in things, as Aristotle taught, but they have a certain impetus towards or away from one another. The sun moves on its axis and varies its position among the stars, of which it is one. The earth's atmosphere rotates with it. He sees that geologically natural forces are in constant operation and produce very slow changes in land and sea. He thought 'a countless multitude of creatures live not only in us but in all composite things.' He surmised that other suns would have planets. Above all, his thinking throughout presupposes the universal rule of scientific law and the conservation of matter-energy.

This sort of citation could be multiplied. Even when his ideas are wrong or only right in part, they show how acutely he was thinking about the new situation he had opened up. Some 19th-century commentators stressed the strong evolutionary element in his thinking:

perpetuity of matter and of force; continuity of slight variations or alterations which, across the immensity of time, are expressed in a more or less marked differentiation; integration of finality [purpose] in the mechanism through the principle of the survival of the 'best-adapted' beings; close relation binding all animated beings together and reposing on their substantial identity; natural transition from the homogeneous to the heterogeneous, from the indistinct, from the simple to the more and more complex compound....[1]

All that is present in his work; but we must beware of calling it evolutionist. Bruno is building on Neoplatonist ideas of the unity and interrelation of all being, and his concept of absolute substance prevents him from releasing his ideas in a clear evolutionary direction. However he has a strong sense of organic being; for instance he sees that if a snake were changed into a man, it would have a man's consciousness. And we can say that his deep sense of organic relationship would at once have filled out the Epicurean picture of growth drawn from Lucretius, and would have moved rapidly

---

[1] Mondolfo summarised by Charbonnel, *Pensée*, 548. Troilo also stresses the evolutionary aspect, and Brünnhofer, *G. B.'s Lehre vom Kleinsten als die Quelle der pratabilirten Harmonie von Leibniz*, 1890, 174ff. Note stress Bruno lays on the formation of the hand in the development of the embryo: see *Op. Ital.*, ii, 275f, and Appendix 5 here.

towards a true concept of evolution, if he had been able to jettison his absolute matter.

But in the last resort it is not any particular anticipations of later scientific work that matter in Bruno. What matters is the whole outlook and direction of his thinking: his extreme mobility of mind, his steady elimination of all idealist notions of imposed purpose or finality in the movement and growth of things, his joyous conviction of having emerged from a small, closed, and fabricated system that has darkened the spirits of men, into the full and open reality, with its enormous possibilities. This makes him the first man of the modern world, the opener-up of the new scientific outlooks that steadily become the basis of the modern consciousness.

He does manage in *The Expulsion* to formulate a theory of forward progress by men, in which the existing divisions will be overthrown; and he has a sense of the development of thought as more than a mere accumulation of the details of knowledge. It is worth while indeed to look in some detail at his formulations; for they show that, while basing himself on Lucretius, he developed his own lines of emphasis; and he does so in a way that brings out the hopeless contradiction between a theory of Leisure, which could only be parasitic in his world, and the actual situation which needed an all-out effort to advance productivity. In the third dialogue of *The Expulsion*, Leisure (*Ocio*) appeals to the original paradise of the Age of Gold, when the products of the earth sufficed the simple beings who had not dispersed their energies in ambitious enterprises and who awaited death in their old age with tranquillity. But Care (*Sollecitudine*) intervened with vain Glory, Pride, and Violence to trouble the Eden. Men shared out the earth; individual property was born. Through trade and industry, resources grew monopolised and flagrant injustices resulted. Concord gave way to division; the right of the stronger became the law of the world, and the world was torn by economic rivalries as much as by wars. (Bruno here, as in several other places, makes a strong attack on colonial expansion and conquest, with the resulting enslavements and corruptions of native peoples.) The different religions played their part in the general process of division and fratricidal conflict.

Momus and Jupiter reply, without disputing Leisure's historical analysis of the fall into social division and injustice, that men have been given reason and hands for action, to create new ways and organisations, to show their inventive faculties, by using their intelligence and freedom. Without activity all human powers remain dead. Our ancestors in the Age of Gold were not more virtuous than today's animals. 'Perhaps even, they were more stupid than many of the latter.' The ardent zeal, the desire to satisfy spiritual desires, the magnificent emulation which has driven men towards the idea of perfection: there are the levers that have progressively brought them into a higher civilisation. The obstacles to be overcome, the new needs putting their ingenuity to the test and causing new discoveries, in short the imperious pressures of necessity have obliged successive generations to multiply prodigies in the domains of art and science. Leisure is a good thing as the reward and aftermath of toil; but as an ideal in itself it is bad. (Bruno uses this point to launch an attack on monasticism.) Morality can draw its sanctions only from practical activity. Thus to the dream of a communal golden age Bruno opposes the reality of a community of socially valuable work; and he sees the struggle in society as between those who belong to this community, and those who exist parasitically through power, privilege, and property.

Where he goes far beyond Lucretius is in stressing class-division and productive activity as forces in history.[1] Indeed, he here stands on his own. He still uses the term contemplation for philosophic activity; but by his attacks on metaphysical abstractions he removes all passive attitudes. Contemplation is simply the exercise of thought in the service of mankind, and to be effective it must be linked at all points with activity and practical application. The second dialogue of *The Expulsion* includes a long and passionate insistence on the supreme value of activity and work. Bruno's test is always social value; and there is no contradiction between this test and the glorification of the 'heroic transports' of the bold and lonely thinkers, which he repeats with such heady eloquence. His thought:

is revolutionary... because it wants to put an end to the alienation of the World, the Mind, and the Truth. And such a conclusion, desired and announced by Bruno, signifies that philosophy, no longer alienated but returned in all things to itself, by contemplating (in the Brunian

[1] It is worth noting that at one point the argument in *The Expulsion* is interrupted. Mercury has been sent to appease a popular sedition that has broken out in Naples. Gentile holds that this is the uprising that protested in May 1547, the year of Bruno's birth, against the introduction of the Spanish Inquisition; Badaloni thinks the reference is to later events and to the fundamental fact of social conflict at Naples.

sense) the world, not only interprets it, but, whether on the theoretical level, or on the ethical and historical, can and must change it. (Troilo)[1]

His philosophy is at all points attuned to what he feels the main objective of history:

The usurpers are worse than grubs, caterpillars, or destroying locusts, and should be treated accordingly....

No institution or law ought to be approved or accepted which does not tend to the highest end: the direction of our minds and reform of our natures so that they produce fruit necessary or useful for human intercourse (*Expulsion*).

Bruno attempts to work out in both the philosophic (scientific) and social spheres a dialectical resolution of the concepts of necessity and freedom. While glorying in a universe of pervasive law, he seeks to define how the consciousness of necessity begets freedom—while at the same time he opposes the rule by Fortune (ultimately money-power, money as an abstract force, as he shows in the *Candelaio*) to the liberations gained by identifying oneself with Nature (law and reason) in its totality. There is a long and deep struggle in his thought around these points, which I can here only thus briefly indicate.[2]

He is the great prophet of the advent of science as the new central force in life. He realises with every fibre of his being that the religious formulations are doomed and that men must fully absorb all the implications of scientific method and discovery. But again here the matter is not so simple as it might seem at first glance. On the one hand Bruno's thought is in accord with the new

[1] Troilo, *Prospetto*, 557. He stresses the popular character of B.'s positions. There are many points of an implied historical attitude in B. (in the same way as there are implied evolutionary attitudes): *e.g.* the fact that for him the supreme philosophic realisations imply an active relationship to a real and concrete (historical) situation, and so on.

[2] Badaloni 157ff for discussion of Bruno's social relations, esp. 172f on Necessity; 188, 250, his notion of the State; 263ff; Machiavelli, 162, 204f. Many of the limitations of Bruno's thought are thus clarified. It seems to me that he remains at root true to the small-producer level, the craftsman; hence his concrete stress on work and on the hand. But the coming expansion that he intuits means the destruction of that level. Hence an inner conflict which in many ways leads on into William Morris. Bruno's historical moment is that when it seemed possible for the free-thinker to capture the directing groups of the new national states (Elizabeth, Henri, etc); but in fact the balances to which he looks are illusory and are to give way rapidly to violent social, political, religious, and economic conflicts. In all respects B. is too extreme for the bourgeois forces of which he is in one sense the prophet.

developments soon to be started off by Galileo, Gassendi, Descartes, Newton, and the others, on the ground he has cleared. His matter with its lack of all essential quality and with its comprehensible constancies is the sphere which the scientists from Galileo onwards to the nuclear physicists were to explore with their purely quantitative methods of analysis. What is metaphysical in Bruno's system thus corresponds to the needs of mechanist science in the coming centuries. Yet his main bias is against mechanism; what he wants is an integrative science such as we have not yet arrived at. To examine this aspect of his thinking would lead us too far into difficult issues; but it is necessary to point out that while the metaphysical issues that he opens up lead on to the line of thinkers running from Spinoza to Hegel, his unitary-materialist side is only now becoming understandable.

One confusing point is that his integrative ideas are often entangled with animist survivals. Thus, his insistence on the universe as throughout organic derives from primitive animist ideas; but nowadays with the breaking-down of the divisions between organic and inorganic Bruno might argue that, however much we need the notion of a dialectical leap between the two levels, there is a problem of unity here that is not so easily settled. The full analysis of Bruno's ideas on nature and the universe has not yet been made; perhaps it cannot yet be made. But we may claim that if from one angle he is the great prophet of the coming (mechanist) scientific break-through, from another angle he looks to a fully dialectical and integrative approach, which is only now on the edge of becoming possible. He is therefore also the prophet of a development in scientific method which is yet to come. His meanings are not exhausted.

A word about his style. His poems hold a high place among the long didactive exposition in Latin verse of the Renascence; but though they have forceful passages and are essential to the full working-out of his thought, they cannot be compared with the Italian works as expressions of his rich and complex personality. The dialogues are not high works of art as Plato's are, in which the speakers keep their diverse characters and are dialectically related. But the conversational form keeps a freshness, an impact, which is lacking in Bruno's direct statements; and there is a genuine dialectical movement in the expression of thought. *Cause* is the best example of this. Bruno continually musters the various medieval positions, brings forward analytic differentiations, and then resolves the oppositions in a higher unity. The comedic element is always ready to break in, as if to remind us that life irrupts on the best-regulated of arguments and has always something fresh to bring forward. Above all, we feel the actual struggle of thought; we are not merely presented with conclusions. And it is in this respect that Bruno does deserve to be put beside Plato.[1] In *The Supper* he tells us that his aim is 'a full and mighty prose, taking its own time; coming, not as of clerkly art, but flowing and strong as are the waters of a mighty current.'

8. His Influence

THE most important influence that Bruno directly exerted was on Spinoza, through whom certain important aspects of his unitary thinking entered the main stream of European philosophy. Spinoza never mentions Bruno, but the relationship cannot be doubted. Kepler reproached Galileo for paying no tribute to Bruno, but again the relationship cannot be doubted. Presumably Galileo, fighting a hard enough battle with the Church, did not want to make things worse by admitting any link with a heretic burnt at the stake. Through Kepler and Galileo Bruno's cosmological ideas entered the main stream of science.[2]

In England his work was known to Hariot and other astronomers, to Gilbert and Bacon. The latter could not be expected to

[1] It is significant that in the last dialogue of *Cause*, where the argument comes to rest on absolute substance, we get long harangues; the dialectical leaven disappears, to revive near the end with the discussion of opposites. In *The Supper* (*Proem. Epistle*) he sets out his stylistic principle of diversity, of natural richness, in unity. Looking at the details of a landscape, the various beasts and birds and so on, 'one criticises, and finally centres one's attention on the main subject.' See Corsano, 1940, ch. iv, 2, for the language and style of the dialogues.

[2] Descartes probably borrowed many arguments from Bruno, *e.g.* his treatment of the relation of finite to infinite substances. Bruno had stressed the need for a readiness to doubt everything: *De min.*, i, 1. For Bruno and Descartes' vortices, Badaloni (a) 298–300. In general: Badaloni (a) and (b), and Salvestrini.

grasp Bruno's tumultuous and dialectical thought in anything like its fullness, although he seems generally influenced by it. However Bruno had considerable effect on the English scientific and literary world, as shown by Bruce and Burton; the idea of a moon-journey was taken from him by Godwin, Wilkins, and others; Spenser perhaps was thinking of Bruno in the introduction to Book II of *The Faerie Queene*. The discussion on immortality in the latter part of the first version of Sidney's *Arcadia* is based on Bruno; but the writer whom he most powerfully affected was the young Donne.[1] *The Expulsion* was the book that had most effect in England. It seems to have influenced Spenser in his Two Cantoes of Mutability. Thomas Carew wrote a masque *Coelum Brittanicum*, played before Charles and Henrietta Maria in 1633, which was based on it; and it was prized by the English deists in the early 18th century, when W. Morehead in 1713 published a translation—the first translation of any of Bruno's works in any language.

It is rare however to find a friendly discussion of Bruno in the 17th century; Kepler is the exception. But this does not mean that Bruno was not well known by all the advanced thinkers. Nobody wanted to cite a man burned at the stake, who was considered a violent atheist. After the death of Henri IV an offensive against the freethinkers, the *libertins*, set in; and the importance that the reaction gave to combating Bruno's ideas can be seen in the work of P. M. Mersenne: his *L'Impiété des Déistes, Athées et Libertins*, 1624. The second part returned to the attack in a Refutation of the Dialogues of Bruno. Mersenne particularly laments the way in which *De la Causa* is widely read. But apart from the needs of prudence, the new thinkers did not want to emulate Bruno's unitary method which insisted on relating thought to action and following ruthlessly out the implications of every idea. Galileo restricted his views in part out of caution, but also because he was the first full-fledged example of the scientist of the new mechanistic era. He did not want to relate thought and life; he wanted to concentrate on his own particular line of narrow though important inquiry. Descartes did not want any head-on collision with authority; the division of mind and body was of the essence of his thinking; and

---

[1] See Appendix 4. No one has noted the close relation of Bruno and Donne (though as far back as June 20th 1936 I wrote a letter in the *T.L.S.* about it: see further July 4th and 11th, D. Yates). In general: Singer, Yates, Badaloni (b). ,

thus prudence and mechanistic outlook combined to resist the full
impact of Bruno's unitary views.

Bayle's *Dictionary* gave the final abusive currency to the idea
of Bruno as an atheist; but a new approach to his work began
with the German romantic thinkers, who stressed the unitary outlook while ignoring its materialistic basis. Jacobi championed him;
Herder was interested in him; and J. F. Abel brought him to
Schiller's notice. Schelling enthusiastically took up Bruno's idealist
side; and Hegel, though repelled by his more vital trends, was
astonished at his dialectic. An important influence was on the young
Goethe. The young Coleridge too was much affected.

In the 19th century, in Italy and Germany, Bruno became a
legendary figure symbolising the struggle for emancipation. The
climax came after the liberation of Italy, when on June 9th 1889
some 30,000 people assembled to honour his monument unveiled
on the Field of Flowers. The Pope fasted and issued an address to
be read in the churches, condemning Bruno as a man of 'insincerity,
lying and perfect selfishness, intolerance of all who disagreed with
him, abject meanness and perverted ingenuity in adulation,' a
charlatan whose 'own writings condemn him of a degraded
materialism and show that he was entangled in commonplace
errors.'

The more one reads and considers Bruno's work in its totality,
the more one feels that all the major trends of European thinking
in the next three centuries are contained somewhere in it. His influence cannot be estimated by counting up the references to his
works in the 17th century; he was then more or less unmentionable
except for a polemist like Mersenne; but his work was certainly
known to Spinoza, Leibniz, Descartes, and underlay their points
of departure, their new contributions. With the 18th century he had
been lost and was rediscovered, helping to confirm or encourage,
but no longer a primary influence. It is in a way then all the more
interesting to watch, for instance, how Hegel seems regaining the
Brunonian positions on the vastly enriched new historical level, but
with a bias to the elements of self-intoxicated idealism rather than
to those of stubborn unitary integration. One feels almost that the
later developments represent a more complicated filling-out of a
script sketched by Bruno, a more expanded dramatisation of roles
through which he passed in his quest for the wholly adequate
dialectic.

The modern study of his work may be said to begin with C. Bartholmèss in 1847. During the latter part of the century valuable contributions were made by Fiorentini, Berti, Carrière, Brünnhofer, Wagner, Cantoni, Clemens, Tocco, and others. While the tendency was to stress pantheist or idealist aspects by ignoring the materialist dialectic, these writers generally saw Bruno as a great liberating force. Tocco argued for the consistency of his thought, but on the whole the idealist approach of Schelling had a devastating effect. However, with the turn of the century, a reaction against the shallowly 'progressive' positions of the 19th century led to an attempt to isolate Bruno as an individualist concerned with problems of God's immanence and the like. Gentile played an important part in distorting Bruno's ideas and attitudes; and other critics did their best to prove that he lacked all consistency and represented an eclectic hurly-burly: *e.g.* Olschki. Under the Fascist regime it became the fashion to argue that he converted philosophy irrationally into magic and theurgy.

These arguments have carried on into the postwar world: Bruno as a magician (Giusso and even Corsano); as wildly lacking continuity in his libertine ideas (Spini or Fraccori); as romantically seeking to unthrone God and put man in his place (Fenu); as setting up a purely inner cult of God (Guzzo). The attacks of Catholic apologists have not ceased, leading to the justification of the Inquisition by Mercati; Cicuttini declares that Bruno's pyre has burnt out, but 'humanity still today bears all the consequences of this thinker.'

On the other hand there has been the effort to carry on from the best of the 19th-century positions, as represented by Spaventa. Troilo, Garin, Horowitz, and others have seen the centrality of his dialectic, and Badaloni (1955) fully clarifies the materialist basis. The positions taken in this essay belong to this latter line. It seems to me that once the materialist dialectic is recognised as the core of Bruno, the other aspects fall into perspective and can be adequately understood and related to his development. Any other method leads to a one-sided confusion or leaves Bruno a cloudy pantheist with his distinctive aspects robbed of all meaning.

JACK LINDSAY

CAUSE, PRINCIPLE, AND UNITY

PREFATORY EPISTLE

Addressed to the Most Illustrious

Messire Michel de Castelnau

Seigneur of Mauvissière, Concressault, and Joinville

Chevalier of the Order of the Most Christian King, Councillor
of his Privy Council,

Captain of 50 men at arms

and Ambassador to the Most Serene Queen of England.

Most illustrious and unique Chevalier, if I direct the eyes of
thought to wonder at the longanimity, perseverance, and solicitude with
which, heaping service on service, benefit on benefit, you have over-
whelmed me, obliged me, and bound me to you, and by which you are
wont to overcome every difficulty, save me from all perils whatsoever,
and successfully conclude all your most honourable designs, I cannot
but remark how excellently appropriate to you are the noble arms
with which you adorn your terrible crest: where a liquid humour in-
flicts gentle wounds, and, falling with a constant and frequent drip,
by force of perseverance softens, hollows, masters, fractures, and
levels a compact, harsh, hard, and rugged rock.

If besides I bring to thought (omitting your other noble deeds)
how you are for me, by divine ordinance, by high providence and
predestination, a sufficient and sure defender among the unjust outrages from which I suffer (so that it is necessary for me to be a soul
truly heroic if I am not to drop my arms, yield to despair, and give
myself up in defeat to the rapid torrent of criminal imposture with
which I have been attacked in full force by the envy of the ignorant,
the presumption of sophists, the detraction of the malicious, the
murmurs of servitors, the insinuations of the mercenary, the contradictions of valets, the suspicions of fools, the apprehensions of reporters,
the zeal of hypocrites, the hatred of the barbarous, the fury of the
mob, the complaints of those nearly-touched, and the laments of those
chastised—not that there has lacked also a discourteous, maddened,
and malevolent female disdain, the false tears of which are often more
redoubtable than the most swelling waves and sternest storm of pre-
sumptions, envies, detractions, whisperings, betrayals, angers, scorns,
hates, and furies)—then you appear to me all the more a solid, stable,
and constant rock, which, rising up and revealing its head above the
swollen sea, is not frightened, moved, or shaken by the raging heaven,

47

by the dread of winter, by the violent shocks of surging waters, by the jarring tempests of wind, or by the furious breath of Aquilo, but rather grows green afresh, recovers its sides with a like substance, and is once more habited. You, endowed with double virtue, through the liquid and gentle drippings are made most powerful, the rough and tempestuous waves most impotent; through which the lordly stone is rendered so weak against the slight drops and the afflicted stone rises up so strong against the billows—you are at the same time the sure and peaceful haven for the true Muses and the ruinous crag against which peters out and fails the sham ammunition of the impetuous schemes of hostile sails.

I then, whom no man has ever been able to accuse of ingratitude or abuse for discourtesy, I against whom no one can justly make complaints, I, hated by the stupid, slighted by the base, blamed by the ignoble, vituperated by the rascals and persecuted by the brutish kind, I, loved by the sage, admired by the learned, magnified by the great, esteemed by the mighty, and favoured by the gods, I who have gained such favour as to be received by you, nourished, defended, liberated, set in safety, sheltered in a haven, like one who has escaped through you from a great and perilous tempest, I consecrate to you this anchor, these shrouds, these worn-out sails, and these wares so dear to me and to the future world more precious yet, in order that, thanks to you, they may not founder in the iniquitous and turbulent Ocean, my foe. Hung up in the sacred temple of Fame, by their power against the impudence of ignorance and the voracity of time, they will provide eternal witness of your unconquerable favour, so that the world may know of this noble and divine offspring, inspired by high intelligence, conceived by tempered sense, and brought forth by the Nolan Muse. Through your aid it has not perished in its swaddling-clothes, but promises to live while this earth with its surface of life goes turning round in the eternal sight of the other shining stars.

Here then is that species of philosophy in which surely and truly is found what is vainly sought in the contrary and diverse ones. And first of all I present to you, in a brief summary of five dialogues, all that seems relevant to the real contemplation of cause, principle, and unity.

Argument of the first dialogue

Here you have an apology or an I-don't-know-what, on the five dialogues of *The Ash-Wednesday Supper*, etc.

Argument of the second dialogue

Here you have first the reason for the difficulty of such cognition: the knowledge of how far the knowable object is removed from the cognitive power.

Second, in what mode, and how far, that which has in it cause and principle comes to clarify the principle and cause.

Third, how far the cognition of the universe's substance helps us to grasp that on which it depends.

Fourth, by what means and what road we try in a particular sense to know the first principle.

Fifth, the difference and concordance, identity and diversity, between the meaning of this term *cause* and this term *principle*.

Sixth, what is the cause that is divided into efficient, formal, and final; the many modes of designating the efficient cause and the many lines of thought by which it is conceived; how this efficient cause is in some ways intrinsic to natural things, as being nature itself, and how in some ways it is extrinsic to them; how the formal cause is united with the efficient and how the efficient works through it, and how the same formal cause is raised up by the efficient from the womb of matter; how the efficient and the form coincide in a subject and principle, and how the one cause is distinct from the other.

Seventh, the difference between the universal formal cause (a soul through which the infinite universe, as infinite, is animated, not positively but negatively) and the particular formal cause, multipliable and multiplied to infinity, which, insofar as it is in a more general and superior subject, is by that much more perfect; whence the great animals such as stars should in a grand comparison be esteemed most divine, *i.e.* most intelligent, without error, and acting without defect.

Eighth, that the first and principal natural form, formal principle and efficient nature, is the soul of the universe: which is the principle of life, vegetation, and sense in all things that live, vegetate, and feel. And further, by way of conclusion, that it is unworthy of a rational subject to believe that the universe and its principal bodies are inanimate, since from the parts and residues of these bodies derive the animals that we call most perfect.

Ninth, that there is nothing whatever so defective, broken down, diminished, imperfect, which, from its ownership of the formal principle, does not similarly own a soul, even when it lacks the kind of external activity that we call animal. And we conclude, with Pythagoras and others, who have not opened their eyes in vain, that an immense spirit, according to diverse manners and degrees, fills out and contains the whole.

Tenth, it is shown intelligibly that the spirit exists permanently together with matter, which the Babylonians and Persians called shadow, and that since both these are indissoluble, it is impossible at any point that anything should be corrupted or perish insofar as substance is concerned, though, according to certain accidents, everything changes its aspect and is transmuted into one or another composition, through one or another disposition, abandoning and taking up again one being or another in turn.

Eleventh, that the Aristotelians, Platonists, and other sophists have not recognised the substance of things; and it is clearly demonstrated that in natural things (apart from matter) what we call substance is nothing but the merest accident; and that the cognition of true form yields us the true notion of what life is and what death is; and that once the vain and childish terror of death is dissipated, we know in part the felicity that is brought by our contemplation, according to the fundamentals of our philosophy: seeing that it destroys the gloomy veil of idiot belief about the Ogre and greedy Charon, by which all that is sweetest in our life is ravished and poisoned.

Twelfth, form is distinguished, not according to its substantial nature, through which it is one, but according to the acts and the exercises of the facultative potencies and the specific degrees of being that it begets.

Thirteenth, the true definitive basis of the formal principle is established: how form is a perfect species, distinct in matter, according to the accidental dispositions which depend on material form—this form consisting, for example, of diverse degrees and dispositions of active and passive qualities. We see how form is variable and how it is invariable; how it defines and limits matter and how it is defined and limited by it.

Finally, it is shown by a similitude, adapted to the vulgar sense how this form, this soul, can be all in all and in any part whatever of the whole.

Argument of the third dialogue

Here (after having previously spoken of form, which has more the nature of cause than of principle) we proceed to the consideration of matter, which is regarded as having more the nature of principle and element than of cause. Ignoring the preambles at the outset, we come first to the demonstration that David of Dinant was not misguided in taking matter as a most excellent and divine thing.

Second, how, with the various roads of philosophising, we can take various views of matter, though in truth there is a single primary and absolute matter; since it is realised in various degrees or is hidden under various species, we each can take it diversely according to the viewpoints that are appropriate to our outlook, just as number is treated by the arithmetician purely and simply, by the musician harmonically, by the cabalist symbolically, by other fools and other sages in their own ways.

Third, the meaning of the word *matter* is brought out through the difference and likeness between the natural and the artificial subject.

Fourth, proposals are made how the obstinate are to be got rid of and how far we should feel obligation to reply and argue.

Fifth, from the true nature of matter it is deduced that no substantial form loses its being; and a forceful proof is offered that the Peripaticians and the other vulgarising philosophers, though they use the term substantial form, have known no other substance than matter.

Sixth, we arrive at a constant formal principle, just as a constant material principle has been recognised; and find that with the diversity of dispositions that exist in matter, the formal principle is transferred to the multiform configuration of diverse species and individuals; and we show how it has happened that some men, bred in the Peripatetic school, have not wanted to recognise any other substance than matter.

Seventh, why it is necessary for reason to distinguish matter from form, potency from act; then is repeated what was set out in the second section: how the subject and principle of natural things can be diversely understood by the various modes of philosophising without incurring blame, but more usefully according to natural and magical modes, more variously according to mathematical and rational modes —especially if these conform to the rule and operation of reason in such a [formalised] way that in the end nothing worth while is realised in act through them and no fruits of practice are gained, without which all contemplation must be estimated as useless.

Eighth, two lines of thought with which it is usual to consider matter are set out: as potency or as subject. And beginning with the first line, we differentiate matter into active and passive; and then, in a certain way, we bring it back to unity.

Ninth, we deduce from the previous section how the supreme and divine is all that it can be, the universe is all that it can be, and particular things are not all that they can be.

Tenth, as a result of this deduction, an explanation, profoundly brief and evident, is given for the existence in nature of vices, monstrosities, corruption, and death.

Eleventh, in what way the universe is in none and in all of its parts: with a resulting excellent contemplation of divinity.

Twelfth, why it comes about that the intellect cannot grasp this absolute act and this absolute potency.

Thirteenth, we conclude with the excellence of matter, which coincides with form as potency coincides with act.

Finally, as much from this conclusion that potency coincides with act and the universe is all that it can be, as well as for other reasons, we decide that all is one.

Argument of the fourth dialogue

After having in the third dialogue considered matter in so far as it is potency, in the fourth we consider it in so far as it is a subject.

First, with Poliinnician diversions, we bring out the meaning of matter according to the vulgar principles of some Platonists as well as of all the Peripatetics.

Second, reasoning out *iuxta* [according to] correct principles, we show that one is the matter of both corporeal and incorporeal things, for several reasons. The first reason is drawn from the potency found in the same genus; the second, from the reason of a certain proportional analogy between corporeal and incorporeal, absolute and contracted; the third, from the order and ladder of nature, which goes up to a first [principle] completing or comprehending all; the fourth, from the fact that there must be something indistinct before matter becomes distinguished into corporeal and incorporeal—something that comes to be represented by the supreme genus of the category; the fifth, from the fact that there must be a basis shared by the intelligible and the sensible, and so there must be [one shared] by the subject of sensibility [and that of intelligibility]; the sixth, from the fact that the being of matter is independent of the being of body, and so with as much reason we can apply this position to incorporeal as to corporeal things;

the seventh, from the order ranging from higher to lower which is found in substances, since, where such an order exists, there is presupposed and understood a certain communion, which, in matter, turns out to be that which is always expressed as the genus (just as form is expressed by the specific difference); the eighth, from a principle extraneous but conceded by many; the ninth, from the plurality of species attributed to the intelligible world; the tenth, from the likeness and concordance of the three worlds of metaphysics, physics, and logic; the eleventh, from the fact that all number, diversity, order, beauty, and ornament are connected with matter.

Third, four opposing arguments are briefly reported and answered.

Fourth, there are shown the diversities of nature existing between this and that matter, and how matter in incorporeal things coincides with act, and how all sorts of dimensions exist in matter and all qualities are comprehended in form.

Fifth, that no sage has ever said that forms are received by matter as from outside, but that matter, sending them out as from her bosom, produces them from within. Hence it is not a *prope nihil*, an almost-nothing, a bare and pure potency, if all forms are as if contained in it, and through it by virtue of the efficient cause (which can even be indistinguishable from it in its being) produced and brought forth; they have no other reasons of actual existence in sensible and explicit being than by accidental existence, for all that appears and is made manifest by accidents based on dimensions is pure accident; only substance remains always undivided and coincident with undivided matter. Hence it is evident that from explication we cannot obtain other than accidents and so the substantial differences are hidden, as Aristotle said, constrained by the truth. As a result if we want to think rightly, we can rightly infer that one is the uniform substance, one is truth and being: revealing itself in innumerable circumstances and individual cases and appearing in so many and such varied states.

Sixth, how far wide of all reason is what Aristotle and his like understand of matter as being in potency—which certainly is not null; for as they themselves admit, matter is so permanent that it never changes or varies its being, though linked with it is every variety and mutation, and that which is, coming after it has been able to be, is always (still according to these men) composite.

Seventh, the question of matter's appetite is dealt with and it is shown how vain is the effort to define matter in such terms without getting away from the reasons (drawn from the principles and suppositions) of those same men who like to proclaim it the daughter of privation and comparable to the insatiable greed of the ardent female.

Argument of the fifth dialogue

In this dialogue, which deals specially with unity, there is completed the basis of the edifice of all cognition natural and divine. Here, first, we bring forward the concept of the coincidence of matter and form, potency and act, so that being, logically divided into what it is and what it can be, is seen as physically [*i.e.* really] undivided, indistinct, and one; and this being is at one and the same time infinite, immobile, indivisible, without difference of whole or parts, principle and principled.

Second, that in the One there is no difference between century and year, year and moment, span and furlong, furlong and mile, and that in their essence this and that specific being are not distinguished; hence there is no number in the universe and the universe is one.

Third, that in infinity point is not differentiated from body, for potency is not one thing and act another; if the point can extend into length, the line into breadth, the surface into depth, then the point is long, the line is broad, the surface is deep; and since everything is long, broad, and deep they are all one and the same, and the universe is all centre and all circumference.

Fourth, from the fact that Jove (as he is called) is more intimately in all than the form of all can be imagined there (because he is the essence through which all that exists has being; and as he is in all, everything possesses the whole more intimately than its own form) it is inferred that everything is in everything and in consequence all is one.

Fifth, a reply is made to the doubt which asks why all particular things change and why the particular matters, to receive this or that being, are constrained to this or that form; and it is shown how in multiplicity there is unity and in unity multiplicity, and how being is many-moded and multi-unique, and in the last resort is one in substance and truth.

Sixth, it is brought out whence proceed this difference and this number [of particular things], and that they are not being but are of being and relative to it.

Seventh, it is noted that who has found this one (I mean the reason of this unity) has found that key without which it is impossible to have access to the true contemplation of nature.

Eighth, in a new contemplation, it is repeated that the one, infinity, being, that which is in all, is that which is everywhere, indeed is the very *ubique*, and that thus the infinite dimension, since it is not magnitude, coincides with the individual, just as the infinite multitude, since it is not number, coincides with unity.

Ninth, how the infinite is not made of part on part, whatever is the case in the unfolded universe; hence all that we see of diversity and difference is only a diverse and different face of the same substance.

Tenth, how in the two extremes that are spoken of at the extremity of nature's ladder, we must contemplate, not two principles, but one; not two beings, but one; not two and various contraries, but a concordant and identical one. Height is there depth, the abyss is inaccessible light, darkness is clarity, the great is the small, the confused is the distinct, discord is friendship, the divisible is the undivided, the atom is immensity; and inversely.

Eleventh, how certain geometrical terms such as point and unit are used to carry us on to the contemplation of being and unity, but are not by themselves capable of expressing them. That is why Pythagoras, Parmenides, Platon should not be stupidly interpreted according to the pedantic criticism of Aristotle.

Twelfth, from the fact that substance, being, is distinct from quality, measure, and number, we infer that substance is one and undivided in the whole and in any particular thing.

Thirteenth, there are introduced the signs and verifications through which [we see how] contraries truly coincide, being born of a single principle and being one in truth and substance, which, after being mathematically considered, is finalised from a physical aspect.

There then, most illustrious Seigneur, you see from what point it is necessary to emerge before attempting to enter into the most special and appropriate cognition of things. Here, as in the right seeds, is contained and implicated the host of natural science's conclusions. Hence derive the interrelation, disposition, and order of the speculative sciences. Without this introduction in vain one attempts, presses in, makes a start. Accept then with a thankful mind this principle, this unity, this source, this head, that its progeny and product may be further stirred as to emerge and move forward, and its rivers and streams be diffused more widely, their number successively multiplied and its members disposed on all sides—until, with the ending of night in its drowsy veil and tenebrous mantle, the clear Titan, parent of the divine Muses, adorned with his family, surrounded by his eternal court, banishes the nocturnal torches, brightens the world with a new day, and sends out again the triumphal chariot from the rosy bosom of this delightful Aurora. *Vale.*

Giordano the Nolan to the Principle of the Universe

Though cleaving to the watery swoln expanse,
let him leave, Titan, Lethaean origins
and seek the stars. You wandering orbs in your courses
I hasten, your twin, if you've unlocked the way.
Yet your gyres grant me uprushing through the void
to find the double doors of sleep thrown wide.
What greedy time for long has hugged obscured
let me now rescue from the heavy dark.
Frail mind, what holds you back? Haste to your birth,
however unworthy the age for what you offer.
While the flux of shadows blurs the earths, your crest
raise, our Olympus, into the clear heavens.

To his Own Spirit

Though deeply rooted you are held by earth,
Mount, lift your summit to the stars in strength.
A kindred force from the height of things is calling,
Mind, making you the bound twixt hell and heaven.

Maintain your rights, lest, sinking to the depths,
assailed, you drown in Acheron's black waters.
Rather go soaring, probing nature's lairs;
For, at God's touch, you'll be a blaze of fire.

To Time

Old Man, you are slow and fast, you open and close,
should we then call you good or call you evil?
You are stingy and prodigal; what you offer, you take;
where you stood as parent you'll as murderer stand.
What comes from your bowels, into your bowels goes.
What's born from your bosom is champed between
    your jaws.
You make all things and wreck them. Then I'm right
to call you good and call you evil, both?
Yet where in rage with cruel stroke you spoil
cease threatening to outstretch that scythe of yours,
where trodden foot-prints of black Chaos show
do not seem good, do not seem evil, either.

Of Love

Through you O Love I see the high truth plain.
You open the doors of diamond and deep night.
Through eyes the godhead enters; and from sight
is born and lives, is fed, holds endless reign.
How much earth, heaven and hell contain, he bares;
true images of absent things he shows;
regathers strength and driving on, with blows,
reveals what's hidden, as the heart he tears.
Then hear, base crowd, the truth which I repeat.
Stretch out your ears to words that own no cheat.
Open, if so you can, mad squinting eyes.
You call him child, so slight and small your mind;
because you veer so fast, you think he flies;
and seeing nothing, you must call him blind.

Cause, principle, eternal unity,
on which all being, motion and life depend:
in length, in breadth, in depth your powers extend
as far as heaven and earth and hell may be—
with sense, with reason, and with spirit I've seen
that reckoning, measure and act can't comprehend
the force, the number and mass, which, with no end,
pass all that's low or high or set between.

3+

Blind error, greedy time, and cruel fate,
deaf envy, menial fury, evil zeal,
strange boldness, impious wit, and heart of hate,
are not enough to darken air and sky,
enough to hang before my eyes a veil
or cut them from my beautiful sun on high.[1]

[1] The first three poems are in Latin; the pair of sonnets, in Italian.

FIRST DIALOGUE

SPEAKERS: *Eliotropio, Filoteo, Armesso*

Eli. It's as with convicts grown used to the gloom: when they are freed from the dungeon of some dark tower and go out into the daylight. In the same way, many men who've been trained in vulgar philosophy, and others as well, become scared and bewildered: unable to sustain the new sunlight of your clear concepts, they are thoroughly disturbed.

Fil. The fault is not in the light, but in the sight. The more beautiful and excellent the sun, the more detestable and harshly unwelcome will it be to the eyes of night-witches.

Eli. The enterprise you've undertaken, Filoteo, is difficult, rare, and singular. For you want to bring us up out of the blind abyss and lead us into the open, tranquil, and serene aspect of the stars, which we see scattered about in such lovely variety on the cerulean mantle of the heavens. Although to men alone you hold out the helping hand of your charitable zeal, the reactions of the ungrateful against you will be as diverse as are the creatures that the benign earth brings forth and nourishes in her maternal and ample bosom. For it's a fact that the human species in its individuals reveals the variety of all the other species put together. Each individual comprises the whole lot more expressly than do the individuals of the other species.

That's why some persons will have scarcely sniffed at the fresh air, like dazzled moles, before they'll be scratching away at the earth and seeking again their native dark lairs. Others, like night-owls, will have no sooner glimpsed the rosy messenger of the sun come up in the shining East than immediately screwing up their weak eyes they'll feel themselves drawn back slinking to their dim retreats. All the creatures, banished from the aspect of the celestial lights and destined to the eternal prison-cages, the ditches and caverns of Pluto—recalled by the terrifying horn of Alecto—will spread their wings and direct their headlong course towards their homes.

But the creatures born to look upon the sun, arriving at the end of hateful night, will thank the goodness of heaven and, preparing to receive in the rounded crystal of their eyes the rays they have so desired and hoped-for, will adore the East with an applause of heart, voice, and hand, which has long gone out of fashion. And when the delightful Titan, from the golden balcony of the East, has sent out the fiery chargers and broken the sleepy silence of the damp night, the men will discourse together, the docile, harmless, and simple flocks of sheep will bleat, the horned herds under the care of coarse bumpkins will bellow, the mounts of Silenus [the asses] will bray on behalf of the hard-pressed gods to put panic into the giants more stupid than themselves. Wallowing in their beds of slime, the tusked swine will deafen us with their importunate grunts; the tigers, bears, lions, wolves, and crafty foxes will stick their heads out of their holes and regard the level field of the hunt from the deserted heights, and they'll pour out from their savage breasts a medley of grunts, screeches, growls, roars, yelps, howls.

In the air and on the leaves of branching plants, the cocks, eagles, peacocks, cranes, turtledoves, blackbirds, swallows, nightingales, ravens, magpies, crows, cuckoos, cicalas, will none of them be behindhand in repeating and re-echoing their stridulant chirrupings. From the liquid and unstable element the white swans, the many-hued ducks, the agitated loons, the marsh ducks, the raucous geese, the querulous frogs, will disturb our ears with their noise. And so the warm light of the sun, diffused in the air of this privileged hemisphere, will find itself accompanied, saluted, and perhaps harassed by as many voices as there are numbers and kinds of spirits who bring them up out of the depths of their chests.

Fil. It is not only normal, it is also natural and necessary, that each creature should emit its own voice; and it isn't possible for beasts to form regulated accents and articulated sounds like men, since the bodily constitutions are contrary, the tastes different, and the foods various.

Arm. Please give me the freedom on speaking in my turn, not about light, but about certain circumstances which do not usually cheer the sense so much as disturb the thought of any man who sees and considers. For your peace and repose, which I wish for with all brotherly charity, I don't want these discussions of yours to be turned into comedies, tragedies, laments, dialogues, or whatever name you prefer, like those that a short while ago, which, themselves being openly broadcast, have obliged you to stay closed-up and secluded at home.

Fil. Speak freely.

Arm. I won't speak like a holy prophet, an abstracted diviner, an apocalyptic visionary, or the angelic she-ass of Balaam. I shall not discourse as if inspired by Bacchus, nor as if swoln-up with wind through the prostituted Muses of Parnassus, nor as a Sibyl impregnated by Apollo, nor as an oracular Cassandra, nor as if packed from my toenails to the tips of my hair by Apollinian enthusiasm, nor as a seer illuminated by the oracle or Delphic tripod, nor as an Oedipus interrogated and faced with the Sphinx's riddles, nor as a Solomon before the enigmas of the Queen of Sheba, nor as a Calchas interpreter of the Olympian Senate, nor as a possessed Merlin, nor as someone come up out of the cave of Trophonius.

No, I'll speak in the everyday and vulgar tongue, like a man who goes on lapping up the juice of the big and little nape till there's only dryness left to the meninges. I'll speak, I say, like a man who has no other brain than his own, and is ignored by even the heaviest-eating and deepest-drinking gods of the heavenly court —those, I mean, who do not gulp down ambrosia or relish nectar, but quench their thirst from the bottom of the barrel and from soured wines, without the least concern for lymph or nymph: those gods who are used to be more at-home, intimate, and sociable with us: gods like Bacchus or the boozy straddler of the ass or Pan or Vertumnus or Faun or Priapus—even these do not consider me worth the gift of a single bit more of straw, though they heap benefactions even on horses.

Eli. Too long a preamble.

Arm. Patience, the conclusion will be brief. I want to remark briefly that the words I'll make you listen to are not the sort that need deciphering, as if they'd had a process of distillation, gone through a retort, been broken-down in a *bain-marie* and sublimated in recipients of the quintessence. No, they'll be the sort of words dinned into my head by my nurse, who was just as brawny, bosomy, big-bellied, broad in the beam and vast in the rump, as was that Londoner I saw in Westminster, a lump of a woman who in the guise of stomach-warmers had a pair of long flabby breasts rather like the halfboots of the giant San Sparagorio—bubs that, tanned into leather, would have surely produced two Ferrara bagpipes.

Eli. Well, that ought to be enough for a preamble.

Arm. To come then to my further comments—leaving on one side the remarks and opinions on the theme of light and the clarification your philosophy may bring us—I'd like you to state the sort of voices with which you'd wish us to greet in particular that brilliance of doctrine emanating from the book *Ash-Wednesday Supper.* What animals are those that perform in the Supper? I ask you: are they aquatic, aerial, earthly, or lunatic? And putting aside the observations of Smith, Prudenzio, and Frulla, I'd like to know if those critics are incorrect who assert you bark like a rabid and demented dog in addition to sometimes playing the role of monkey, sometimes of magpie, sometimes of parrot, now this creature and now that, mixing up all kinds of discourses, grave and serious, moral and natural, ignoble and noble, philosophic and comic?

Fil. Don't be astounded, brother. For the setting was none other than a supper, where brains are controlled by the states of the body brought about by the effectiveness of the savours and smells of the food and drink. Such as the material and corporeal supper is, so consequently develops the verbal and spiritual one. Thus the dialogued supper has its diverse and contrasted sections, just as the other is used to have. The latter has its proper conditions, circumstances, and means, which the former also in its turns should have.

Arm. Please explain your meaning.

Fil. At the meal, as is customary and correct, there are normally served salads and solid dishes, fruits and the usual courses, kitchen snacks and spiceries, food for the healthy and for the out-of-sorts, cold food and hot, raw and cooked, sea-things and earth-things, cultivated and wild, ripe and green, nourishing food and food only for the taste, substantial and light, salted and insipid, tart and sweet, bitter and mild. Similarly, in the dialogue, by a certain analogy, there have shown up its own contradictions and oppositions, accommodated to the contrary and various stomachs and tastes that may wish to put in an appearance at our symbolic banquet. Thus nobody can complain of a pointless invitation, and he who doesn't like one thing may take another.

Arm. That's so. But what's your answer if at your party, your supper, there turn up as well things that aren't any good as salads or solid dishes, fruits or the usual courses, cold or hot, raw or cooked things, things that don't serve to stir appetite or allay hunger, are useless for the healthy or the out-of-sorts, and would better have never left the hands of cook or expert confectioner?

Fil. You'll see that our supper doesn't differ, in this, from any other kind of supper whatever. Here too, at the most pleasant moment of eating away, you burn yourself with a scalding mouthful and you've no choice but to spew it out at once or to push it to and fro on your palate, with tears and moans, till you can get it down your gullet into the depths with a cursed gulp; or else some tooth is jarred or your tongue is caught so that you bite it together with the food, or a small fragment of grit is broken up and ground between your teeth, so that you have to spit the mouthful out, or some bristle or hair of the cook sticks to your palate and almost makes you vomit, or a fish-bone lodges in your throat and produces a low coughing, or a bit of bone scraping down your gullet puts you in danger of suffocation.

At our other supper, to our common disgrace, there happen corresponding and comparable matters. All this occurs through the sin of the ancient first-formed man Adam, on whose account our perverse human nature is condemned always to find the pleasant joined to the unpleasant.

Arm. A pious and holy observation. But what's your answer to what they say: that you're a raging cynic?

Fil. I'll concede the point readily: if not wholly, at least in part.

Arm. But don't you know that it's less dishonourable for a man to undergo outrages than to inflict them?

Fil. It's sufficient that mine are called revenges and those of the others outrages.

Arm. Even the gods are liable to receive insults, suffer defamation, and be the subject of blame. But to blame, to defame, to insult are the deeds of the base, the ignoble, the worthless, and the villainous.

Fil. True. But we don't indulge in insults, we rebutt those cast at us, or rather not at us but at despised philosophy, and we proceed in such a way that new troubles won't be added to those already experienced.

Arm. You want then to seem a dog that bites, so that no one will dare to molest you?

Fil. That's it. Because I want quiet and unpleasantness displeases me.

Arm. Yes, but men consider you carry on with too much rigour.

Fil. To stop them having another try and to daunt their fellows from coming to dispute with me and others when they want to treat our conclusions with similar half-measures.

Arm. The offence was private, the retaliation public.

Fil. None the less just for that. Many errors are committed in private and then justly chastised in public.

Arm. But that way you stain your reputation and make yourself more to blame than they. The world will declare that you're impatient, fantastic, eccentric, giddy-witted.

Fil. I don't care, as long as they or others don't harass me further. That's why I shake my cynic staff at them—to force them to leave me in peace with my own affairs; and if they don't want to make overtures, they shouldn't work off their barbarism upon me.

Arm. Still, do you think it suits a philosopher to take a stand on vendettas?

Fil. If those who annoy me were Xanthippes, I'd be a Socrates.

Arm. Don't you know that long-suffering and patience sit well on everyone and that they're the cause of our becoming like the heroes and eminent gods, who, according to some, take vengeance only tardily, and according to others, never take it at all or give way to anger?

Fil. You're mistaken in thinking I take my stand on vendettas.

Arm. What else then?

Fil. My aim has been correction, by exercising which we equally resemble the gods. You know that poor Vulcan was ordered by Jove to work even on holidays, and that his cursed anvil never leaves off untiringly receiving the blows of endless fierce sledgehammers. Scarcely is one hammer raised up than the other is crashed down, so that the righteous thunderbolts, by which the guilty and the criminal are punished, may never be in short supply.

Arm. There's a difference between you and the smith of Jove, the husband of the Cyprian goddess.

Fil. It's enough that I'm not unlike the gods in patience and long-suffering, which I've put to the test on this occasion by not altogether letting go the rein of my scorn or using a stronger prick of the spur.

Arm. It's not every man's place to set himself up as corrector, especially of the multitude.

Fil. Add to that: above all when the multitude doesn't touch him.

Arm. Men say you shouldn't let yourself be provoked in a foreign country.

Fil. To that I make two answers. First, it's not right to kill a foreign physician for trying to carry out cures which none of the natives manage; and second, I say that to a true philosopher every country is his fatherland.

Arm. But if the people don't accept you as a philosopher, as a physician, or as a fellow countryman?

Fil. That doesn't make me any the less so.

Arm. Who makes you believe that?

Fil. The divinities who have set me here, I who find myself here, and those who have eyes and see me here.

Arm. You have very scanty and little-known witnesses.

Fil. Very scanty and little-known are the true physicians, almost all of them are in fact sick men. I repeat that no one has the liberty of inflicting, or permitting others to inflict, such treatment on men who bring honest wares, whether or not they're foreigners.

Arm. Few know those wares.

Fil. Gems are no less precious on that account, and no less should we with all our might defend them and help their defence, free and vindicate them, from the trampling of swine. And as the gods may be propitious to me, my dear Armesso, I swear I've never practised such retaliations out of any sordid self-love or any low care for my individual self. I've acted solely out of love for my beloved mother, philosophy, and zeal for her affronted majesty. By her false friends and sons—for there's no abject pedant, no phrase-mongering slug, no boor of a faun, no ignorant hack, who doesn't hope to be enrolled in her family by presenting himself loaded-up with books, lengthening out his beard, or adopting other mannerisms of pretentious masquerade—she is reduced to such a state that among the commonfolk to call anyone a philosopher is tantamount to insulting him as a quack, a good-for-nothing, a howling pedant, a charlatan, a mountebank, a mere

3*

cheat, good only as entertainment at home and as scarecrow in the fields.

Eli. To tell you the truth, the race of philosophers is rated by the general run of men as more despicable than that of chaplains. The latter, raised up out of every sort of riffraff, have brought the priesthood into contempt; the former, designated out of all sorts of brutes, have dragged philosophy down into disrepute.

Fil. So let's praise antiquity for its ways. Then philosophers were such that from their ranks men were elevated to be legislators, counsellors, and kings. And such were the counsellors and kings that they promoted philosophers to be priests. But in our times, most of the priests are sunk so low as to be despised, and through their fault the divine laws are despised in turn. On the same level are almost all the philosophers we see: fallen so low in men's eyes that the sciences have become contemned as well. What's more, the host of crooks among them are accustomed for their part, like nettles, with their opposing visions to sting and impede the rare virtue and truth, which are revealed to the few.

Arm. I don't know any philosopher, Eliotropio, who gets so worked up at the contempt for philosophy, nor anyone so enthusiastic for his science as this Teofilo. What would happen if the others were similarly constituted—I mean as impatient?

Eli. Those other philosophers have not made such discoveries as he; they don't have so much to protect, so much to defend. One can easily hold cheaply philosophy which is of no value or not worth much, or which one doesn't know; but a man who has found the truth, which is a hidden treasure, kindled by the beauty of that divine face, becomes just as jealous a guardian against fraudulence, negligence, or contamination, as another man, miserly obsessed with gold, rubies, and diamonds, or with the carrion of feminine beauty.

Arm. But let's return to our theme and come to the *quia* [why]. It's reported of you, Teofilo, that in this Supper of yours you have criticised and insulted a whole city, a whole province, a whole kingdom.

Fil. That I have never meant, never wished, never done. And if I'd meant, wished or done it, I'd condemn myself most of all. I'd be prepared to make a thousand retractions, a thousand disavowals, a thousand palinodes. Not only if I'd insulted a noble and ancient kingdom such as this, but if I'd done it to any other one, however barbarous in reputation—not only to any city whatever, however uncivilised it was considered, but also to any breed of men, however savage they were esteemed, or even any family, however inhospitable it was said to be. For there cannot be a kingdom, city, breed, or whole household, in which everyone must be assumed to be of the same humour and in which there cannot be contrary and opposing manners, so that what pleases one person displeases another.

Arm. Certainly. As for myself, I've read and re-read and thoroughly pondered all your statements, and, though in some places I find you for some reason or other too effusive, in general you seem to me to proceed soberly, reasonably, and thoughtfully. But the rumour has spread in the way I've reported to you.

Eli. That rumour and others have been spread through the baseness of certain persons who feel themselves touched to the quick. Anxious to take revenge and aware of the weakness of their reasons, doctrine, wit, and force, they fabricate such lies as they can, to which no one except their fellows gives credit, and they further look round for partisans by making their individual chastisement appear a collective insult.

Arm. No, I believe there are persons, not without judgment or counsel, who consider the attack to be general, because you clearly define the manners in question as belonging to our nation.

Fil. But what are these alleged manners? Are not similar ones, worse and much more peculiar—in genus, species, and number—to be found in the most excellent parts and provinces of the world? Would you perhaps call me denigratory and ungrateful towards my homeland if I said that similar and yet more criminal customs are to be found in Italy, in Naples, in Nola? Would I perhaps belittle this region, blessed by heaven and set at the same time at the head and at the right hand of the globe, governor and ruler of all the other nations, and always esteemed by us as mistress, nurse, and mother of all the virtues, disciplines, humanities, modesties, and courtesies—if I go on to amplify in addition those same poets of ours have sung about it in poems that make it no less the mistress of all vices, errors, greeds, and cruelties?

Eli. All this is certainly in accord with the fundamentals of your philosophy, which lays down that contraries coincide both in the principles and in the related subjects. Thus the same wits, which are most apt for lofty, virtuous, and noble enterprises, are liable, if they turn perverse, to throw themselves into extreme vices. More, we usually find the rarer and choicer wits turning up where the commonfolk are very ignorant and bumble-headed, and where in general people are less urbane and courteous—so that, in different ways, it seems, the many nations are each given the same measure of perfection and imperfection.

Fil. You speak the truth.

Arm. Despite all this, Teofilo, I and many others regret that in our friendly country you have come up against the sort of persons who provided you with the material for your complaints at an Ash-Supper, rather than the others—and there are many of them—who would have made you realise how much our land, though declared by your compatriots to be *penitus toto divisus ab orbe* [utterly cut off from the whole world], is inclined to all the studies of fine letters, arms, chivalry, humanities, and courtesies. In which matters, to the best of our ability, we strive not to fall below the level of our ancestors and not to be surpassed by other nations—above all by those who believe themselves endowed with nobilities, sciences, arms, and civilised ways by nature.

Fil. On my faith, Armesso, in all you've remarked there's nothing I should or could contradict with word, reason, or conscience; for you defend your case with every skill of modesty and argument. Therefore, on your account and because you haven't accosted me with barbarous arrogance, I begin to regret and deplore that I was drawn into the misadventure and grieved you and others of an honourable and humane character. And so I wish that those dialogues had never been published, and if it please you, I'll take care that none other such ever see the light.

Arm. My grief, together with that of other noble persons, derives so little from the circulation of those dialogues that I'd readily do all I could to have them translated into our tongue. They'd serve as a lesson for those among us who are poorly or badly educated. Perhaps when the latter learned with what a stomach their discourteous rejoinders are received, with what a delineation they are set down, and what a bad impression they provide, it might come about that even if they didn't want to budge out of their chimney-nook, to follow the good discipline and example of the best and greatest men, yet at least they might make an effort to change and to imitate them from the mere shame of being counted among the others. They'd then discover that honour and courage do not consist in knowing how to molest and in being able to do it, but in the diametrically opposed positions.

Eli. You show yourself very discreet and shrewd in the cause of your homeland, and you aren't ungrateful or forgetful about the good offices of others, as is commonly the fault of men poor in argument and counsel. But Filoteo does not seem to me as adroit in preserving his reputation and defending his person. For, just as nobility and rusticity are different, so contrary effects are to be expected and apprehended from them.

A Scythian boor will appear a wise man and find himself celebrated for his good fortune if, by leaving the banks of the Danube and going to try the Roman Senate's authority and majesty with a bold rebuke and justified complaint, he provides the occasion with his censure and invective for the Senate to act with the highest prudence and magnanimity, and to set up a statue and monument in honour of his sharp reprehension.

However a Roman gentleman and senator to his misfortune would not in the least emerge as a wise man if, abandoning the pleasant margins of his Tiber, he departed even with a just complaint and reasonable reproach to try the Scythian boors. For the latter would seize the chance to erect towers and babels of arguments of the utmost baseness, infamy, and boorishness; they'd pelt him with stones, giving full rein to popular fury—so that other nations might come to know what a difference there is in intercourse and contacts between human beings and those who are merely made in the image and likeness of them.

Arm. Never let it be said, Teofilo, that I should or could consider it proper for me, or for anyone possessed of more salt than myself, to take up the cause and defence of those who are the objects of your satire, as if they were the people and the persons of this country, to whose defence we are driven by a common natural law. For I'll never admit, and I'll always remain the enemy of anyone who asserts, that they are parts and members of our country, which comprises only persons as noble, civilised, well brought-up, disciplined, discreet, humane, and reasonable as those of any other nation.

Hence, though they exist within our bounds, they are present only in the same way as ordure, scum, dung, carcasses are. They could be called a part of the kingdom or the city only in the same way as the bilge is part of a ship. For such reasons we should all the less resent them, since in our resentment we ourselves ought to be blamed.

I do not exclude a large number of doctors and priests from this group. Thanks to their doctorate, some of them turn into gentlemen. But the majority who do not dare first to spread themselves in their rude sense of power, later on, becoming hardier and more presumptuous through the assumption of the title of lettered man and priest, boldly and vaingloriously bring it fully into the open.

It's no wonder then to see such crowds who with all their doctorate and their priesthood are more acquainted with herd, flock, and stable than is an actual horse-groom, goat-herd, or cow-herd. For this reason I'd have preferred you not to have assailed our university so harshly, as if allowing it no excuses, even in general, and without taking into account what it once was, what it will or can be in the future, and what in part it already is today.

Fil. Don't be upset. Even if it has been submitted on this occasion to detailed examination, still it doesn't commit worse errors than other universities which are considered superior and where the larger part of the graduates, under the doctor's title, conceal fools bedizened with rings and asses adorned with diadems.

I do not however deny how well your university has been organised since its origin, the fine programme of studies, the gravity of ceremonies, the system of training, the decorum of traditions, and many other circumstances that meet the needs and ornamenting of an academy. Hence, without any doubt, everyone must proclaim it the first in Europe and consequently in the whole world. And I don't deny that as far as fineness of spirit and acuity of wit are concerned—things which one part or another of Britain naturally produces—it is comparable with, and on the same level as, the most truly excellent academies anywhere. Nor is it forgotten that speculative letters, before they were found in other parts of Europe, flourished in this spot. Thanks to its princes of metaphysics, barbarous though they may be in tongue and cowled in profession, the splendour of a most noble and rare section of philosophy (which in our day is almost extinct) has been propagated through all the academies of the non-barbarous regions.

But what has troubled me, what has seemed to me at one and the same time irksome and comical, is that today's doctors, than whom I know none others more Roman or Attic in speech, for the rest (I speak of the generality) vaunt themselves as being wholly unlike and even the contrary of their predecessors who, with little care for eloquence and grammatical rigour, gave themselves up exclusively to the speculations which the men of today call sophisms. Still, I have a higher opinion of the metaphysics of these latter, in which they advanced their leader Aristotle—despite impurities and blots, with certain empty conclusions and theories, which are neither philosophic nor theological, but suitable only for idle and wrongly-employed wits—than I have of that which the doctors of the present age can contribute with all their Ciceronian eloquence and their declamatory arts.

Arm. Those arts are not to be despised.

Fil. I agree, but as we must make a choice, I set the culture of the mind, however mean it may be, above the most eloquent flow of words and languages.

Eli. Your remark brings Fra Ventura to my mind. Commenting on the Gospel passage: *Reddite quae sunt Caesaris Caesari* [Render unto Caesar that which is Caesar's], he collected in explanation all the names of the coins that were circulating in Roman times, together with their stamps and their weights—over a hundred and twenty of them, pieced together from I-don't-know-what devil of annals or scribbling-books, to demonstrate how studious he was and how retentive his memory. At the sermon's end, a good man accosted him with the request: Reverend father, please lend me sixpence. To which the friar replied that he belonged to the mendicant order.

Arm. What's the point of this tale?

Eli. I want to bring out that those who are well-versed in phrases and names, but who don't concern themselves with the things, are riding the same mule as this reverend father of mules.

Arm. It's my belief that, apart from the study of eloquence in which they excel all their predecessors and do not yield to other moderns, they are also not destitute in philosophy and the rest of the speculative fields. Without ability in them, they cannot be promoted to any academic degree; for the university statutes, to which they are bound by oath, lay down that *nullus ad philosophiae et theologiae magisterium et doctoratum promoveatur, nisi epotaverit e fonte Aristotelis* [no one is to be promoted to the degree of master and doctor of philosophy and theology unless he has drunk from the fountain of Aristotle].

Eli. O, I'll tell you what they've done to avoid committing perjury. There are three fountains in the university, and they've baptised one *Fons Aristotelis*, the second *Fons Pythagorae*, the third *Fons Platonis*. As they draw from these three fountains the water used for making beer and ale—the same water as the cattle and horses are used to drink—the result is that no one spends three or four days in those faculties and colleges without drinking not only at the Aristotelian fountain but also at the Pythagorean and the Platonic.

Arm. Alas, it's all too true. And so it happens, Teofilo, that doctors are as cheap in the market as pilchards; for, as they're made, found, and hooked with little effort, they are buyable at a low price. Such then being the host of doctors in this age—without any imputation on the fame of some celebrated alike for eloquence, doctrine, and high courtesy, for example, a Tobias Matthew, a Culpepper, and others I cannot name—it has come about that the possession of a doctorate, far from elevating a man to a new level of nobility, brings him under suspicion of owning a contrary nature and condition, unless he is personally known. Hence it happens with men who are noble by birth or some other accident, even when the principal part of nobility is added to them, the part that comes through deep learning, they are ashamed to graduate and assume the title of doctors. So they content themselves with 'being learned.' And you will find a larger number of these in the courts than you can encounter among the pedants of the university.

Fil. Don't complain, Armesso; for in all places where there are doctors and priests, you'll discover both these breeds. Those who are true doctors and true priests, even if they have come up from a low origin, cannot help being civilised and ennobled; for knowledge is a most profound way of making the human soul heroic. But the other sort show themselves all the more expressly rustic in wanting to thunder from on high with *divum pater* [the Father of the Gods] or with the giant Salmoneus, when, like satyrs or fauns dressed up in purple, they promenade in that horrible and imperial masquerade, after having determined from their magistral chair to what declension belong *hic, et haec, et hoc nihil.*

Arm. Now let's leave these questions. What is the book you hold in your hand?

Fil. Some dialogues.

Arm. The Supper?

Fil. No.

Arm. Which then?

Fil. Others, where the theme is Cause, Principle, and Unity, according to our system.

Arm. Who are the speakers? Perhaps we shall have another devil, like Frulla or Prudenzio, who will involve us afresh in some broil.

Fil. Don't doubt that with one possible exception they are peaceable and very honest people.

Arm. And so, from what you say, we shall have some prickly stuff to unhusk from these dialogues?

Fil. Don't doubt that either. You will be scratched where it itches rather than pricked where it hurts.

Arm. What more?

Fil. Here as first speaker you'll meet that learned honest lovable wellbred and ever-so-faithful, Alexander Dicson, whom the Nolan loves as his own eyes and who is responsible for the bringing of this theme into discussion. He is introduced as the person proposing to Teofilo the subject to be dealt with. For the second speaker, Teofilo, who is myself, and who, according to the occasions, proceeds to distinguish, to define, and to demonstrate the proposed theme. For third speaker you have Gervase, who is not a philosopher by profession but who likes attending our discussion as a pastime. He is a person who's neither scented nor stinking, who treats the actions of Poliinnio as mere comedy and from time to time seizes the occasion for making him let loose his folly.

That sacrilegious pedant is the fourth speaker, one of the rigid censors of philosophers, a man through whom Momus expresses himself, strongly attached to his own flock of students, so that he is reputed to follow the Socratic way of love, a fellow who is the ceaseless foe of the female sex; whence, so as not to be sensual, he considers himself like Orpheus, Musaeus, Tityros, and Amphion. He is one of those who when they have concocted a Beautiful Construction, produced an elegant Little Epistle, cadged a fine phrase from the Ciceronian cookhouse, are at once Demosthenes revived, inspired by Tullius, a reincarnation of Sallust: here is an Argus with an eye for every letter, every syllable, every word, here a Rhadamanthus *qui umbras vocat ille silentium* [who calls the shadows of the silent dead], here a Minos, king of Crete, who *urnam movet* [moves the urn]. Such a pedant closely scrutinises discourses and builds up a discussion round each phrase, saying·

These belong to the poet, those to a comic author, this to an orator; this is grave, this is light, that is sublime, that other is *humile dicendi genus* [a humble manner of speaking]; this harangue is harsh, it would be smoother if it were composed in such and such a way; this writer is an infant, little read in the ancients, *non redolet Arpinatem, desipit Latium* [he doesn't smack of Cicero's home-town, he doesn't know Latium]; this word isn't Tuscan, it isn't used by Boccaccio, Petrarch, and other approved authors, it's incorrect to write *homo*, it should be *omo*; *honor* should be *onor*, Polihimnio should be Poliinnio. With that the fellow triumphs, he is smugly self-satisfied, nothing pleases him so much as his own doings.

He is a Jove who from his lofty vantage-point, looks down and ruminates on the life of other men, who are subject to so many errors, calamities, miseries, and vain strivings. He alone is blessed, he alone lives a celestial life, contemplating his own divinity in the mirror of a Spicilegium, a Dictionary, a Calepinus, a Lexicon, a Cornucopia, a Nizzolius. He is endowed with such sufficiency that, while each of us others is a unit, he alone is everything. If he happens to laugh, he calls himself Democritus; if he happens to moan, he calls himself Heraclitus; if he has an argument, he becomes Chrysippus; if he discourses, his name is Aristotle; if he invents chimeras, he turns into Plato; if he bellows out a small sermon, he takes the name of Demosthenes; if he grammatically analyses Virgil, he is himself Maro. Thus he corrects Achilles, approves Aeneas, reprehends Hector, exclaims against Pyrrhus, condoles with Priam, puts the case against Turnus, excuses Dido, praises Achates, and finally, while *verbum verbo reddit* [he gives back word for word] and heaps up his barbarous synonyms, *nihil divinum a se alienum putat* [he thinks nothing divine alien to himself].

Then he haughtily descends from his chair, as if he had put the heavens in order, organised the Senate, tamed armies and reformed worlds; assured that if it were not for the injustice of the times he would translate into act what he has performed in thought. *O tempora O mores* [O times O manners], how few are those who understand the nature of participles, adverbs, conjunctions. How much time has run away before one has delved out the reason and true cause for the adjective agreeing with the noun, the relative coming together with the antecedent, and the rule according to which it comes at the head or the tail of a sentence, also in what measure and order are to be inserted those interjections *dolentis, gaudentis* [of someone grieving or rejoicing] such as *heu, oh, ahi, ah, hem, ohe, hui,* and other condiments without which the whole discourse is quite insipid?

Eli. Say what you like, understand it as you like, but I hold that for felicity in life it is better to imagine oneself Croesus and yet be poor than to imagine oneself poor and yet be Croesus. Isn't it more likely to produce bliss if one possesses a slattern whom one thinks beautiful and finds satisfying, than to have a Leda, a Helen, who bores you and begets tedium? What then does it matter to these people if they are ignorant and ignobly occupied as long as they are the happier to the extent that they are solely satisfied with themselves? Thus it is that fresh grass is good for the ass, barley for the horse, just as oatmeal bread and partridge are for you. Thus it is that the pig finds a repast in acorn broth, just as Jove does in ambrosia and nectar. Do you want perhaps to deprive them of their pleasant folly when in return for the cure you'll get your head broken? I leave aside the question: who knows whether the illusion or the cure is the folly? A Pyrrhonist has said: Who knows whether our state is not death, and that of the alleged dead is not life? In the same way, who knows whether all felicity and true beatitude doesn't consist in the due conjunction and apposition of the members of an oration?

Arm. Thus the world is constituted. We act Democritus at the pedants and grammarians, the assiduous courtiers act Democritus at us, the monks and priests, who are little concerned with thinking, act Democritus at everyone. Reciprocally the pedants ridicule us, we the courtiers, and everyone the monks; and in conclusion, as each of us is a fool to the others, we are all fools, differing in species but concordant *in genere et numero et casu* [in kind, number, and case].

Eli. The species and manners of censure are thus various, diverse too are its grades; yet hardest, harshest, most horrible and most terrifying are the censures of our archdidascals. So we must bend our knees and bow our heads before them, turn our eyes their way and raise up our hands, sighing, crying, calling out and begging for mercy. It is therefore to you I address myself, to you who bear in your hand the caduceus of Mercury, so you may decide the controversies and settle the questions stirred up among men and gods: to you, Menippi, who, seated on the globe of the moon, look down at us with sidelong and narrowed glances, noting with repugnance and scorn our actions; to you, shield-bearers of Pallas, standard-bearers of Minerva, stewards of Mercury, councillors of Jove, foster-brothers of Apollo, officials of Epimetheus, cupbearers of Bacchus, grooms of the Euhan-criers, scourgers of the Edonides, impellers of the Thyiads, seducers of the Maenads, suborners of the Bassarids, riders of the Mimallonides, copulators of the nymph Egeria, correctors of enthusiasm, demagogues of the wandering people, disk-bearers of Demogorgon, Dioscures of the fluctuating disciplines, treasurers of Pantamorphus, and scapegoats of the highpriest Aaron—to you we recommend our prose, we submit our Muses, our premises, our minors, our digressions, our parentheses, our applications, our clauses, our periods, our constructions, our adjectives, and our epithets.

O you most gentle go-betweens, who with your lovely little elegancies ravish our senses, bind fast our hearts, fascinate our minds, and put our voluptuous souls in brothels, deliver a wise judgment on our barbarisms, demolish our solecisms, bung up our stinking chasms, castrate our Silenes, clap our Noahs into breeches, eunuchise our macrologies, patch up our ellipses, curb our tautologies, moderate our acrilogies, forgive us our ecrilogies, pardon our perissologies, excuse our cacophonies.

I next conjure you all in general and you in particular, severe, supercilious, and savage master Poliinnio, to cast off this contumelious rage and this criminal hatred of the noble female sex, and not to disturb what the world has of beauty and the heavens with so many eyes stare down upon. Return, return to yourselves and recover the wit by which you may recognise your rancour as nothing but the expression of mania and fanatical zeal. What is more insensate and stupid than a man who doesn't see the light? What folly can be more abject than that which on account of sex is an enemy of nature itself, like that barbarous king of Sarza, who, repeating what he'd learned from you, declared:

> No perfect thing can Nature e'er design
> since Nature's of the gender feminine.

Consider a little the truth, raise up your eyes to the tree of the knowledge of good and evil, and note the antithesis and opposition between one thing and another. Regard what men are and what women are. Here you see as subject the body *corpo*, which is your friend, masculine, and there the soul, *anima*, which is your enemy, feminine. Here chaos, *caos*, masculine; there organisation, *disposizione*, feminine. Here, sleep, *sonnio*, masculine; there, vigil, *vigilia*, feminine. Here, lethargy, *letargo*, masculine; there memory, *memoria*, feminine. Here, hate, *odio*, masculine; there, friendship, *amicizia*, feminine. Here, fear, *timore*, masculine; there, security, *sicurtà*, feminine. Here, harshness, *rigore*, masculine; there, tranquillity, *quiete*, feminine. Here, scandal, *scandalo*, masculine; there, peace, *pace*, feminine. Here, error, *errore*, masculine; there, truth, *verità*, feminine. Here, defect, *defetto*, masculine; there, perfection, *perfezione*, feminine. Here, hell, *inferno*, masculine; there, felicity, *felicità*, feminine. Here, the pedant Poliinnio; there, the muse Poliinnia. To sum up, all the vices, defects, and crimes are masculine; and all the virtues, excellencies, and goodnesses are feminine. Hence, prudence, justice, fortitude, temperance, beauty, majesty, divinity, as they are named, as they are imagined, as they are described, as they are painted: so they are feminine all.

And now, leaving these theoretical, verbal, and grammatical reasons, which are appropriate to your argument, and coming to what is natural, real, and practical: should not this single instance have sufficed to bridle your tongue, shut up your mouth, and confound you as well as your fellows? I mean, if someone should ask you where you can find a man superior or equal to this Divine Elizabeth who reigns in England. She is so highly endowed, exalted, favoured, protected, and sustained by the heavens, in vain the words or forces of others will strain to overthrow her. There is none more worthy in all the kingdom, I say, than this lady; none more heroic among the nobility; none more learned among those who wear the gown; none wiser among the counsellors. Compared with her, as much for her bodily beauty as for her knowledge of both vernacular and learned tongues, as much for her grasp of the sciences and the arts as for her prudence in government, as much for the felicity of her great and long-held authority as for all other civil and natural virtues, how paltry indeed are the Sophonisbas, the Faustinas, the Semiramises, the Didos, the Cleopatras, and all the queens in whom Italy, Greece, Egypt, and the other parts of Europe and Asia in past time, can glory?

My witnesses are the deeds and the happy success that the present age admires, not without a noble wonderment. While across the surface of Europe, there flows the wrathful Tiber, the menacing

Po, the violent Rhone, the bloody Seine, the turbid Garonne, the maddened Ebro, the tumultuous Tagus, the agitated Meuse, the unquiet Danube, she with the splendour of her eyes has been able for five lustres and more to calm the great Ocean which with unceasing ebb and flow, joyous and serene, gathers the beloved Thames to its broad bosom—the Thames which, far from every dread and trouble, rolls on securely and gaily, serpentining this way and that between its grassy verges.

Arm. Stop there, stop, Filoteo. Don't strain yourself to add water to our Ocean, light to our sun. Leave off showing yourself so abstract, not to say worse, in your polemic against the absent Poliinnio. Communicate rather something of those dialogues you have here, so that we don't pass today and its hours unprofitably.

Fil. Here, take them and read.

SECOND DIALOGUE

SPEAKERS: *Arelio Dicson, Teofilo, Gervase, Poliinnio*

Dics. Please, Master Poliinnio, and you, Gervase, don't interrupt our discussions again.

Pol. Fiat. [So be it.]

Gerv. If that man, who is the *magister*, butts in, assuredly I won't be able to hold my tongue.

Dics. You state then, Teofilo, that everything which isn't first principle and first cause, owns a principle and a cause?

Teo. Beyond doubt, beyond any controversy.

Dics. Do you consequently believe that the man who knows the things thus caused and ruled by a principle, knows the cause and the principle?

Teo. Not at all easily the proximate cause and principle; and with great difficulty, even in their vestige, the first cause and principle.

Dics. Then how do you think that things which own both first and proximate cause and principle can be truly known, if as far as the efficient cause is concerned—and that is one of the things contributing to the real cognition of things—they remain hidden?

Teo. I admit it's easy to construct a theory of proof, but difficult to make proof itself. It's practicable enough to classify causes, circumstances, and methods of doctrines; but our method-builders and analysts make a defective application of their *organum*, their methodological principles, and their art-of-arts.

Gerv. It's like men who know how to make fine swords, but not how to wield them.

Pol. Ferme. [Aye, aye.]

Gerv. Firmly close your eyes, please, so that you can't open them again.

Teo. That's why I say a natural philosopher isn't to be expected to bring out all causes and principles, but only the physical ones, and of them, the principal and appropriate ones. Although then, dependent as things are on the first principle and first cause,

77

they can be said to possess that cause and that principle, yet there is not invariably such a necessary relation that from the cognition of one we can infer a cognition of the other. Consequently we shouldn't ask for both of them to be set out in the same system.

Dics. How is that?

Teo. Because from the cognition of all dependent things we cannot infer other notion of the first principle and cause than by the rather inadequate method of vestiges: all things being derived from the will or goodness [of the first cause], which is the principle of its operation and from which proceeds the universal effect. The same situation can be made out in our relation to works of art, insomuch as the man who sees the statue does not see the sculptor. He who sees Helen's portrait doesn't see Helen, but he does see the effect of the operation which comes out of the goodness of Apelles' genius; and this effect is wholly the result of the accidents and circumstances of the substance of a man who, as far as his absolute essence is concerned, is not in the least known.

Dics. So that to know the universe is like knowing nothing of the being and substance of the first principle, since it's like knowing the accidents of the accidents.

Teo. Exactly, but I wouldn't want you to imagine I put accidents into God or think he can be known by his accidents.

Dics. I don't attribute to you such a crude wit, and I know it's one thing to say: These are accidents—and another thing to say: These are his accidents—and yet another to say of everything foreign to the divine nature: These are as his accidents. By the last way of speaking I take you to mean the effects of the divine operation, which, insofar as they are the substance of things and even the natural substances themselves, are still like accidents too remote to enable us to touch the cognition which apprehends the divine supernatural essence.

Teo. Well put.

Dics. And so we see that of the divine substance—both because it is infinite and because it is extremely distant from its effects, which represent the furthest bound of our discursive faculty's range —we can know nothing, except by means of vestiges, as the Platonists say, of a remote effect, as the Peripatetics say, of outer garments, as the Cabalists say, of mere shoulders and behinds, as the Talmudists say, of a mirror, a shadow, and an enigma, as the Apocalyptics say.

Teo. No, even more: because we do not perfectly see this universe of which the substance and the master are so hard to understand, we have far less ground for knowing the first principle and cause through its effect than we have of knowing Apelles through the statues he has made. For we can view them as wholes and also examine them part by part, but not so the grand and infinite effect of the divine power. This analogy, then, must be understood as involving no proportional comparison.

Dics. So it is and so I understand it.

Teo. It will then be as well for us to abstain from speaking on so lofty a matter.

Dics. I agree, since it is enough, morally and theologically, to know the first principle insofar as the supernatural deities have revealed it and divine men have declared it. Beyond this point, not only every law and theology whatever, but also all reformed philosophies, hold it the expression of a profane and turbulent spirit to rush into demanding reasons and wanting definitions for things beyond the sphere of our intelligence.

Teo. Excellent. But these are not so much deserving of reproach as those who struggle towards the knowledge of this principle and cause, deserve to be loaded with praise: men who apprehend its grandeur as far as is possible by wandering with the eyes of their well-regulated minds among those magnificent stars and luminous bodies which are so many habitable worlds, great animals, and most excellent deities, and which both seem and are innumerable worlds not much unlike that which contains us. It is impossible for them to have being out of themselves, considering that they are composite and dissoluble: not that they are therefore deserving of disintegration, as has been well said in the *Timaeus*. It is necessary for them to know principle and cause, and consequently with the grandeur of their being, their life, and their operation, they reveal and proclaim in infinite space with countless voices the infinite excellence and majesty of the first principle and cause.

Leaving aside then, as you say, such a consideration insofar as it goes beyond the reach of all sense and intellect, let us inquire into principle and cause through the vestiges, which are either nature herself or the light shining in her expanse and bosom. Put your questions then to me if you want me to reply in order.

Dics. I'll do so. But first of all, as you keep on speaking of cause and principle together, I'd like to know if these words are for you synonyms,

Teo. No.

Dics. Then what is the difference between the two terms?

Teo. I answer that when we speak of God as first principle and first cause we mean the same thing from divergent points of view. When we speak of principles and causes in nature, we speak of diverse things from different points of view. We speak of God as first principle inasmuch as all things come after him, in a definite system of before and after, according to their nature or their duration or their value. We speak of God as first cause insofar as all things are distinct from him, as the effect from the efficient cause, the thing produced from that which produces.

And these two viewpoints differ, since not everything that is prior and more valuable is the cause of what comes after it and is less valuable; and not everything which is a cause is prior and more valuable than what is caused, as is quite clear to any careful reasoner.

Dics. Then tell me, as far as natural things are concerned, what difference is there between cause and principle?

Teo. Although at times one term is used in the other's place, yet all the same, properly speaking, not everything which is a principle is a cause. For the point is the principle of the line, but not its cause; the instant is the principle of activity; the position-whence is the principle of motion, but not its cause; the premises are the principle of any argument, but not its cause. So principle is a more general term than cause.

Dics. Then, restricting these two terms to certain exact meanings, as is the custom of men who systematise their speech, I believe you take principle to be what intrinsically contributes to the constitution of a thing and remains in the effect. For example, matter and form, which remain in the composite; or again, the elements out of which things have been formed and into which they come to be resolved. But cause you call what contributes to the production of things from outside and has its being outside the composition, as is the case with the efficient cause and with the end for which the thing produced is destined.

Teo. Very good.

Dics. Now, as we have agreed on the difference of these things, first I want you to turn your attention towards causes and then towards principles. And as to causes, first I'd like to learn about the first efficient, about the formal which you say is associated with the efficient, and lastly about the final, which is understood to be the efficient's motive power.

Teo. I very much like the order you propose. As for the efficient cause, I declare that the universal physical efficient cause is the universal intellect, which is the first and principal faculty of the world-soul. The world-soul in turn is the universal form.

Dics. Your view seems to me not only to agree with that of Empedocles, but also to be more trustworthy, more precise, and more explicit—and further, insofar as I can tell from your previous statements, more profound. So you will do me a favour if you proceed to the explanation of it all in more detail, beginning with an account of just what this universal intellect is.

Teo. The universal intellect is the innermost, most real and essential faculty and the most efficacious part of the world-soul. It is the one and the same thing, which fills the whole, illumines the universe, and directs nature in producing her species in the right way. It plays the same role in the production of natural things as our intellect does in the parallel production of rational systems. The Pythagoreans call it the mover and agitator of the universe, as the Poet sets out in these words:

totamque infusa per artus
Mens agitat molem, et toto se corpore miscet.

[Infused through the members, mind
stirs the whole mass and with the whole body is mingled.]

The Platonists call it the world-artificer. This builder, they assert, proceeds from the higher world, which is indeed one, to the sensible world, which is multibly divided and over which there reigns, not only harmony, but also discord, through the breaking-up into parts.

This intellect, infusing and bringing something of its own into matter, and itself remaining restful and immobile, produces all things. The Magi call it most fruitful in seeds, or the sower, since it is that which impregnates matter with all forms, and, according to their type and condition, succeeds in shaping, forming, and inter-relating it in such admirable systems as cannot be attributed to chance or to any principle unable to distinguish and set in order.

Orpheus calls this intellect the world's eye, since it beholds both the inside and the outside alike of all natural things, in order that all things may succeed in producing and maintaining themselves, intrinsically as well as extrinsically, in their proper symmetry. Empedocles calls it the differentiator, since it never tires of unfolding the forms confused within the bosom of nature and of calling out the generation of one thing from the dissolution of another. Plotinus calls it father and progenitor, since it distributes seeds in the field of nature and is the proximate dispenser of forms.

As for us, we call it the inner craftsman, since it forms matter and shapes it from within, as from within the seed or root is sent forth and unfolded the trunk, from within the trunk are thrust out the branches, and from within the branches the formed twigs, and from within these the buds are unfurled, and there within are formed, shaped, and interwoven, like nerves, the leaves, flowers, and fruits. As from within, at certain times, the sap is recalled from the leaves and fruits to the twigs, from the twigs to the branches, from the branches to the trunk, and from the trunk to the root.

Similarly in animals: its work proceeds from the original seed, and from the centre of the heart, to the outer members, and from these finally gathers back to the heart the unfolded faculties, knotting up as it were the already spun-out threads.

Now, if we believe that forethought and intellect are required to beget even inanimate works, which we know how to shape on the surface of matter with a certain order and imitative effect—as when, cutting and carving a piece of wood, we reproduce the image of a horse—how much superior must we esteem that creative intellect which from the interior of the seminal matter solders the bones together, extends the cartilage, hollows out the arteries, breathes out the pores, interweaves the fibres, branches out the nerves, and disposes the whole with such admirable mastery?

How much greater an artificer, I say, is he who does not restrict himself to a single part of matter, but works continuously in wholeness everywhere. There are three sorts of intellect: the divine which is all things, the mundane which makes all things, and the particular ones which become all things. For it is necessary to find between the extremes the middle which is the true efficient cause, not only extrinsic but also intrinsic, of all natural things.

Dics. I'd like to hear you distinguish, as you understand them, extrinsic cause and intrinsic.

Teo. I call a cause extrinsic when as an efficient it does not form a part of things composed and things produced. I call a cause intrinsic insofar as it does not operate around matter and outside it, but in the manner just described. Hence a cause is extrinsic through being distinct from the substance and the essence of its effects, and because its being does not resemble that of things capable of generation and decay, although it embraces them. A cause is intrinsic with regard to the action of its own workings.

Dics. I think you've spoken enough about the efficient cause. Now I'd like to make out what you mean by the formal cause, joined to the efficient. Is it perhaps the ideal basis? For every agent that operates in accordance with the rule of intellect will fail to produce effects unless in accordance with some intention, and that intention cannot exist without the apprehension of something, and that something is no other than the form of what is to be produced.

Hence intellect, which has the power to produce all species and to send them forth with such beautiful construction from the potency of matter into act, must previously contain them all, according to certain principles of form, without which the agent could not proceed to his work of manufacture—just as it is not possible for a sculptor to model various statues without having first conceived the various forms.

Teo. You understand it excellently. For what I want is the consideration of two sorts of form. One which is cause, not actually the efficient, but through which the efficient does its work; and the other which is the principle, called forth from matter by the efficient.

Dics. The aim, and the final cause which the efficient sets before itself, is the perfection of the universe: which implies that in diverse parts of matter all the forms have an actual existence. In this end the intellect delights and takes such pleasure that it never tires of calling forth all sorts of forms from matter, as Empedocles seems also to believe.

Teo. Quite right. And I add that just as this efficient is omnipresent in the universe, and is special and particular in that universe's parts and members, so also are its form and its purpose.

Dics. Now we've discussed causes enough. Let's go on to reason about principles.

Teo. Well, to get at the constitutive principles of things, first I'll discuss form. For form is in some sort identical with the efficient cause we've defined, since the intellect, which is a potency of the world-soul, has been called the proximate efficient cause of all natural things.

Dics. But how can the same subject be at once principle and cause of natural things? how can it have the nature of an intrinsic part and not of an extrinsic one?

Teo. I deny that there's any impropriety in that, if we consider that the soul is in the body like the pilot in the ship, and the pilot, insofar as he shares the ship's motion, is part of it; yet, insofar as he is understood as the ship's guide and mover, he is seen, not as a part, but as a distinct efficient cause. Likewise the soul of the universe, insofar as it animates and informs, comes to be an intrinsic and formal part of the universe; yet insofar as it directs and governs, it is not a part, it does not rank as a principle, but as a cause.

Aristotle himself admits all this, since, though he denies that the soul has the same relation to the body as the pilot to the ship, yet in considering it with regard to its power of understanding and knowing, he does not dare to call it an act and form of the body, but looks on it as an efficient cause separate in its being from matter. And he states that it is a thing which comes from outside, according to its own existence, separated from the composite.

Dics. I approve of what you say; for, if an existence separated from the body belongs to the intellectual power of our soul, and if this power has the value of an efficient cause, all the more should we affirm the same of the world-soul. Plotinus, writing against the Gnostics, says that 'the world-soul rules the universe with greater ease than our soul its body.' Besides, there is a great difference in the way in which each one rules. The first, as if unfettered, rules the world in such a way that what it controls does not hamper it, and it does not suffer through other things or with them. It raises itself without impediment to higher things. In giving life and perfection to the body, it does not itself take back any smutch of imperfection; and therefore it is eternally conjoined with the same subject.

As for our souls, obviously they are in quite the contrary condition. Since then, according to your principle, the perfections which exist in inferior natures should be attributed to, and recognised in, superior natures in a far higher degree, we should without any doubt support the distinction which you have brought out.

And this point must be affirmed, not only of the world-soul, but also of all the stars. For, as the aforesaid philosopher holds, it is the case that they all have the power of contemplating God, the principles of all things, and the way in which the arrangement of the universe is carried out. He holds that this does not happen by means of memory, reasoning, and reflection, since each of their works is an eternal work and no action can be new for them, and so they do nothing which is not harmonious with the whole, perfect, with a certain and predetermined order which does not involve an act of cogitation.

Aristotle demonstrates this by the example of a perfect writer or lutanist. Here, while nature does not reason and reflect, he doesn't wish the conclusion to be drawn that she works without intellect and final intention, because profound writers and musicians pay less attention to what they create, and yet do not go astray like the more inexpert and clumsy, who, though giving more thought and attention, produce a less perfect result and show no lack of faults.

Teo. You understand me. Let us now move to the more particular. In my opinion those thinkers who will not understand or affirm that the world with its members is animated, are detracting from the divine goodness and from the excellence of this great animal and simulacrum of the first principle. How should God feel envy of his own image or the architect fail to love his own individual work—he of whom Plato remarks that he is pleased in his creation because of the likeness to himself which is reflected in it? And indeed what thing more beautiful than this universe could be presented to the eyes of the divinity? And since the universe is composed of its various parts, to which of these should more be attributed than to the formal principle? I leave for a better and more particular discussion the thousand natural reasons beyond this topical or logical one.

Dics. I do not care to have you straining over this point, since there is no philosopher of any reputation, even among the Peripatetics, who does not hold that the world and its spheres are in some way animated. I'd like now to learn how you conceive this form comes to insert itself into the matter of the universe.

Teo. It links itself there in such a way that the nature of the body, which in itself is not beautiful, participates as far as it is capable in beauty; for there is no beauty which does not consist of some species or form, and there is no form which is not produced by the soul.

Dics. I seem to be hearing something very unusual. You hold perhaps that not only the form of the universe, but all forms of natural objects whatever are soul.

Teo. Yes.

Dics. All things are then animated?

Teo. Yes.

Dics. But who will agree with you on this?

Teo. Who with reason can disprove it?

Dics. Common sense tells us that not all things are alive.

Teo. Common sense isn't the truest sense.

Dics. I readily believe that your view can be defended. But the fact that a view can be defended isn't enough to make it true; it must be also proved.

Teo. That's not hard. Aren't there philosophers who declare that the world is animated?

Dics. There are certainly many, and they the leading ones.

Teo. Then why don't these same philosophers say that all the world's parts are animated?

Dics. They indeed do say it, but only of the principal parts and those which are the true parts of the world; for with as much reason they hold that the soul is entire in the whole world and entire in any one of its parts, as that the soul of the living creatures perceptible to us is entire throughout them all.

Teo. Then what do you think are not true parts of the universe?

Dics. Those which are not, in Peripatetic terms, primary bodies: the earth, together with the waters and other parts, which, according to your statement, constitute the complete organism: the moon, the sun, and other like bodies. Beyond these principal organisms there are those which are not primary parts of the universe and some of which, it's said, possess a vegetative soul, others a sensitive, others an intellective one.

Teo. But if the soul is in the whole and also in the parts, why do you refuse to allow it in the parts of the parts?

Dics. I do allow it, but in the parts of the parts of animate things.

Teo. Now what things are there which aren't animate or don't make up the parts of animate things?

Dics. Don't you think we have a few of them here before our eyes? All things that lack life.

Teo. And what are the things that lack life, at least the vital principle?

Dics. To come to the point, do you assert that there is nothing not endowed with life and owning a vital principle?

Teo. That's exactly what I do assert.

Pol. Then a dead body has a soul? Then my shoes, my slippers, my boots, my spurs, my ring, and my gloves are animated? my gown and my cloak are animated?

Gerv. Yes, sir, yes, Master Poliinnio, why not? I certainly believe that your gown and cloak are fully animated when they contain such an animal as you. The boots and spurs are animated when they cover your feet; the hat is animated when it holds your head, which is not lacking in soul; and the stable is also animated when it takes in the horse, the mule, or your lordship. Don't you think so, Teofilo? Don't you consider I've understood you better than the *dominus noster*?

Pol. Cujum pecus? [Whose cattle?] As if there weren't asses *etiam et etiam* [also and also] subtle! Do you dare, you ignoramus, you ABCD-arian, to compare yourself with an archididascal and director of the School of Minerva such as me?

Gerv. Pax vobis, domine magister, servus servorum et scabellum pedum turorum. [Peace be with you, lord master, I am your servants' servant and your feet's footstool.]

Pol. Maledicat te Deus in secula seculorum. [God curse you, world without end.]

Dics. No brawling there. Leave us to settle this argument.

Pol. Prosequatur ergo sua dogmata Theophilus. [Then let Teofilo continue his teaching.]

Teo. I'll do so. I say then that the table as table is not animated, nor the clothes, nor the leather as leather, nor the glass as glass; but as natural things and composites they have within themselves matter and form. Let a thing be as small and diminutive as you like, it still possesses in itself a part of spiritual substance which, if it finds a suitable subject, becomes plant, becomes animal, and receives the members of one or other of the bodies that are commonly called animate; for spirit is found in all things and there is not the least corpuscle that doesn't contain internally some portion that may become alive.

Pol. Ergo, quidquid est, animal est. [Then whatever is, is an animal.]

Teo. Not all things that possess soul are called animate.

Dics. Then, at least, all things have life.

4+

Teo. I grant that all things have soul in them, have life, according to the substance they possess; but I do not hold that they are alive in terms of the act and operation recognisable as life by all the Peripatetics and those who define life and soul in a certain overgross way.

Dics. You disclose to me a plausible way of maintaining the opinion of Anaxagoras that all things are in all things; for since the spirit or soul or universal form is in all things, all can be produced from all.

Teo. I don't call it plausible, I call it true. For spirit is found in all things, which, if they are not living creatures, are still organisms. If not according to the perceptible presence of animation and life, yet they are animate according to the principle and a sort of primordial activity of animation and life. I don't elaborate this point as I want to pass over the properties of many small stones and gems, which, broken and recut and set in irregular pieces, possess a certain virtue of altering the spirit and engendering new affections and passions in the soul, not only in the body. And we know that such effects do not proceed, and cannot come forth, from a purely material quality, but are necessarily to be referred to a symbolic principle of life and animation. Besides, we see the same principle sensibly at work in withered stubs and roots which, by purging and gathering humours, by altering their spiritual state, manifest what are unmistakably the effects of life.

I pass over also the fact that not without good cause do necromancers hope to accomplish many things by means of the bones of the dead, and believe that those bones retain, if not the thing itself, at least a definite vital activity, which turns out competent to produce extraordinary effects. Other occasions will give me the chance to discourse at more length on the mind, the spirit, the soul, the life, which penetrates all, is in all, and moves all matter, fills the bosom of matter and dominates it rather than is dominated by it. For the spiritual substance cannot be overpowered by the material, but rather manages to embrace it.

Dics. That seems to me to conform not only with the outlook of Pythagoras, whose position the Poet recites when he says:

Principio caelum ac terrae camposque liquentes,
lucentemque globum lunae Titaniaque astra
spiritus intus alit, totamque infusa per artus
mens agitat molem, totoque se corpore miscet.

[In the beginning, heaven, earth, and fields of the waters
the moon's shining orb and the Titanian stars
the spirit within sustains; infused through the members, mind
stirs the whole mass and with the whole body is mingled.]

but also to conform with the outlook of the theologian who says:
The spirit overbrims and fills the earth, and is what contains all
things. Also, another thinker, speaking perhaps of the commerce
of form with matter and with potency, remarks that the dominating
factors are act and form.

Teo. If then spirit, soul, life, is found in all things and in
various degrees fills all matter, the certain deduction is that it is
the true act and the true form of all things. The world-soul, it
follows, is the formal constitutive principle of the universe and all
contained in it. I say that if life is found in all things, the soul must
be the form of all things: that which presides throughout over
matter, holds sway over composite things, and determines the composition and consistency of their parts. And hence such form is
no less enduring than matter is.

I understand it to be one in all things. But, according to the
diversity of matter's dispositions and the power of the material
principles, active and passive, it comes to produce diverse con-
figurations and to bring about the different faculties, sometimes
showing the effect of life without sense, sometimes the effect of
life and sense without intellect, and at other times achieving an
appearance of the total suppression of the faculties, their repression
by weakness or some other condition of matter.

Thus, while the form changes place and circumstance, it itself
cannot possibly be annihilated, since spiritual substance is no less
real than material. So, only outer forms change and are even
destroyed, since they are not things, but of things; they are not
substances, but accidents and circumstances of substances.

Pol. Non entia sed entium. [Not entities, but of entities.]

Dics. Certainly, if any part of substance were to be annulled,
the whole world would be emptied out.

Teo. We then have an intrinsic formal principle, eternal and
subsistent, incomparably superior to that imagined by the Sophists,
who, ignorant of the substance of things, play about with accidents
and come to posit corruptible substances. For what they call
chiefly, primarily, and principally substance is what results from

composition: which is only an accident, does not contain in itself any stability and truth, and is resolved into nothing.

They declare that that is truly man which is the result of composition, and that the soul is truly no more than the perfection and act of a living body, or at least something that emerges from a certain symmetry of complexion and members. So it is not surprising that they make such an ado and are so greatly terrified of death and dissolution, like men who feel the loss of their being is imminent. Against this madness nature cries out in a loud voice and assures us that neither bodies nor soul need fear death, since matter and form alike are absolutely constant principles.

> O genus attonitum gelidae formidine mortis,
> quid Styga, quid tenebras et nomina vana timetis,
> materiam vatum falsique pericula mundi?
> Corpora sive rogus flamma seu tabe vetustas
> abstulerit, mala posse pati non ulla putetis:
> morte carent animas domibus habitantque receptae.
> Omnia mutant, nihil interit.

> [O race confounded by the icy terror of death,
> why do you dread the Styx and the empty names,
> mere tales for poets, the dangers of an invented world?
> Whether the pyre burns up our bodies or age
> wastes them away, death holds no evils to suffer.
> Souls cannot die, they leave their previous dwelling
> and live in new homes, which they forever inhabit.
> All things change, but nothing perishes.]

Dics. That seems to me to agree with what was said by Solomon, esteemed the wisest of men among the Hebrews: *Quid est quod est? Ipsum quod fuit. Quid est quod fuit? Ipsum quod est. Nihil sub sole novum.* [What is the thing that is? That which was. What is the thing that was? That which is. There is no new thing under the sun.] And so this form which you posit is not existent in, nor adhering to, matter according to its being, and does not depend on body or matter for its existence?

Teo. That is so. And more, I do not decide if all form is accompanied by matter, whereas I already definitely assert of matter that no part of it is ever destitute of form, unless form is defined in an abstractly logical way, as in Aristotle, who never tires of dividing by reason what is indivisible according to nature and truth.

Dics. Don't you hold that there may be another form than this eternal companion of matter?

Teo. Yes, and one more natural still: the material form about which we shall later reason. For the moment, note this distinction of form. There is a sort of primary form which informs, is extended, and is dependent; and since it informs everything, is in everything. And since it is extended, it communicates the perfection of the whole to the parts. And since it is dependent and has no activity through itself, it communicates the operation of the whole to the parts; likewise the name and the being. Such is the material form, for example, that of fire. Because each part of fire warms, it is called fire, and is fire.

Secondly, there is another sort of form, which informs and is dependent, but is not extended; and such form, since it perfects and actuates the whole, is in the whole and in every part of it. Since it is not extended, the result is that the action of the whole is not attributed to the parts. Since it is dependent, the action of the whole is communicated to the parts. Such is the vegetative and sensitive soul, since no part of the animal is an animal, yet all the same each part lives and feels.

Thirdly, there is another sort of soul, which actuates and perfects the whole, but is not extended and is not dependent as to its operation. Since this form actuates and perfects, it is in the whole, and in all and every part. Since it is not extended, the perfection of the whole is not attributed to the parts. Since it is not dependent, it does not communicate the operation of the whole to the parts. Such is the soul insofar as it can exercise intellectual power, and it is called the intellective soul; it does not make any part of a man which can itself be called a man, or be a man, or be described as possessing intelligence.

Of these three sorts of form, the first is material, and cannot be conceived or cannot exist without matter. The other two sorts, which in fact come together as one according to their substance and being, and are distinguished by the above-mentioned method, we denominate that formal principle which is distinct from the material principle.

Dics. I follow you.

Teo. Further, I want you to take note that although in common terms we say that there are five grades of form: namely, the elemental, the mixed, the vegetative, the sensitive, and the intellective, we do not however understand this in the vulgar sense; for the distinction has validity according to the operations which appear with the subjects and proceed from them—but not from the view-point of the primal and fundamental essence, the essence of the form and spiritual life, which, the same in all things fills all things, but not according to the same mode.

Dics. I understand. Inasmuch as this form which you posit as principle is a subsistent form, it constitutes a perfect species, is of its own genus, and is not, like that Peripatetic form, a part of a species.

Teo. That's so.

Dics. The determination of forms in matter is not according to the accidental dispositions which depend on material form.

Teo. True.

Dics. Hence also this separated form is not multiplied in the sense of number; for all numerical multiplication depends on matter.

Teo. Yes.

Dics. Further, invariable in itself, it is variable through the subject's and matter's diversity. And such form, though it differentiates the part from the whole in the subject, yet itself does not differ in the part and in the whole: though one ground suits it as subsistent on and by itself, another insofar as it is the act and perfection of some subject, and yet another in relation to a subject with dispositions of one kind, another with those of another kind.

Teo. Precisely.

Dics. This form is not to be taken as accidental or as like the accidental, as mixed with matter or as inherent in it, but as indwelling, associated, assistant.

Teo. That's my position.

Dics. More, this form is defined and determined by matter, since, owning the capacity of constituting the particulars of innumerable species, it restricts itself to constituting an individual; and on the other hand, the potency of indeterminate matter, which is able to receive any form whatever, finds its delimitation in a species. And so the one is the cause of the definition and determination of the other.

Teo. Very good.

Dics. Then in some sort you approve of the opinion of Anaxagoras, who calls the particular forms of nature latent—as to some extent that of Plato, who deduces them from ideas, and to some extent also that of Empedocles, who makes them issue from the intelligence—and again in some sort that of Aristotle, who makes them emerge, as it were, from the potency of matter?

Teo. Yes. For, as we have said, where there is form, there is, in a certain sense, everything. Where there is soul, spirit, life, there is everything. The creator of ideal species is the intellect; and even if it does not bring forms out from matter, it still does not go begging for them outside of it, since this spirit fills the whole.

Pol. Velim scire quo modo forma est anima mundi ubique tota [I'd like to know in what way form is the world-soul everywhere entire], if it is indivisible? It must then be very large, even of infinite dimensions, if you say the world is infinite.

Gerv. There's good reason for its being large. The same thing was said of Our Lord by a preacher at Grandazzo in Sicily. There, as a sign that he is present everywhere in the world, he ordered a crucifix as big as the church, in the image of God the father, who has the empyrean for canopy, the starry heavens for throne, and such long legs that they reach down to the earth, which serves him as footstool. To this preacher there came a certain peasant, who questioned him: Reverend father, now how many ells of cloth would it take to make his hose? And another added that all the peas, haricots, and broad beans of Melazzo and Nicosia wouldn't be enough to stuff his belly. Look to it then that this world-soul isn't made in the same fashion.

Teo. I don't know how to answer your doubt, Gervase, but that of master Poliinnio I can handle. However, to meet the question of you both, I'll make use of a comparison, since I want you too to gather some fruit from our reasonings and discussions. You must then realise in brief that the world-soul and the divinity are not omnipresent through the whole and through every part as some material thing could be. For that is impossible to a body of any kind and a spirit of any kind. But they are present in a way which isn't easy to explain except along some such lines as the following.

You must note that if the world-soul and the universal form are said to be everywhere, we do not mean in a corporeal and dimensional sense; for such they are not, and such they cannot be in any part. But they are spiritually everywhere in their wholeness. To take an example, even though a crude one, you can imagine a voice which is entire inside a room and in every part of it, since every-where there it is entirely heard—just as these words I utter are entirely heard by every one of you and would still be heard if there were a thousand present. And my voice, could it reach throughout the whole world, would be everywhere entire.

I say then to you, master Poliinnio, that the soul is not in-divisible as a point is, but in some sort as a voice is. And I reply to you, Gervase, that the divinity is not everywhere in the sense that the God of Grandazzo is in the whole of his chapel, because, though he is present everywhere in the church, he is not wholly present everywhere, but his head is in one part, his feet in another, his arms and chest in yet other parts. But the divinity is entire in any part whatever, just as my voice is heard entire from all parts of this room.

Pol. Percepi optime. [I understood perfectly.]

Gerv. I have at least comprehended your voice.

Dics. I believe that's so of the voice, but as to the argument, I think it's gone in one ear and out of the other.

Gerv. I think it hasn't even gone in; for the hour is late and the clock in my stomach has struck suppertime.

Pol. Hoc est, idest [this is what it is], to have your brains in the platter.

Dics. Enough then. We'll meet again tomorrow to carry on with the material principle.

Teo. I'll wait for you or you wait for me here.

THIRD DIALOGUE

Gerv. It's time already and they haven't turned up. As I have nothing else in mind to attract me, I wish to amuse myself by listening to their discussion. Apart from being able to pick up a smattering of philosophy, I pass the time agreeably by noting what fads and fancies skip about like crickets in the heteroclite brain of the pedant Poliinnio. First he sets himself up as judge of who speaks well, who discourses better, who commits incongruities and errors in philosophy; yet when his own turn comes to speak and he doesn't know what to advance, he proceeds to extract from the sleeve of his windy pedantry a trivial salad of proverbialities, of Latin and Greek phrases, with no relation at all to what the others are saying. So any blind man could see without too much difficulty what a fool he is for all his letters, and how sage the others are in their plain vernacular.

But here he is, on my faith; and as he struts on this way, you can tell by his very manner of walking that he takes literate steps. Good day, *dominus magister*.

Pol. I don't care much for that *magister*. In our topsy-turvy and outrageous epoch it comes to be attributed as much to any barbering fellow, cobbler, or swine-cutter, as to my peers. Hence the counsel was given: *Nolite vocari Rabbi* [Be not ye called Rabbi].

Gerv. How then do you want me to address you? Do you like Very Reverend?

Pol. Illud est presbiterale et clericum [that's priestly and clerical].

Gerv. How then Most Illustrious?

Pol. Cedant arma togae [arms yield to the toga]. That is for those of knightly station, such as the purple-clad.

Gerv. Your Imperial Majesty?

Pol. Quae Caesaris Caesari [what is Caesar's, give to Caesar].

Gerv. Accept then the *domine*! Take to yourself the title of Loudthunderer, of *divum pater*!—But let's come to facts: why are you so late?

Pol. I believe that the rest are held up by some other business. Myself, so as not to lose this day with no occupation, I have given myself up to contemplating that kind of globe which is called a map of the world.

Gerv. What have you to do with a map of the world?

Pol. I contemplate the parts of the earth, the zones, the provinces and regions. I have traversed them all in ideal reason, and many I have covered also with my feet.

Gerv. I'd like you to do a little travelling back inside yourself; for that it seems to me is what you most need and what I think you care least for.

Pol. Absit verbo invidia [all boasting apart], in this way I come much more effectively to know myself.

Gerv. And how will you convince me of that?

Pol. Because from the contemplation of the macrocosm, easily, *necessaria deductione facta a simili* [after the necessary process of deduction, by means of comparison] we can arrive at the cognition of the microcosm, in which the particulars correspond to the various parts of the macrocosm.

Gerv. So you'll find inside yourself the Moon, Mercury, and the other stars, France, Spain, Italy, England, Calicut, and the other countries?

Pol. Quidni? per quamdam analogiam. [Why not? by a certain analogy].

Gerv. Per quamdam analogiam I believe you're a great monarch. But if you were a woman, I'd ask you if you had a place for lodging a baby or for sticking-in one of those plants that Diogenes mentions.

Pol. Ah, ah, *quodammodo facete* [a joke of sorts]! But such a request does not square with a sage and a scholar.

Gerv. If I were a scholar and held myself a sage, I wouldn't come here to learn at the same time as you.

Pol. You, yes—but I do not come here to learn; for *nunc meum est docere; mea quoque interest eos qui docere volunt iudicare* [my office is to teach, my concern is also to pass judgment on those who wish to teach]; hence I come with another purpose than that which must bring you—you to whom it befits to be tiro, isagogue, and disciple.

Gerv. What is your purpose?

Pol. To pass judgment, I tell you.

Gerv. Indeed it suits your sort more than others to pass judgment on sciences and doctrines, since you are the only ones to whom the liberality of the stars and the munificence of fate have accorded the ability to extract the sap from words.

Pol. And consequently also from the meanings which are associated with the words.

Gerv. As soul with body.

Pol. Which words, being properly understood, beget a right comprehension of their meanings. That is why from the knowledge of tongues, in which I more than anyone else in this city am expert and in which I do not count myself less learned than any of those who hold open schools of Minerva, there proceeds the knowledge of any science whatsoever.

Gerv. Then all those who understand the Italian tongue will grasp the Nolan's philosophy?

Pol. Yes, but they need also to possess some dexterity and judgment.

Gerv. For some time I have thought this dexterity the main thing; for even if one does not know Greek, one can still understand all the meaning of Aristotle and recognise many errors in him. One sees clearly that the idolatry surrounding the authority of that philosopher, especially in natural science, has been quite abolished among those who grasp the ideas of this other school [the Nolan]. Also, a man who knows no Greek, no Arabic, and perhaps no Latin, like Paracelsus, can yet have a better knowledge of medicaments and medicine than Galen, Avicenna, and all the others who were acquainted with the Roman tongue. Philosophers and laws fall into perdition, not through the lack of interpreters of words, but through the lack of men who are profound thinkers.

Pol. So you then count a man like me among the number of the witless crowd?

Gerv. The gods forbid, since I know that by the knowledge and study of tongues—which is a rare and remarkable thing—you as well as those like you are most capably equipped for assessing doctrines, after having sifted through the opinions of those who uphold them.

Pol. As you hit the mark of truth, I can easily persuade myself that you don't speak without good reason; and so, as you don't find it difficult, you won't find it disagreeable to explain it all.

Gerv. I'll do so, submitting myself at all points to the judgment of your prudence and learning. It is a common proverb that those who watch a game understand it better than those engaged in it. In the same way those looking on at a spectacle can better judge of the performance than those persons who are on the stage; and one can better sample music when one is not of the chapel or the concert. And again the same thing applies to a card-game, chess, fencing, and the like.

So with you others, gentleman pedants, outsiders and strangers to every activity of science and philosophy, who have never been drawn into the systems of Aristotle, Plato, and their like—you can better judge and condemn them in your grammatical self-sufficiency and your presumptuous reliance on your natural powers than the Nolan who finds himself on the same stage and in such familiarity and intimacy with them, that he easily combats them after having come to know their innermost and deepest ideas. You others, I repeat, by standing outside every profession of honoured men and rare wits, can better judge them.

Pol. I don't know how to make a point-blank reply to this impudent fellow. *Vox faucibus haesit* [the voice is stuck in my throat].

Gerv. Thus your sort are so presumptuous, unlike those who have their feet inside the problem. And in consequence I assure you that worthily you usurp the right of approving this, reproving that, glossing the other, making here a concordance and collation of texts, and there an appendix.

Pol. This total ignoramus wants to infer from the fact of my being versed in humane letters that I am ignorant in philosophy.

Gerv. Most learned sir, Poliinnio, I'd like to inform you that if you had all the tongues, which our preachers declare are seventy-two——

Pol. Cum dimidia.

Gerv. —it still would not only fail to follow that you are capable of judging philosophers, but also it would show that you couldn't help being the biggest blundering creature that exists in human form. Besides, there is nothing to stop anyone with the mastery of scarcely one of these tongues, even a bastard one, from being the wisest and most learned man in the whole world.

Now, consider what success has been achieved by two such writers as I shall mention—the one [Pierre de la Ramée], a French archpedant, who has composed dissertations on the liberal arts and animadversions against Aristotle; the other [Francesco Patrizzi], an Italian, an excrement of pedantry, who has soiled many quires with his Peripatetic Discussions. Anyone can easily see that the first man with much eloquence displays his lack of understanding; the second, to speak bluntly, gives away that he has much of the beast and the ass in him.

Of the first we can remark that he understood Aristotle, but understood him badly; and if he had understood him well, he would perhaps have possessed the wit to wage honourable war with him—as has been done by the most judicious Telesio of Cosenza. Of the second we cannot assert that he has understood Aristotle well or ill, we can only say that he has read and reread him, sewn him up and torn him to bits, compared him with a thousand other Greek authors, his allies and opponents alike. And so in the end he has achieved an enormous boredom, not only without any advantage, but *etiam* [even] with the greatest disadvantage. If anyone wants to see into what folly and presumptuous vanity a pedantic character can precipitate and engulf a man, let him read this one book before his seed is quite lost. But here comes Teofilo and Dicson.

Pol. Adeste felices, domini [welcome]. It is thanks to your arrival that my state of glowing wrath doesn't issue in thunderbolts of judgment hurled against the vain statements made by this garrulous ejaculator of immature seed.

Gerv. And for the same reason I am cut short in my jesting with the majesty of this most reverend owl.

Dics. All is well as long as you haven't lost your temper.

Gerv. Everything I say, I say in jest, because I love the master.

Pol. Ego quoque quod irascor, non serio irascor, quia Gervasium non odi [I too, insofar as I'm angry, am not angry in earnest, because I don't hate Gervase].

Dics. Good, then let me resume the discussion with Teofilo.

Teo. Democritus then and the Epicureans assert that what is not body is nothing, and that in consequence matter alone is the substance of things and is the divine nature, as an Arab named Avicebron has stated in a book entitled *The Spring of Life.* These philosophers, together with the Cyrenaics, the Cynics, and the Stoics, hold that forms are only accidental dispositions of matter.

And I myself for a long time adhered to this view, only because it has a basis more in correspondence with nature than that of Aristotle. But after riper reflection and after taking more things into consideration, we find that it is necessary to recognise in nature two sorts of substance: one that is form and one that is matter. For a substantial act is needed, in which is the active potency of everything, as well as a potency and a substratum in which there is an equal passive potency of all things. In the first is the power to make, in the latter the power to be made.

Dics. Anyone who reasons correctly will find it obviously impossible that the former can always make everything if there were not always present that which can be made everything. How can the world-soul (I mean, the totality of forms), which is indivisible, set about acting as shaper without the substratum of dimensions or quantities, which is matter.

And how can matter be shaped? Perhaps by itself? Clearly we can say that matter is shaped by itself if we wish to consider the universal formed body as matter and to call it matter—just as we'd describe an animal with all its faculties as matter, if we distinguished it, not by the form, but by the sole efficient cause.

Teo. No one can prevent you from using the term matter along those lines: just as for many schools the self-same reasons are used to bring out different meanings. But the manner of approach you sketch, I know, can suit only a mechanist or physician who takes his stand on practice—such as the man [Paracelsus] who reduced the universal body into mercury, salt, and sulphur: a declaration that reveals less the divine genius of a physician than the stupidity of a man who wants to claim the name of philosopher.

For the aim of philosophy is not to arrive simply at this distinction of principles that is obtained physically through the separation brought about by the virtue of fire, but also at that distinction of principles which cannot be achieved through any material efficient cause—because the soul, which is inseparable from the sulphur, mercury, and salt, is the formal principle, and that principle is not subjected to material qualities, but is in everything the master of matter. It is not touched by the experiments of the chemists, whose work of dividing ends in the three aforesaid things and who know another sort of soul than that of the world, and which we need to define.

Dics. Excellently said. This consideration pleases me very much. For I see some persons who so lack in judgment that they don't distinguish the causes of nature taken absolutely in accordance with the total extension of their being—as philosophers do—and those taken in a limited and adapted sense. The first mode is useless and vain for physicians as such; the second is defective and restricted for philosophers as such.

Teo. You have touched on the very point for which Paracelsus, who has treated philosophy medically, is praised, and Galen, who has approached medicine philosophically, is censured. The latter has produced such an irksome mixture, such a tangled web, that in the last resort he comes out as a shallow enough physician and a very confused philosopher. I make these comments however with some reserve, as I have not had the leisure to examine all aspects of his work.

Gerv. Please, Teofilo, do me this favour first, as I am not very competent in philosophy. Expound to me what you mean by this term matter, and just what matter is in natural things.

Teo. All who want to distinguish matter and consider it in itself, apart from form, have recourse to the analogy of art. That is what is done by the Pythagoreans, the Platonists, the Peripaticians. Take one sort of art, that of the carpenter. It has wood as subject for all its forms, all its work—as the blacksmith's subject is iron and the tailor's is cloth. All these arts, in their own particular material, produce various images, orders, and figures, none of which is proper or natural to the material. Thus, nature, which art resembles, needs a material for its operations, since it is impossible for any agent to want to make something and yet have nothing out of which to make it, or to want to work and yet have nothing on which to work.

There is then a sort of substratum, from which, with which, and in which, nature effects its operations, its work, and which is endowed by nature with so many forms that such a host of various species is presented to the eyes of consideration. And just as in itself it has no artificial form, but can have them all through the operations of the carpenter, so matter, of which we speak, has no natural form in itself but can have all forms through the operations of the active agent, the principle of nature.

This natural matter is therefore not as perceptible as artificial matter, because the matter of nature has absolutely no form, but the matter of art is something already formed by nature. For art cannot operate except on the surface of things formed by nature, such as wood, iron, stone, wool, or the like. But nature works, so to speak, from the centre of its subject or matter, which is throughout formless. As a result, the subjects of art are many, but one is the subject of nature. For the former, through being diversely formed by nature, are different and various; the latter, through not being in any way formed, is throughout identical, since all difference and diversity proceed from form.

Gerv. So the things formed by nature are the matter of art and a single formless thing is the matter of nature.

Teo. That's so.

Gerv. Is it then possible for us to know the substratum of nature, just as we can see and know clearly the substrata of the arts?

Teo. Assuredly, but with different principles of cognition. In the same way as we don't know colours and sounds by the same sense, so we cannot see the substratum of the arts and that of nature with the same eye.

Gerv. You mean that we see the first with the eyes of sense and the second with the eye of reason?

Teo. Exactly.

Gerv. Would you please develop this line of argument?

Teo. Gladly. The relation and reference that the form of art has to its matter is the same as that which the form of nature has to its matter, allowing for the due differences. In art the forms vary to infinity (if that were possible), but the same matter always persists under them. Thus, the form of the tree becomes the form of a trunk, then of a beam, then of a table, a stool, a chest, a comb, and so on; but the wood remains all the while identical in its being. So it is in nature, where forms vary to infinity and succeed one another, yet matter always remains identical.

Gerv. How can this analogy be confirmed?

Teo. Don't you see that what was seed becomes stalk, and what was stalk becomes corn, and what was corn becomes bread—that out of bread comes chyle, out of chyle blood, out of blood the seed, out of the seed the embryo, and then man, corpse, earth, stone, or something else in succession—on and on, involving all natural forms?

Gerv. I see that easily.

Teo. There must then exist an unchanging thing which in itself is not stone nor earth nor corpse nor man nor embryo nor blood nor anything else in particular, but which, after it was blood, became embryo, receiving the embryonic being; and after it was embryo, received the human being and became man. In the same way, in that which is formed by nature and constitutes the subject of art, what was tree becomes table and receives the being of table; that which was table, receiving the being of door, becomes door.

Gerv. Yes, that I understand quite well. But this substratum of nature, it seems to me, cannot be body, nor of a certain quality. For, escaping as it does into one form and natural being, and then into another, it does not manifest itself corporeally, like wood or stone, which always appear what they materially are, or serve as a subject, no matter what the form.

Teo. You put it well.

Gerv. What then shall I do if I happen to be discussing this idea with some obstinate person who refuses to agree that there is one matter underlying all the formations of nature, just as there is one under all the formations of art? For the latter are to be seen with one's eyes and so cannot be denied; but the former are visible only to the eyes of reason and so can be denied.

Teo. Dismiss him and don't reply.

Gerv. But what if he is importunate in his demand for evidence, and if he is someone of respect who is more in a position to dismiss me than I am to dismiss him, and who takes as an insult my refusal to answer?

Teo. What would you do if a blind demigod, worthy of heaven-knows-what honour and respect, were insistent, importunate, and obstinate in wanting to acquire cognition of, and to demand evidence for, colours—not to mention the external figurations of natural things—as for instance: What is the form of a tree? what is the form of mountains? of stars? or again, what is the form of a statue, a robe, or other artificial things, which for those who can see are so plain?

Gerv. Why, I'd tell him that if he had eyes he wouldn't ask for evidence, but would be able to see for himself; but as he's blind, it's also impossible for others to show him these things.

Teo. In the same way you'll be able to answer those others: that if they had intellect, they wouldn't ask for further evidence, but would be able to see them by themselves.

Gerv. That reply would make some feel ashamed, others would regard it as too cynical.

Teo. Then you will speak to them in a more covered-up way: Most illustrious sir, or your Sacred Majesty, just as some things become evident only through the hands and the sense of touch, others only through hearing, others through taste, and others through the eyes, so this matter of natural things cannot become evident except through the intellect.

Gerv. Perhaps he'll understand the stroke, which after all isn't so hidden or obscure, and he'll reply: But you're the one who has no intellect, I have more of it than all your sort.

Teo. You'll credit him no more than if a blind man retorted that it's you who are blind and that he sees more than all those who think they see like you.

Dics. You have said enough in demonstrating more plainly than I've ever heard, what the term matter signifies and what we must understand by matter in natural things. So Timaeus the Pythagorean teaches us to find, through the transmutation of one element into another, the matter which is hidden and can be known in certain analogical terms. Where the form of earth was, he says, there afterwards appears the form of water. And we cannot assert that there one form receives the other since a contrary does not accept or receive another: *i.e.* the dry does not receive the wet, or rather dryness does not receive wetness, but the dryness is expelled from a third thing and into that third thing the wetness is introduced—and this third thing is the substratum of both the contraries and is itself not contrary to anything.

It follows that since we must not think the earth has disappeared into nothing, we must consider that something which was in the earth has subsisted and survives in the water. Similarly, when the water is transmuted into air (because the virtue of the heat comes to extenuate it into smoke and vapour), this something will persist and will be there in the air.

Teo. Hence we may conclude (again in spite of the Peripaticians) that nothing is ever annihilated and loses its being, apart from the accident form, material and corporeal. Then the matter and the substantial form alike, of any natural thing whatever—that is, the soul—are indissoluble and indestructible, and cannot lose their being in anything, anywhere. Such certainly cannot be all the substantial forms of the Peripatetics and others like them, which consist of nothing apart from a certain complexion and a certain order of accidents. And for these philosophers, all that they are able to designate outside their primary matter is nothing but an accident, a complexion, a disposition of qualities, a principle of definition, quiddity.

That is why some cowled and subtle metaphysicians among them, wishing to excuse rather than accuse the insufficiency of their deity Aristotle, have invented Humanity, Bovinity, Oliveness, to take the place of specific substantial forms. This Humanity, for example Socratiety, this Bovinity, this Horsiness, constitute for them the substance of plurality.

All this they have fabricated in order to provide a substantial form which merits the name of substance—just as matter [deservedly] owns the name and being of substance. Yet they have never profited in the least. If you ask them, starting from the beginning: In what does the substantial being of Socrates consist? they'll reply: In Socratiety. If you then follow up: What do you mean by Socratiety? they'll reply: The proper substantial form and the proper matter of Socrates. Well, let's leave aside this substance which is matter, and ask: What is the substance as form? Some will reply: Its soul. Ask them: What is its soul? If they say: An entelechy or perfection of a body capable of life, remark that this is an accident. If they say: It is the principle of life, sense, vegetation, and intellect, remark that, though this principle is a substance when fundamentally considered, as in our system, they themselves always present it solely as an accident.

For to be the principle of this or that thing is not the same as being the substantial and absolute reason [for its existence]. It means rather to be an accidental and relative reason of that in which the principle exists—just as no one can express my being and substance by stating what I am doing or can do; an absolute definition can be made only by stating what I myself, considered absolutely, am.

You see then how they treat this substantial form, which is the soul. Even if by chance they have recognised it as substance, they have never defined or considered it as such. This conclusion you can see yet more plainly brought out, if you ask them in what consists the substantial form of an inanimate thing, e.g. that of wood. Those with the greatest subtlety will imagine that it lies in Woodiness.

Now take away this matter which is common to iron, wood, stone, and say: What substantial form of iron remains? They'll never adduce anything but accidents. These however are among the principles of individuation and give particularity; they cannot be contracted to the particular except through some form, and this form, to be the constituent principle of a substance, should be substantial—but then they cannot show it physically [in its reality] except as something accidental.

Finally, when they've done all they can with the means at their disposal, they are left with a substantial form, yes, but not one that exists in nature, only a logical construction. And thus at the end a logical concept comes to be put as the principle of natural things.

Dics. Aristotle doesn't realise this?

Teo. I think he realised it fully, but couldn't remedy it. So he declared the ultimate differences to be indefinable and unknown.

Dics. Then he seems to me to have made an open confession of his ignorance; and therefore I'd judge it yet better to embrace those philosophic principles which in this important question do not plead ignorance: such as those of Pythagoras, Empedocles, and your Nolan, whose opinions we yesterday touched on.

Teo. Here is the viewpoint of the Nolan. There is one intellect which gives being to everything, called by the Pythagoreans and the *Timaeus* giver-of-forms: a soul and formal principle which becomes and informs everything, called by the same thinkers the fountain-of-forms: a single matter out of which everything is produced and formed, called by everyone the receptacle-of-forms.

Dics. This doctrine gives me much satisfaction, for there seems nothing lacking to it. And indeed it is necessary, just as we can posit a constant and eternal material principle, that we posit a similar formal one. We see all natural forms fall out of matter and afresh arise out of matter; and so in reality nothing is constant, stable, eternal, and worthy of being esteemed a principle except matter.

Besides the fact that forms have no being without matter, in which they are generated and into which they are resolved, it is out of her bosom that they come forth and into it that they are gathered. Hence matter, which always remains identical and fertile, ought to have the principal prerogative of being recognised as the sole substantial principle, as that which is and which forever remains. And

forms, all of them together, are to be taken only as varied dispositions of matter, which come and go, which cease and renew themselves—so that they cannot, any of them, have the value of a
principle.

And so we find philosophers, who, after thoroughly considering the reason of natural forms and being able to turn away from
Aristotle and his like, have decided in the end that those forms are
only accidents and circumstances of matter. As a result the prerogative of action and of perfection should be referred to matter
and not to things, of which we can truly say that they are not substance or nature, but belong to substance and nature, which (these
philosophers say) are matter. And matter in their view is a necessary principle, eternal and divine, just as it is to that Moor Avicebron, who calls it God-who-is-in-everything.

Teo. They have been led into this error because they do not
recognise any other form than the accidental. And this Moor,
though accepting the substantial form of the Peripatetic doctrine
in which he had been bred, yet in all his work considered it as a
corruptible thing, not only changeable in relation to matter. As that
which is produced but does not itself produce, established but not
stable, thrown out but not itself throwing anything out, he despised
it and held it worthless in comparison with matter, which is stable,
eternal, progenitor, and mother. And this position is inevitably
reached by those who do not know what we know.

Dics. That was very well thought-out. But it's time to turn
from this digression back to our problem. We now know how to
distinguish matter from form—as much from accidental form
(taking that any way you like) as from substantial form. What
remains is to look into its nature and reality. But first I'd like to
know whether, in view of the great union that the world-soul and
universal soul has with matter, we ought not to accept the other
mode of philosophising—that of thinkers who do not separate the
act from the nature of matter and who understand matter as a
divine thing, not as something so bare and formless that it cannot
form and clothe itself.

Teo. Not easily, since nothing works absolutely in itself alone,
and there is always some distinction between the agent and what
is produced or on which the action and the operation play. So it is
as well in the body of nature to distinguish matter from soul, and
in the soul to determine the reason of species.

Hence we declare that there are three things in nature's body: first the universal intellect inherent in things, secondly the soul which vivifies all, and thirdly the substratum. But for all that we shall not refuse the name of philosophers to those who, following their own bent, take this formed body (or, as I'd prefer to say, this rational organism) and then in some way begin by accepting as first principles the members of this body, such as air, earth, fire, or the ethereal region and stars, or spirit and body, or indeed the void and the plenum (meaning by the void however something other than Aristotle did), or in fact any convenient grouping.

Such a philosophy does not seem to me to deserve rejection, above all when, no matter what basis is presupposed or what form of edifice is reared, the work helps in bringing about the perfection of speculative science and the cognition of natural things, as indeed has been done by many of the most ancient philosophers.

For it's a sign of an ambitious and presumptious brain, vain and envious, to want to convince others that there is only a single road for investigating and reaching the cognition of nature; and it is a sign of a madman, a man without discourse, to give way to a belief in oneself alone. Then, although we should prefer, honour, and cultivate the most consistent and steady way, the most contemplative and clear way, the mode of loftiest thought, yet there is no need to find fault with another way which is not without good fruit, though they may not be from the same tree.

Dics. So you approve of the study of different philosophies?

Teo. Indeed, for those who have plenty of time and wit. For others I approve of the study of the better way, if the gods will that they fathom it.

Dics. I'm sure however that you don't approve of all the philosophies, only of the good and the better ones.

Teo. That's so. As again among the various orders of medicine, I don't condemn that which is carried on magically by the application of roots, suspension of stones, and the murmuring of incantations, if the rigour of the theologians permits me to speak as a mere natural philosopher. I approve of what is done physically and executed by the apothecary's prescriptions to treat or dispel choler, blood, phlegm, and melancholia. I accept that other mode which proceeds chemically, which abstracts the quintessence, and which through the action of fire on all composite bodies volatilises the mercury, deposits the salt, and makes the sulphur grow luminous or dissolve.

However, as regards medicine, I have no wish to establish among so many good methods which is the better. If the epileptic, over whom the physician and the chemist have lost so much time, happens to be cured by a magician, he will approve of the latter more than of this or that brand of physician. We must apply the same line of argument to all the other kinds of treatment, of which none will be less good than the other if one as well as another attains the end it has set itself. In a particular case the physician who cures me is better than the others who murder and torture me.

Gerv. What's the reason for the large number of enemies among these medical sects?

Teo. Greed, envy, ambition, and ignorance. Generally the practitioners scarcely understand their own system of treatment, so it's all the less likely they'll get the hang of someone else's. Besides, most of them, unable to raise themselves to honour and profit through their own merits, seek to get preference by depreciating the others and making a show of contempt for what they can't attain. But the best and truest of them all is the man who is not only a physicist but is also a chemist and mathematician.

But to come back to our theme: among the kinds of philosophy, that is best which most serviceably and eminently effects the perfection of the human intellect and most closely corresponds with the truth of nature and co-operates as fully as possible with it —whether by divination (I mean through natural order and the laws governing change, not through an animal instinct as with the beasts and those who resemble them, not through the inspiration of good or bad demons, as prophets do, and not through melancholic enthusiasm, as poets and other contemplatives do), or whether by ordering laws and reforming customs, by healing, or somehow knowing and living a more blessed and divine life.

You see then that there's no sort of philosophy that has been elaborated by a regulated system of thought, which does not contain in itself some good property not to be found in the others. I apply the same attitudes to medicine, when it derives from such principles, which presuppose a not-imperfect habit of philosophy: as the activity of foot and hand presupposes that of the eye. And so it is said that no one can own a good medical principle unless he first has a good philosophic grounding.

Dics. You please me greatly and I give you back an equal measure of praise. Not being as uncultured as Aristotle, you are also not as offensive or pretentious. He wanted to disparage the opinions of all other philosophers with their own ways of philosophising.

Teo. Of all the philosophers that exist, I know of none more based on fantasies or more removed from nature than he is; and if at times he says excellent things, one recognises that they do not derive from his principles but are always propositions borrowed from other philosophers. We see many such divine things in his book *On Generation,* in the *Meteors,* and in the books *On Animals and Plants.*

Dics. Coming back then to our theme: do you assert that one can give diverse definitions of matter without error and without running into contradictions?

Teo. Yes, just as different senses can each deliver a judgment on the same object. Also, as we have already touched on, the consideration of a thing can be grasped under diverse heads. Though not rising above material quality, the Epicureans have said many good things. Though failing to mount above the soul, Heraclitus has given us knowledge of many excellent things. Anaxagoras manages to draw profit from nature, though not only in her, but perhaps also outside and above her, he recognises an intellect, which Socrates, Plato, Trismegistus, and our theologians have called God.

So, a man who starts off from the experimental knowledge of simple things (as they call them) can proceed on the discovery of nature's mysteries as effectively as those who begin with rational theory. And among such, those who start off from complexions as much as those who start off from humours; and among the latter, those who descend from sensible elements as much as those who start higher up, from absolute elements or from the one matter which is of all principles the highest and most distinct.

Sometimes the man who takes the longest way round does not make the best journey, especially when his end is not so much contemplation as operation. As for the manner of philosophising, it will not be less convenient to unfold forms as from a principle that involves them, than to distinguish them as from a chaos, or to distribute them as from an ideal source, or to bring them out into act from a state of possibility, to draw them out as from a womb, or to exhume them into the light as from a blind and dark abyss. For every foundation appropriate to its superstructure is good;

every seed is welcome when the trees and the fruits are desirable.

Dics. To come now to our purpose, please inform us of your distinct doctrine on this principle.

Teo. Certainly. This principle, called matter, can be considered in two ways. First, as potency; second, as substratum. Insofar as we take it as potency, there is nothing in which, in a certain way and according to its own specific nature, it cannot be found. The Pythagoreans, Platonists, Stoics, and others have placed it in the intelligible world as well as in the sensible. But we, who do not understand it in exactly the same way as they do, but in a higher and more explicit sense, speak in the following way of potency and possibility.

Potency is commonly divided into active potency, by means of which the subject is able to operate, and passive potency, by means of which it is able to exist or to receive or to possess or to be the subject of the efficient cause in any way. For the moment we shall not reason about active potency. I'll go on to say that potency regarded in its passive aspect—although it is not always passive—may be considered either relatively or absolutely.

Therefore, there is nothing which can be said to exist, if it cannot also be said to own the capacity of existing. And this aspect corresponds so precisely with active potency that passive and active cannot exist in any way without one another—so that, if there has always been the potency to make, produce, create, there has also always been the potency to be made, produced, created. One potency implies the other. I mean that in positing one we necessarily posit the other. And this [passive] potency does not indicate any weakness in that of which it is affirmed; rather it confirms its virtue and efficacy. Thus we find in the end that it is one with, and indeed the same thing as, active potency. Hence there is no philosopher or theologian who hesitates to attribute it to the first supernatural principle. For the absolute possibility, through which the things that are in act are able to be, does not precede the actuality nor does it come after it. Further, the capacity-to-be co-exists with the being-in-act, and does not precede it. For, if what is able to exist were able to make itself, it would exist before it was made.

Now, contemplate the supreme and best principle, which is all that it can be: it could not be all if it lacked the capacity to be all. In it then act and power are the same thing.

This is not the case with other things, which, however much they are what they can be, could perhaps however cease to be, and certainly could become something other, or something in a different way, than what they now are. For there is no thing which is all it can be. Man is what he can be, but not all he can be. A stone is not all it can be, since it isn't lime or vase or dust or grass. That which is all it can be is a unity which in its being comprehends every being.

Every other thing is not like that. Hence potency is not equal to act in them, since act is not absolute but limited. More, potency is always limited to a single act, since it never has more than one specific and particular being. And if it aspires to every form and act, it does so by means of certain dispositions and a certain succession of one being after another. Every potency and act then, which in the principle are as enfolded, united, and one, are unfolded, dispersed, and multiplied in other things.

The universe, which is the great simulacrum, the great image and sole-begotten nature, is also all that it can be, through the same species and principal members and contents of the whole of matter, to which nothing can be added, from which nothing can be taken away, and which consists of an entire and single form.

But it is not however all that it can be through the same differentiations, modes, properties, and particulars. Hence it is only a shadow of the first act and first potency; and in it potency and act are not absolutely the same, since no part of it is all that it can be. Further, in that specific mode that we have mentioned, the universe is all that it can be—in an unfolded, dispersed, and distinct way. Its first principle is all it can be, in a unified and undifferentiated way, since all is there all and identical in the utmost simplicity, without difference or distinction.

Dics. What is your explanation of death, corruption, vices, defects, monstrosities? Is it your meaning that these also have a place in that which is all it can be and which is in act all it is in potency?

Teo. These things are not act and potency, but defect and impotency, which are found in unfolded things because these latter are not all they can be, and are constrained into becoming what they can be. And so, unable to be several things all at once, they lose one being in order to possess another, and sometimes they confound one being with another; then they are diminished, made deficient, mutilated, through the incompatability of one being with another, and the sharing of the same matter by the two.

Now back to our theme. The first absolute principle is grandeur and magnitude; and this magnitude and grandeur is such that it is all it can be. It is not great in its grandeur in such a way that it can be made greater or lesser, or that it can be divided like every other grandeur which is not all it can be. Hence it is both the maximum grandeur and the minimum too, infinite and indivisible and of every measure. It is not the maximum because it is the minimum; it is not the minimum because it is that same maximum; and it is beyond every equality because it is everything it can be.

And what I say about its grandeur is to be understood of everything that can be asserted about it. It is similarly the goodness which is every goodness that can be. It is the beauty which is everything beautiful that can be; and there is no other beauty, except this one, which is all that it can be. One is that which is all and can be all absolutely.

In natural things, moreover, we do not see anything which is other than what it is in act; and through the act it is what it can be, as a result of owning a specific kind of actuality. But all the same in this unique specific being there is never all that any particular thing can be.

Take the sun there. It is not all the sun can be, it is not everywhere the sun can be. When it is east of the earth, it is not in the west, nor in the north, nor in the south, nor in any other aspect. Now, if we want to show the way in which God is the sun, we'll say (since he is all that he can be) that he is in the east, west, south, north, and any other point whatever in the earth's globe. And so if we want to understand of this [absolute] sun whether it moves or changes place (through its own revolution or through that of the earth), we'll say that it is not actually at a single point without the potency of being in all the others and hence has the ability to be there—and that therefore if it is all that it can be, and possesses all that it is apt to possess, it will be simultaneously everywhere and in all things; it is so completely mobile and fast-moving that it is also the most stable and immobile.

That is why, among the divine sayings, we find it described

as stable in eternity and yet most rapid in its course from one end to the other. For we call motionless that which in the same instant leaves the eastern point and returns to the eastern point, and which further is not seen any more in the east than in the west and at every other point of its circuit.

There is therefore no more reason for saying that it goes and returns or has gone and returned from one point to another than from any other of the infinity of points to the same point. It follows that it will be whole and pervading the whole circle as well as present in any of its parts; and consequently every individual point of the ecliptic contains the whole diameter of the sun. Thus an indivisible comes to contain the divisible; and this is brought about, not through natural possibility, but through supernatural. I mean, if one supposes the sun to be this sun which in act is all it can be.

But absolute potency is not only what the sun can be. It is what everything is and what everything can be. Potency of all potencies, act of all acts, life of all lives, being of all beings. That is why the Revealer has profoundly said: 'He who is, sends me. He who is, speaks thus.' And so what is elsewhere contrary and opposed, in him is one and the same, and everything in him is the same. And along similar lines you may argue about the differences of times and durations, as we did about differences of actuality and possibility. He is however neither an ancient nor a new thing, so that the Revealer has well said: First and Last.

Dics. This absolute act, which is the same as absolute potency, cannot be comprehended by the intellect, except by way of negation. It cannot be comprehended, I say, either insofar as it can be all things or insofar as it is all things. For the intellect, when it wants to understand, must form an intelligible species, must assimilate and measure itself and equalise itself with that species. But this is here impossible, since the intellect is never so great that it cannot be greater—while the absolute act, being immeasurable from all sides and in all ways, is as great as it can be. There is then no eye capable of approaching it or gaining access to so lofty a light and so deep an abyss.

Teo. The coincidence of this act with absolute potency has been clearly described by the divine spirit when it says: *Tenebrae non obscurabitur a te. Nox sicut dies illuminabitur. Sicut tenebrae eius, ita ut lumen eius* [Yea, the darkness hides not from you, but the night shines as the day: the darkness and the light are both alike to you].

To conclude then, you see how great is the excellence of this potency, which if you like you can call the essence of matter, into which the vulgar philosophers have not penetrated, and which, without detracting from the divinity, you can treat with a higher meaning than Plato has done in his *Republic* and his *Timaeus*. These works, through exalting too much the essence of matter, have scandalised certain theologians. This has happened, either because these works were not well enough expressed or because the theologians have not understood them well enough, since, bred solely on the opinions of Aristotle, they take matter always as meaning no more than the subject of natural things. And they do not consider that matter, according to their opponents, is such as to be common to both the intelligible and the sensible worlds—to use the terms of the latter, who adopt an equivocal definition based on an analogy.

That is why opinions should be thoroughly examined before being condemned; and the terms used should be as much distinguished as the ideas, considering that, though at times various thinkers come together in a shared concept of matter, they then proceed to their own particular application of it.

And as for what belongs to our line of argument, it is impossible that any theologian should be found, however captious and malevolent his wit might be, who, with the term matter suppressed, would impute impiety to me for what I say and mean about the coincidence of potency and act, taking both terms in an absolute sense.

I would thence like to conclude, in the permitted measure, with a comment on the simulacrum of this act and this potency (which is in specific act all that it is in specific potency, since the universe in this way is all that it can be—let it be as it will with regard to particularising act and potency): it comes to possess a power which is not separable from act, a soul which is not separable from what is animated—I speak not of the composite but of the simple.

And so the universe owns a first principle, which is to be taken as a single principle indistinctly material and formal, and which can be inferred on the analogy of the aforesaid principle, which is absolute potency and act. It is then not difficult or hazardous to accept, finally, that the whole in its substance is one, as perhaps Parmenides, ignobly treated by Aristotle, meant.

Dics. You mean that though in the descent of nature's ladder we encounter a duality of substance: one spiritual, one bodily—yet in sum they are both reducible to one being and one root.

Teo. Yes, if you think that such a conclusion can be tolerated by those who cannot penetrate far into the problem.

Dics. It's easy enough as long as one does not raise oneself above the limits of nature.

Teo. That has been already noted. If we do not have the same conception and method of defining the divinity, as are generally used, we have a particular point, which, without being contrary to or alien from the viewpoints of others, is yet perhaps clearer and more explicit—in accordance with reason, which does not go above the head of our argument and from which I did not promise you to abstain.

Dics. Enough has been said of the material principle from the angle of possibility and potency. Will you please then tomorrow go on to deal with the same, viewed as substratum?

Teo. I shall.

Gerv. Goodbye.

Pol. Bonis avibus [may the omens be good].

FOURTH DIALOGUE

Pol. (alone). Et os vulvae nunquam dicit: sufficit; id est, scilicet, videlicet, utpote, quod est dictu: materia [And the mouth of the womb never says: Enough. That is, namely, to wit, so to speak, what is to be said: Matter], which is expressed by this thing: *recipiendis formis numquam expletur* [it is never filled up by the forms it has to receive]. Well, since there is no one else in this lyceum, *vel potius* [or rather] Antilyceum, *solus (ita, inquam, solus, ut minime omnium solus) deambulo, et ipse mecum confabulor* [I alone, thus, I say alone, though really the least alone of men, take my stroll and discourse with myself].

Matter, then, has been denominated by the prince of the Peripaticians and by the topless genius of the great Macedonian controller, *non minus* [no less] than by the divine Plato and others, as *chaos*, or *hyle*, or *sylva*, or mass, or potency, or aptitude, or *privationi admixtum* [admixture with privation], *peccati causa* [cause of sin], or *ad maleficum ordinata* [ordained to evil], or *per se non ense* [in itself non-being], or *per se non scibile* [in itself unknowable], or *per analogiam ad formam cognoscibile* [knowable by analogy with form], or *tabula rasa* [a blank tablet], or *indepictum* [indescribable], or *subiectum* [subject] or *substratum*, or *substerniculum* [bed bespread], or *campus* [field] or *infinitum*, or *indeterminatum*, or *prope nihil* [almost nothing] *or neque quid, neque quale, neque quantum; tandem* [neither something nor quality nor quantity; at last] after having made comparisons of varied and diverse nomenclatures, to define the nature of this thing, *ab ipsis scopum ipsum attingentibus* [by attributes pertinent to the set aim] I have succeeded in naming it Woman. *Tandem, inquam (ut una complecantur omnia vocabula) a melius rem ipsam perpendentibus foemina dicitur* [at length, I say, to express the whole matter in one word, it is called Woman by those pondering the question more effectively].

Et mehercle [and by Hercules] not without some important cause did the senators of the realm of Pallas decide to collocate on an equal footing these two things: Matter and Woman. For they

117

have been brought to that transport and frenzy by their experience of the creature's flat inflexibility—and here there occurs to me a precise rhetorical flourish. Women are a chaos of irrationality, a *hyle* [wood] of wickedness, a forest of ribaldry, a mass of uncleanliness, an aptitude for every perdition—another rhetorical figure here, called by some Complexion! Where existed in potency, *non solum remota* [not only far-off] but *etiam propinqua* [also near-at-hand], the destruction of Troy? In a woman. Who was the instrument enfeebling the strength of Samson, that hero, I say, who, with the famous jawbone of an ass that he found, became the unconquerable triumpher over the Philistines? A woman. Who mastered at Capua the impetus and might of the great captain and perpetual foe of the Roman republic, Hannibal? A woman. (*Exclamatio!*)

Tell me, O lutanist prophet, the cause of your fragility? *Quia in peccatis concepit me mater mea* [because my mother conceived me in sin]. How, O ancient first-made man, being gardener of paradise and cultivator of the tree of life, did you turn so wrongheaded as to precipitate yourself with all the human seed into the deep gulf of perdition? *Mulier quam dedit mihi; ipsa, ipsa me decepit* [the woman whom he gave me, she, she deceived me].

Procul dubio [without doubt], form does not sin and error is engendered by no form unless it is conjoined to matter. That's why form, signified by the male, when placed in a position of intimacy with matter and come into composition or copulation with it, replies in these words to *natura naturans*, or rather in this sentence: *Mulier, quam dedit mihi, idest* [the woman whom he gave me, that is] matter, which was given me as consort, *ipsa me decepit: hoc est* [she deceives me: that is] matter is the cause of all my sin. Consider, consider, divine spirit, how the egregious philosophers and the discriminating anatomists of nature's bowels, in their efforts to set fully before our eyes the nature of matter, have found no more suitable way than to confront us with this equation: which shows that the state of natural things is to matter as the economic, political, and civil state is to the female sex. Open, open your eyes, *etcetera.*

O, I see that colossus of indolence, Gervase, coming to snap the thread of my elaborate speech. I fear he has overheard me; but what does it matter?

Gerv. Salve, magister doctorum optime [Good-day, master, best of doctors].

Pol. If you don't mean *tuo more* [according to your custom] to jeer at me, *tu quoque, salve* [good-day to you, too].

Gerv. I'd like to know what you ruminated as you strolled about on your own.

Pol. As I was studying in my little temple of the muses, *in eum, qui apud Aristotelem est, locum incidi* [there I came upon a passage in Aristotle], in the first book of the *Physics*, where he sets out to elucidate what primary matter is, and takes as mirror the female sex: the sex, I mean, capricious, frail, inconstant, soft, petty, infamous, ignoble, base, abject, negligent, unworthy, reprobate, sinister, abusive, frigid, misshapen, vacuous, vain, rash, mad, perfidious, lazy, fetid, nasty, ungrateful, garbled, mutilated, imperfect, inchoate, inadequate, curt, amputated, attenuated, rusty, vermin, tares, plague, disease, death,

> By Nature and by God among us sent,
> a burden and a heavy punishment.

Gerv. I know you say this more to exercise yourself in the oratorical art and demonstrate how copious and eloquent you are, than because you own such thoughts as you set out in the words. For it's a normal thing for you humanists, who call yourself professors of the liberal arts, on finding that you're replete with concepts you can't hold back, to go and discharge them on poor womenfolk, just as when some other irritation inflames you, you vent it on the first offender among your pupils. But beware, you Orpheuses, of the furious wrath of the Thracian women.

Pol. I am Poliinnio, not Orpheus.

Gerv. Then you don't truly censure women?

Pol. Minime, minime quidem [very very little indeed]. I speak truly and I don't think otherwise than I speak, because I don't, *sophistarum more* [like the sophists] make a profession of demonstrating that white is black.

Gerv. Why then do you dye your beard?

Pol. But *ingenue loquor* [I speak freely] and I say that a man without woman is like one of the intelligences. He is, I say, a hero, a demigod, *qui non duxit uxorem* [who doesn't take a wife].

Gerv. And he is like an oyster, a mushroom also, and a truffle.

5+

Pol. Whence the lyric poet has divinely said: *Credite Pisones, melius nil caelibe vita* [Believe me, Pisones, nothing is better than a bachelor life]. And if you want to know the cause, listen to the philosopher Secundus. Woman, says he, is an obstacle to quiet, a continual damage, a daily war, a life-prison, a storm in the house, the shipwreck of man. And the man from Biscay properly confirmed all that when he was stirred to impatience and anger at his horrifying fortune and the raging of the sea, and turned on the waves with a grim and choleric face. Ah sea, sea, he cried, if only I could marry you off!—meaning to infer that woman is the tempest of tempests. Hence, too, Protagoras, asked why he had given his daughter to an enemy, answered that he could do him no worse turn than to provide him with a wife. What's more, it wasn't to refute me that a good Frenchman, who—like all the others suffering a very perilous sea-tempest—was ordered by Cicala, the master of the ship, to throw his heaviest burden overboard, and at once heaved his wife out first.

Gerv. You omit to cite the opposite cases of the numerous men considered blest through their wives. Among whom—not to send you too far afield—here, under this very roof, is Monsieur de Mauvisser. He has encountered one who is not only endowed with uncommon bodily beauty as embellishment and wrap of her soul, but who further, with the triumvirate of her discreet judgment, her careful modesty, and her virtuous courtesy, holds her consort's soul enthralled with an indissoluble knot and is able to captivate all who know her.

And what will you say of her noble daughter, who has seen the light for scarcely a lustre and one year? From her speech you couldn't tell whether she comes from Italy, France, or England; and from her touch on musical instruments, you couldn't make out if she is of corporeal or incorporeal substance. From her habits of mature goodness you would be uncertain whether she has dropped from the heavens or sprung from the earth. Everyone sees that as in the harmony of her beautiful body the blood of her two parents has mingled, so also in the fabric of her singular spirit the virtues of the heroic soul of them both has been fused.

Pol. Rara avis like Marie de Bochetel; *rara avis* like Marie de Castelnau.

Gerv. This rarity that you declare of women can also be applied to men.

Pol. After all, to return to our theme, woman is no more than a matter. If you don't know what woman is, because you don't know what matter is, then study a little the Peripatetics, who, by teaching you what matter is, will teach you what woman is.

Gerv. I see plainly that with that Peripatetic brain of yours you have grasped little or nothing of what Teofilo said yesterday about the essence and potency of matter.

Pol. Of the rest, let it be as you like. But I hold fast to this point: I censure the appetite of both matter and woman, which is the cause of all evil, suffering, defect, ruin, corruption. Don't you believe that if matter were to be satisfied with its present form, no alteration or suffering would have dominion over us—we'd never die, we'd be incorruptible and eternal?

Gerv. And if it had been satisfied with the form it had fifty years ago, what would you say? Would you be yourself, Poliinnio? If it had stopped dead in the form it had forty years ago, would you be so adulterous—I mean so adult, so perfect, so learned? In the same way as you are pleased that previous forms have yielded to that now seen in you, so it is the will of nature which orders the universe that all forms should yield to each other in turn. I omit that there is greater dignity in this our substance being made everything, receiving all forms, than in being incomplete, holding fast to one form. Thus, insofar as it is possible for it, it has a likeness to that which is all in all.

Pol. You begin to turn out learned, pushing past your habitual nature. Come on, then, apply all this, if you can, to show the dignity to be found in woman.

Gerv. I'll do that with the utmost ease—but look, here is Teofilo.

Pol. And Dicson. Another time then. *De iis hactenus* [enough of these matters].

Teo. We have seen, haven't we? that the Peripatetics, like the Platonists, divide substance by differentiating between corporeal and incorporeal. Then, just as these differences are reduced to an identical potency, so it is necessary for the forms to be of two sorts. Some are transcendent (that is, superior to genus) and are called principles, such as entity, unity, one, thing, something, and their like. Others are of a genus distinct from another genus, such as substantiality and accidentality.

The first sort of forms do not make distinctions in matter and do not constitute different potencies out of it; but, as universal terms, they include corporeal as well as incorporeal substances, signifying the most universal, most common, and single substance of them both.

After this, what prevents us, asks Avicebron, just as before recognising the matter of accidental forms (that is, the composite) we recognise the matter of the substantial form (which is part of the composite)—what prevents us, before knowing the matter that is contracted so as to be under corporeal forms, from coming to know a single potency, which is distinguishable through the form of corporeal and incorporeal nature, the one dissoluble, the other indissoluble?

Besides, if all that is (beginning from the sovran and supreme being) owns a certain order and shows a system of dependencies, a ladder on which one climbs from the composite to the simple, and thence to the most simple and absolute, through proportional intermediaries which bind together and participate in the nature of the one and the other extreme, while separating themselves out according to their particular essence—then there is no order where there is not a certain participation; there is no participation where a certain union is not found; there is no union without some participation. It is therefore necessary that all things which subsist should have a single principle of subsistence.

Add to this that the same line of reasoning cannot help presupposing, before anything capable of being distinguished, something indistinct. I speak of things which exist; for the distinction between being and non-being, in my view, is not real, but is merely verbal and logical.

The something indistinct is a common essence, to which is joined the difference and the distinctive form. And surely one cannot deny that, as everything sensible presupposes a substratum of sensibility, everything intelligible presupposes a substratum of intelligibility. It is necessary then for something to exist which corresponds to the common essence of the one and other subject; for every essence is necessarily founded on some being, except the first one, which is identical with its own being, since its potency is its act and it is all it can be, as we said yesterday.

Further, if matter (according to the same adversaries) is not body, and if it precedes by its nature the corporeal being, who then can make it out as so alien from the substance called incorporeal?

Also, there are not lacking Peripatetics who declare that just as in corporeal substances is found something that is formal and divine, so in divine substances it is fitting for there to be something material, so that lower things may have their conformity with the higher and the order of the one depend on that of the other.

And the theologians, though some of them are nourished on Aristotelian doctrine, ought not to be hostile to me in this, if they are ready to accept a greater indebtedness to their own Scriptures than to philosophy and natural reason. Do not adore me, said one of their angels to the patriarch Jacob, for I am your brother. Now, if the speaker is an intellectual substance, as they take him to be, and he affirms by his words that both man and he concur in the reality of a shared substratum, whatever may be the formal difference between them, it follows that the philosophers have as proof an oracle of these theologians.

Dics. I know that you say this with reverence; you're aware that it's not suitable for us to appeal to texts that are outside our domain.

Teo. You speak correctly and truly. But I did not bring in that reference as reason and confirmation. I did it simply to spare myself a scruple as far as possible. I fear no less to appear, than actually to be, opposed to theology.

Dics. Discreet theologians are always ready to admit natural reasons, whatever may be the direction they take, as long as they do not come to conclusions opposed to divine authority, but submit themselves to it.

Teo. Such is my position and always will be.

Dics. Good. Carry on.

Teo. Plotinus also in his book on matter remarks that if in the intelligible world there is a multitude and plurality of species, it is necessary for something common to exist, beyond the property and difference of each one of them. That which is common has the function of matter; that which is individual and brings about the distinction, has the function of form.

He adds: If the sensible world is an imitation of the intelligible, the composition of the one is an imitation of the composition of the other. Besides, if the intelligible world lacks diversity, it lacks order; if it lacks order, it owns no beauty and ornament. All that is related to matter.

And so the superior world should not be solely regarded as throughout indivisible; it must also be regarded as divisible and distinct in some of its aspects; and its division and distinction cannot be grasped without some substratum, matter. And though I assert that all that multiplicity comes together in a single indivisible being, which is outside any sort of dimension, I would declare that it is matter in which so many forms are united. That, before being conceived as varied and manifold, was in a uniform concept; and before being in a formed concept, it was in an unformed one.

Dics. In what you have stated with brevity, you have adduced many strong reasons for coming to the conclusion that there is one matter and one potency through which everything that is, is in act, and that matter belongs to incorporeal substances no less than corporeal—since the former have their existence through their capacity to be as much as the latter through their capacity to be have their existence; and since, as well, you have proved your point by other powerful reasons for anyone who powerfully considers and understands them—yet, if not for the doctrine's perfection so much as for its clarification, I'd like you to specify in some other manner how it is that in the most excellent things, the incorporeal, something unformed and indefinite is found.

How can the essence of a common matter exist? And how is it that the incorporeal things are not similarly described as bodies, when there is an accession of form and act? How, when there is no mutation, generation, or corruption, can you call it matter, seeing that matter has never been posited for any other end than mutation and so on? How can we say that intelligible nature is simple, and yet add that in it is matter and act?

I don't ask these questions on my own behalf; for the truth [of your doctrine] is plain to me. I ask perhaps for others, who may be more exigent and difficult, as, for example, Master Poliinnio and Gervase.

Pol. Cedo [I accept].

Gerv. I accept and thank you, Dicson, for considering the needs of those who lack the hardihood to ask—as suits with the courtesies of transalpine tables, where those occupying the second seats are not allowed to extend their fingers outside of their own squares and circles, but are expected to wait for the food to be placed in their hands so that they won't take a bite unpaid-for by a Many-thanks.

Teo. I'll answer, in full resolution of your questions, that man in his specific human nature is different from a lion in its specific lion-nature, but that in their shared animal nature, their shared bodily substance and the like, they are indifferent and identical. In the same way, the matter of corporeal things, in its specific nature, is different from that of incorporeal things.

All your comments then about matter as the constitutive cause of corporeal nature, as the substratum of all sorts of transmutations, and as a part of composite things, agree with matter taken in its specific meaning. For the same matter—I want to bring out this point more clearly—the same matter (which can be made or can exist): either it is made and exists as a result of dimensions and extensions of the substratum, and those qualities that have their existence in quantity; and this is called corporeal substance and presupposes corporeal matter—or else it is made (if it indeed has newly come into being) and is without those dimensions, extensions, and qualities; and then it is called incorporeal substance and similarly presupposes incorporeal matter.

Thus to an active potency—as much of corporeal as of incorporeal things—or rather to a being as much corporeal as incorporeal, there corresponds a passive potency, as much corporeal as incorporeal, and a capacity to exist, as much corporeal as incorporeal.

If then we wish to speak of composition in one nature as much as in the other, we must understand it in two different manners and must consider that in eternal things we are dealing with matter which is always under the same act, while in variable things it always contains now one, now another act. In the former case, matter simultaneously always, and altogether, possesses everything it can possess, and is everything it can be; in the latter case, it possesses all things and is all things, not in a simultaneity, but at different times, and in a certain succession.

Dics. Some men, though admitting matter in incorporeal things, understand it in a very different sense.

Teo. Whatever may be the diversity according to specific aspects, through which one thing descends to corporeal being and the other does not, the one thing receives sensible qualities and the other does not—and it seems there cannot be a common nature between that matter which is contrary to quantity and to being the subject of those qualities that have their being in dimensions. and the nature which is not contrary to either—yet it remains that both [matters] are one and the same.

As has been said several times, the whole difference depends on whether there has been contraction to corporeal being or contraction to incorporeal.

Thus, in animal being, everything sensitive is one; but when the genus is contracted to particular species, being a man is opposed to being a lion, and so on with each animal species. And I add, if you like, since you'll tell me that what is never found should be regarded as impossible and unnatural rather than natural—that, as [incorporeal] matter is never found with dimensions, corporeality is to be regarded as unnatural to it; and if this is true, it is not likely that the two matters should have a common nature before one of them is contracted to corporeal being—I add, I say, that we can less attribute to matter [as absolute potency] the necessity of all dimensional acts than (as you would have it) their impossibility.

This matter is all that it can be; and so it has all measures, has all species of figures and dimensions; and because it has them all, it has none of them. For that which is simultaneously so many diverse things, is necessarily not any one of them in particular. It is proper for that which is all to exclude every particular existence

Dics. Do you then argue that matter is act? do you hold also that matter in incorporeal things coincides with act?

Teo. Yes, as the capacity to be coincides with being.

Dics. Is there then no difference in form?

Teo. Not in absolute power and absolute act. That [level] therefore exists in the extreme of purity, simplicity, indivisibility, and unity, because it is absolutely all. If it possessed particular dimensions, particular being, a particular figure, a particular property, a particular difference, it would not be absolute, it would not be all.

Dics. Then everything which comprises any genus is indivisible.

Teo. Exactly. For the form which comprises all the qualities is not itself any one of them; what comprises all the figures does not itself possess any of them; what possesses all sensible being is not itself therefore sensible. More highly indivisible is that which possesses all natural being; and yet more highly so is that which possesses all intellectual being; highest of all that which possesses all that can be.

Dics. You then hold that, analogous to this ladder of being, there is a ladder of the capacity-to-be? And you hold that, just as the formal essence ascends, so does the material essence?

Teo. That is true.

Dics. Both in depth and in height you then apply this definition of matter and potency.

Teo. True.

Dics. But here is a truth that cannot be laid hold of by all. It's indeed a difficult task to understand the way in which all the species of dimensions are possessed, and yet none of them; formal being, and yet no form.

Teo. You yourself understand how this can be?

Dics. I believe so. I realise very well that the act, as it is all things, cannot be any specific thing.

Pol. Non potest esse idem totum et aliquid; ego quoque illud capio [the same thing cannot be both the whole and a bit of it; I too understand that].

Teo. Then you'll be able to understand how it follows that if we wanted to posit dimensional existence as the essence of matter, such an essence would not be contrary to any kind of matter. But one matter is differentiated from the other solely in that the one is quite freed from dimensions and the other is contracted to them. As for absolute being, it is above all dimensions and comprehends them all; as for contracted being, it is comprehended by some and is under some.

Dics. You rightly say that matter in itself has no particular dimensions and hence is indivisibly extended, receiving dimensions according to the nature of the form it receives. It has some dimensions under the human form, others under that of the olive, others under that of the myrtle. Then, before it exists under any of such forms, it potentially owns all those dimensions, just as it has the potency of receiving all those forms.

Pol. Dicunt tamen propterea, quod nullas habet dimensiones [yet they say on that account that it has no dimensions].

Dics. And now we say that *ideo habet nullas, ut omnes habeat* [therefore it has none, in order to have all].

5*

Gerv. Why do you hold that it includes rather than excludes them all?

Dics. Because it doesn't come to receive dimensions as from without, but sends them out, brings them forth as from its womb.

Teo. Well said. Further, the Peripatetics themselves too have a customary way of stating that all dimensional activity and all forms emerge and proceed out of the potency of matter. Averroes partly meant this. An Arab and ignorant of the Greek tongue, he yet understood the Peripatetic doctrine better than any Greek we have read, and he'd have understood it still better if he had not been so dedicated to his deity Aristotle.

He says that matter in its essence comprises the indeterminate dimensions—wanting to indicate that the latter come to be determined sometimes by this figure and dimensions, sometimes by such and such others, according to the changes in natural forms. In this sense, we see that matter emits them as from itself and does not receive them as from outside.

Plotinus too, prince of Plato's school, has partly understood all this. In establishing the difference between the matter of higher things and that of lower, he says that the former is everything at the same time, and that as it is all it can be, it has nothing into which it can change; but that the latter, with certain changes in the parts, becomes everything, and in a temporal succession becomes thing after thing, so that it is always under diversity, alteration, and movement. As a result the former is never formless any more than the latter is, though each is formed in a different way—one, in the instant of eternity, and the other in the instants of time; one, in simultaneity, and the other in succession; one, in enfolding, and the other in unfolding; one, as a unity, and the other as a multitude; one, as all and everything, and the other through each and every thing.

Dics. So you wish to infer that, not only according to your own principles but also according to those of other philosophies, matter is not that *prope nihil,* that pure bare potency without act, without virtue and perfection.

Teo. That is so. I call it deprived of forms and without them, not as ice lacks warmth and the abyss is deprived of light, but as a pregnant woman lacks her offspring, which she brings forth and draws out of herself, and as the earth in this hemisphere at night is without light, which in its ceaseless movement it has the power to regain.

Dics. So we find that even in these inferior things act comes largely if not altogether to coincide with potency.

Teo. I leave you to decide.

Dics. And if this potency from below became finally one with that from above, what would happen?

Teo. Judge for yourself. You can hence rise to the concept, I do not say of the highest and perfect principle (which is excluded from our consideration), but of the world-soul, insofar as it is act of all and potency of all and itself all in all. And so at last (given the existence of innumerable individual existences) everything is one and the knowledge of this unity is the purpose and term of all philosophies and natural contemplations—leaving in its own limits the highest contemplation of all, which soars above nature and which, for him who does not believe, is impossible and null.

Dics. True, for the ascent there is by supernatural, not natural, light.

Teo. Such light is not possessed by those who consider that everything is a body, simple like the ether, or composite like the stars and astral things—and who do not seek for divinity outside the infinite world and infinite things, but in that world and in those things.

Dics. Here is the sole point, it seems to me, where the faithful theologian differs from the philosopher.

Teo. That's my opinion too. I think you've understood what I want to say.

Dics. Very well, I think. And so I infer from your remarks that though we do not allow matter to be set above natural things and take our stand on the common definition which the most vulgarised philosophy yields, yet we'll find matter retaining a better prerogative than that definition recognises. The definition does not finally attribute to it anything but the idea of being a substratum of forms and of a potency receptive of natural forms, without name, without definition, without determination because without any actuality.

This idea seemed difficult to certain monks, who, wanting to excuse rather than accuse the doctrine, assert that matter has only the act of entity, which differentiates it from that which simply does not exist, from that which does not have any being in nature, such as some chimera or fictional thing. For this matter in the end does possess being; and this is sufficient for it, even if it lacks mode and dignity, which depend on actuality—in fact a mere nothing.

But then you should insist on an answer from Aristotle: Why do you hold, prince of the Peripatetics, that matter is nothing through not having any act of its own, rather than that it is all through having all acts, even if they are confused and confounded as you like to say? Is it not you who, continually speaking of the new being of forms in matter or of the generation of things, declare that the forms proceed and emerge from the interior of matter? Is it not you who has never been heard to say that through the working of the efficient cause they come from without—stating rather that the efficient brings them forth from within? I omit that the efficient cause of these things (dubbed by you with the common name of nature) you make also an inner principle, and not an external one, as happens with artificial things. If then it seems to me appropriate to say that matter does not possess in itself any form or act, when it receives such things from outside it also seems appropriate to say that it has them all, when it is described as sending them all forth from its own bosom. And yet is it not you who, if not constrained by reason, at least carried along by the usage of language, in defining matter, prefer to call it 'that thing from which each natural species is produced,' and do not ever say that it is 'that in which things are made,' as would be correct if acts did not come out of it and if it consequently did not possess them?

Pol. Certe consuevit dicere Aristoteles cum suis potius formas educi de potentia materiae, quam in illam induci, emergere potius ex ipsa quam in ipsam ingeri [certainly Aristotle was accustomed to say with his pupils that forms are brought out from the potency of matter rather than brought into it, emerge from it rather than are put into it]; but I'd say that he preferred to call act the explication of form rather than its implication.

Dics. And I say that the expressed, sensible, and unfolded being is not the principal essence of actuality, but is a thing consequent on and resulting from it. In the same way the principal being of wood and the essence of its actuality do not consist in being a bed, but in its being of such a substance and such a consistency that it can arrive at being a bed, a bench, a beam, an idol, and anything formed out of wood. I omit that it is a higher reason which demonstrates that all natural things are made of natural matter than that which demonstrates artificial things are made of artificial matter. For art begets forms out of matter by subtraction, as when it makes a statue out of stone, or by apposition, as when by joining stone to stone, earth, and wood, it constructs a house; but nature makes everything out of its matter by means of separation, birth, effluxion: as the Pythagoreans understood, Anaxagoras and Democritus comprehended, and the sages of Babylonia confirmed.

Moses too subscribed to this position in his description of the generation of things ordered by the universal efficient cause, when he employs this mode of speech: let the earth produce its animals, let the waters produce living beings—as if he said: Let matter produce them. For, according to him, the material principle of things is water. That's why he says that the efficient intellect (called spirit by him) brooded on the waters. That is, it gave the waters a procreative virtue and produced from them the natural species, all of which he afterwards calls, in substance, waters. Thus, speaking of the separation of lower bodies and higher, he says that the mind separated the waters from the waters: by which means he infers that dry earth appeared.

All then hold that things come into existence out of matter by way of separation and not by way of apposition and reception. We should hence speak rather of matter containing forms and implicating them than think of it as void and excluding them. And matter which unfolds what it holds folded-up should be called a thing divine, the best parent, generator, and mother of natural things—indeed, nature entire in substance. Isn't this what you say and mean, Teofilo?

Teo. Certainly.

Dics. Also, I am greatly surprised that our Peripatetics have not further worked out their art-analogy. Among the many materials that it knows and employs, art accounts that to be better and more worthy which is less subject to corruption, more constant in its lasting qualities, and from which more things can be made. Hence it accounts gold nobler than wood, stone, and iron, because it is less subject to corruption, and because all that can be made of wood and stone can be made of gold, and also many other things, greater and better for their beauty, constancy, malleability, and nobility.

Well, what then must we say of that matter from which are

made man and gold and all natural things? Should we not hold it to
be worthier than the material of art and to possess an essence of
higher actuality?

Why, O Aristotle, in dealing with that which is the foundation
and basis of actuality—of that, I say, which is in act and which you
declare to exist forever, to last through eternity—why don't you
confess that it is more in act than your forms, than your entelchies,
which come and go in such a way that if you should wish to find
out the permanence of the formal principle——

Pol. Quia principia opportet semper manere [because principles
should always remain].

Dics. —and yet refused to have resort to the fantastic ideas
of Plato, as so contrary to your own viewpoint, you'd be constrained and forced to say that these specific forms have their
permanent actuality in the hand of the efficient cause—which you
can't do, as you call that cause the investigator and extractor of
forms from matter's potency—or else to say that they have their
permanent actuality in the bosom of matter. And that indeed is
what you can't escape saying; for all forms appearing as in the
superficies of matter, which you call individuals, and in act—as
much those that were, as those that are and will be—are things
embodying a principle, not the principle itself.

(And certainly I believe that the particular form is in the
superficies of matter in the same way as the accident is in the superficies of the composite substance. Whence it follows that the expressed form should be accorded a less degree of actuality with
regard to matter, just as the accidental form has a less degree of
actuality with respect to the composite.)

Teo. Indeed Aristotle concludes lamely by saying, together
with all the ancient philosophers, that principles must always remain permanent; and later, when we search through his doctrine
for the point where natural form has its ceaseless permanence, we
do not find it in the fixed stars, since these particular stars we
see do not descend from their height [into the earthly sphere]. And
we do not find it in the ideal signs, separate from matter, since these
are certainly, if not monsters, worse than monsters—I mean,
chimeras and vain fantasies.

What then? The forms are in the bosom of nature. And what
then? Matter is the source of actuality.

Do you want me to carry on further and make you see into

what great absurdity Aristotle has fallen? He says that matter exists in potency. But ask him at what moment it will be in act. He'll reply, and a large host with him: When it has form. Now go further and ask: What is that which possesses the new being? They'll reply in their own despite: The composition, and not matter, since the latter is always the same, it doesn't renew itself, it doesn't change. As with artificial things, when a statue is made of wood, we do not say a new being is added to the wood, because it is in no way more or less wood than it was before. What receives the being and actuality is the new thing that is produced, the composition, I mean the statue.

How then can we attribute the potency to that which will never be in act or possess act? It follows [from the Aristotelian system] that it is not matter which exists in potency of being, since it is always identical and immutable, since it is that about which and in which the mutation takes place rather than that which is changed. What is altered, enlarged, diminished, changed in location, corrupted, is always (according to you, Peripatetics) the composition and never matter itself. Why then do you say that matter is now in potency, now in act? Certainly no one should doubt that matter, whether receiving forms or sending them out of itself, does not in either case receive any more or less actuality as far as its essence and substance are concerned. And therefore there is no reason at all for declaring that it exists in potency.

A state of potency squares with what is in continual movement in relation to matter, and with what is in eternal rest and is even more the cause of that eternal rest. For if form, in accordance with its fundamental and specific being, is of simple and invariable essence, not only logically in the concept and reason, but also physically in nature, it will need to exist in the perpetual potency of matter, which is a potency undifferentiated from act, as I have explained in many ways during my various discussions of potency.

Pol. Quaeso [I beg you], say something on matter's appetite so that we find some resolution of a certain dispute between me and Gervase.

Gerv. Please do so, Teofilo. This man has broken my head with the comparison of woman and matter, and his assertion that woman is less satisfied with men than matter is with forms, and all the rest of his chattering.

Teo. Since matter doesn't receive anything from form, why do you hold that it desires it? If, as we've said, matter sends forms out of its bosom and consequently has them in itself, how argue that it desires them? It doesn't desire those forms which daily change on its surface; for what every well-ordered thing desires is that from which it receives perfection. What can a corruptible thing give to an eternal thing? an imperfect thing, such as the ceaselessly-moving form of sensible things, to something so perfect that if it is well contemplated it is seen as a divine being in things: as perhaps David of Dinant, misunderstood by those who reported his opinions, meant to say.

Matter does not desire form for its preservation, since the corruptible thing does not preserve the eternal thing; further, it is evident that matter preserves form—so that such form should rather desire matter in order to perpetuate itself. For, separated from matter, form loses its being, and not matter, which has all it had before the form was found, and still can have other forms.

I leave aside the fact that when the cause of corruption is given, one does not say that the form flees from matter or abandons it, but rather that matter throws off one form in order to take on another. And I leave also the point that we have no more reason for saying that matter desires forms than for saying on the contrary that it holds them in hate—I refer to forms that are engendered and corrupted. The source of forms, which is in matter, cannot feel desire, as nothing which is already possessed is desired—because by the same line of reasoning, by which it can be said to desire what it sometimes receives or produces, it can be said to detest what it rejects and discards. More, it can be said to detest more potently than it desires, since it eternally throws off the individual form which it retains for a moment of time. If then you remind yourself of this—that matter rejects as many forms as it assumes, you must permit me to say that it is motivated by loathing, as I in turn give you leave to say it is motivated by desire.

Gerv. There go crashing to earth the castles, not only of Poliinnio, but of many another besides.

Pol. Parcius ista viris . . . [more sparingly should these scandals be charged on men].

Dics. We've learned enough for today. Till tomorrow.

Teo. Goodbye then.

FIFTH DIALOGUE

Teo. The universe is then one, infinite, immobile. One, I say, is absolute possibility, one is act, one is form or soul, one is matter or body, one is being, one is the maximum and the best. It is not capable of comprehension and therefore is endless and limitless, and to that extent infinite and indeterminable, and consequently immobile.

It does not move itself locally, since it has nothing outside itself to which it may be transported: seeing that it is the whole. It does not engender itself, since there is no other being which it could desire or look for: seeing that it has all being. It is not corrupted, since there is no other thing into which it can change itself: seeing that it is everything. It cannot diminish or increase: seeing that it is infinite, so that nothing can be added, nothing subtracted—the infinite having no proportional parts. It cannot be altered into any other disposition, since it has nothing external to which it can take a passive relation and by which it can be effected.

More, as it comprehends all contradictions in its being in unity and harmony; and as it can have no inclination towards another and new being, or yet for any other mode of being, it cannot be subject to change according to any quality, nor can it have any contrary or different thing which can alter it, since in it everything is concordant. It is not matter, since it is not configured or figurable; it is not determined or determinable. It is not form, since it does not inform or figure anything else, seeing that it is all, is maximum, is one, is universal.

It is not measurable, nor is it measured, it is not contained, since there is no greater than itself. It does not contain, since there is no less than itself. It is not comparable, since it is not one thing and another, but is one and the same. Being the same and one, it does not have being and other-being; and since it does not have being and other-being, it has no parts and yet more parts; and having no parts, it is not a composition. It is an end in such a way that it is no end; it is form in such a way that it is not form; it is matter in such a way that it is not matter; and it is soul in such a

135

way that it is not soul. For it is all indifferently, and hence is one, the universe is one.

In it, certainly, the height is no greater than the length and the depth; and so, by a certain analogy, it is called a sphere, though it is not one. In the sphere, length is the same as breadth and depth, since they have the same limit; but in the universe breadth, length, and depth are the same, because they all similarly lack any limit and are infinite.

If they have no halves, quarters, and other kinds of measure, if they lack measure altogether, they lack proportional parts, and there is absolutely no part which differs from the whole. For if you want to speak of parts of the infinite, you must speak of the infinite; if it is infinite, it coincides in one being with the whole. Then the universe is one, infinite, indivisible.

And if in the infinite is found no differentiation, as of part from whole and as of one thing from another, certainly the infinite is one. In the comprehension of the infinite, no part is greater and no part is lesser, since any part however large conforms no more to the infinite's proportion than does any other part however small. In infinite duration hour does not differ from day, day from year, year from century, century from moment, since the moments and the hours are not more than the centuries, and the former have no less proportion than the latter to eternity.

Similarly, in the immensity, the foot is not different from the furlong, the furlong from the mile, since miles do not conform to the proportion of immensity more than feet do. Then, infinite hours are no more than infinite centuries, and infinite feet are not a number superior to infinite miles. You do not come any nearer to proportion, likeness, union, and identity with the infinite by being a man than by being an ant, by being a star than by being a man; for you do draw any closer to that being by yourself being a sun or a moon than by being a man or an ant. And so in the infinite these things are indifferent. And what I say of them I mean of all things of particular substance.

Now, if all these particular things in the infinite are not differentiated, are not species, by an inevitable consequence they are not number. Therefore the universe is again a unity that is motionless. Because it comprises all and does not suffer multiple beings, it does not admit of any change with itself or within itself. As a result, it is all that it can be; and in it (as I said the other day) act does not differ from potency.

If act does not differ from potency, in it necessarily the point, the line, the surface, and the body do not differ. For then that line is surface, since a line by moving can become surface; then that surface is moved and becomes a body, since a surface can be moved and by its flowing can become body. Necessarily it follows that in infinity point does not differ from body, since the point, departing from its point-existence, becomes a line; departing from its line-existence, becomes a body. And so the point, since it exists with the potency of being a body, does not differ from being a body, where potency and act are one and the same thing.

Therefore the indivisible does not differ from the divisible, the most simple from the infinite, the centre from the circumference. As then the infinite is all it can be. It is immobile; in it everything is indifferent, is one; and since it has all the greatness and perfection that it can attain beyond all limits, it is the maximum and the supreme immensity.

If point does not differ from body, centre from circumference, finite from infinite, maximum from minimum, we can securely declare that the universe is all centre, or that the universe's centre is everywhere and the circumference is nowhere insofar as it differs from the centre—or rather the circumference is everywhere, but the centre is not to be found insofar as it differs from it.

Here then we see how it is not impossible, but is necessary, for the best, the greatest, the maximum, the incomprehensible, to be all, because, as simple and indivisible, it can be all, is everywhere, is in all. And thus it has not been vainly said that Jove fills all things, inhabits all parts of the universe, is the centre of all that has being—one in all and that through which one is all. Which, being all things and comprising all being in itself, brings about that everything is in everything.

But you will say to me: Why then do things change? why does particular matter constrain itself to other forms?

I reply that there is not a change which seeks another being, but a change which seeks another mode of being. And this is what makes the difference between the universe and the things of the universe. The former comprises all being and all modes of being. Through the latter each thing has all being but not all the modes of being. And it cannot actually have all circumstances and accidents; for many forms are incompatible in the same subject, because they are contrary or because they belong to diverse species. For example, there cannot be the same individual basis under the accidents of horse and man, under the dimension of a plant and an animal.

More, the universe comprises all being in a totality; for nothing that exists is outside or beyond infinite being, as the latter has no outside or beyond. Each individual thing that exists comprises all being, but not totally, as beyond each there are infinite others. Therefore, understand that all is in all, but not totally, and in all modes in each case. So understand how everything is one, but in the same mode as other things.

Therefore he makes no mistake who declares that being, substance, and essence are one being. This being, as infinite and indeterminate as to substance as to duration, as to greatness, as to vigour, does not own the nature of a principle or of that which depends on a principle; for, as all things coincide in unity and identity (I mean, in the same being), they come to have an absolute essence and not a relative one.

In the one, infinite and immobile, which is substance, which is being, if one finds multiplicity and number, which are modes and multiformity of being and which come to denominate specific things, it yet doesn't follow that being is more than one, but that it appears in a many-moded, many-formed, and many-figured way. And so, if we think deeply with the natural philosophers and leave the logicians to their fantasies, we find that all which makes difference and number is pure accident, is pure figure, is pure complexion. Every production of any sort whatever is an alteration, with the substance remaining always the same; for there is only one substance, one being divine and immortal.

Pythagoras, who did not dread death, but looked for a transformation, was able to understand all this. All philosophers, vulgarly called physicists, have been able to understand it; for they say that, as far as substance is concerned, nothing is engendered or corrupted—unless we wish to define in this way the changes that go on.

Solomon too has understood, in his saying that there is nothing new under the sun, but that which is, always was.

You have then this fact: that all things are in the universe and the universe is in all things; we in it and it in us—and that therefore all things concur in a perfect unity.

See how we should not afflict our spirit. See how there is nothing that should alarm us. For this unity is sole and stable, and remains for ever. This oneness is eternal. Every aspect, every face, everything else is vanity, is as nothing—nay, all that is outside of this one is nothing.

Those philosophers who have found this unity have found their beloved, Wisdom. Identical things indeed are wisdom, truth, unity. All philosophers have been able to assert that the true, the one, and being are the same thing; but not all have understood. Some have taken over the sages' manner of speaking, without comprehending their manner of meaning. Aristotle, among others, did not grasp the one, did not grasp being, did not grasp the true, because he never realised how being is one; and though he was free to adopt a significance for being common to both substance and accident, and further to distinguish his categories according to so many genera and species, so many differentiations, he has not avoided being any the less ignorant of the truth, through a failure to deepen his cognition of this unity and lack of differentiation in constant nature and being. And, as a thoroughly arid sophist, by his malignant explanations and his frivolous persuasions, he perverts the statements of the ancients and sets himself against the truth—not so much perhaps through weakness of intellect as through force of jealousy and ambition.

Dics. And so this world, this being, truth, universe, infinity, immensity, is in every part of itself, so that it is itself the *ubique*. Hence, that which is in the universe, with regard to the universe (whatever it is in respect of other particular bodies), exists everywhere according to the mode of its capacity. For it is above, is below, right, left, and so on according to all local differences, since in the whole infinite there are all these differences and none of them.

Everything we take in the universe has in itself that which is entire everywhere; and so it comprehends in its mode the whole world-soul (though not totally, as we've already pointed out). That soul is entire in any part whatever of the universe. Therefore, as act is one and constitutes a single being, wherever it is, we are not to believe there is in this world a plurality of substance and of that which is truly being.

Next, I know that you hold as a manifest thing that each of all these innumerable worlds, which we behold in the universe, are not there so much as if in a containing area or in a gap or [cut-off] space, as they are rather in a single comprehensive, conserving, moving, and efficient whole, which thus comes to be comprised in its wholeness in each of the worlds, just as the [world]-soul is entire in each part of the universe.

Therefore, though a particular world moves itself towards or around another, as the earth moves to and around the sun, still, with respect to the universe as a whole, nothing is moved towards or around it, but is moved inside it.

Further, you hold that—just as the soul (and common parlance backs you up) pervades the great mass to which it gives being, and is itself at the same time altogether indivisible, similarly existent throughout and intact in the whole and any part—so the universe's essence is one in the infinite and in anything taken as a member of it: with the result that the whole and every part of it come to be one in terms of substance. Hence Parmenides has, not unsuitably, remarked that the universe is one, infinite and immobile: whatever may have been his intention, which, reported by a not-particularly-faithful commentator, is uncertain.

You say that all the differences we see in bodies as to their formations, complexions, figures, colours, and other properties and relationships, are nothing else than the varying face of the same substance: a fugitive, mobile, and corruptible face of a single immobile, persistent, and eternal being, in which all forms, figures, and members exist, but indistinctly and as if conglomerated— exactly as in the seed, where the arm is not distinct from the hand, the bust from the head, the nerve from the bone. The distinction and separation-out does happen to produce another and new substance, but brings into action and fulfilment certain qualities, differences, accidents, and orders related to that one substance.

And what is said of the seed as regards the members of animals, is similarly to be said of food as regards its being chyle, blood, phlegm, flesh, seed; and similarly of any other thing that precedes its being food or something else. Similarly too of all things whatever—going up from the lowest level of nature right to the highest, going up from physical universality (which philosophers know) to the height of the archetype (in which theologians believe), if you like: until you arrive at a single original and universal sub-

stance identical for all, which is called being, the basis of all species
and diverse forms—just as in the art of carpentry there is a substance of wood, subject to all measures and figures, which are not
wood, but are of wood, in wood, about wood.

Thus, all that makes for diversity of genus, species, differences,
properties, all that consists in generation, corruption, alteration,
and change, is not being, is not essence, but is condition and circumstance of being and existence, which is one, infinite, immobile,
subject, matter, life, soul, truth, and goodness.

You hold then that as being is indivisible and wholly simple
(since it is infinite and is act entire in all things and is entire in
every part, in the same way as we speak of a part in the infinite,
not a part of the infinite), we cannot think in any way that the earth
is a part of being, the sun a part of substance—seeing that the
latter is indivisible. But it is quite legitimate to speak of the substance of the part, or better still, the substance in the part: just as
it isn't legitimate to speak of a part of the soul being in the arm,
a part of it in the head, but it is legitimate to speak of the soul in
the part that is the head, or of the substance of the part, or in the
part, which is the arm.

To exist as portion, part, member, the whole, equal-to, greater-
than, or less-than, like-this or like-that, of-this or of-that, concur-
ring or differing, and so on, does not express an absolute and hence
cannot be referred to as substance, as one and being, but implies
an existence through substance, in the one, and relative to being, as
modes, conditions, and forms.

Thus it is commonly said that quantity, quality, relation,
action, passion, and other circumstances of genus, are relative to
substance; and thus the one supreme being, in which act is undifferentiated from potency and which can be all absolutely and is
all that it can be, is involvedly one, immense, infinite, which comprehends all being and exists unfoldedly in these sensible bodies
and in the distinct potency and act which we see in them.

Hence you hold that that which is generated and generates
(whether it's a question of an equivocal or an unequivocal agent,
as the vulgarising philosophers say), and that of which the generation is made, are always of the same substance. That is why the
statement of Heraclitus will never jar in your ear, when it declares
all things to be a unity, which through mutability has all things in
itself. And because all forms are in it, in consequence all definitions

agree with it, and equally all contradictory propositions are true. And what makes for multiplicity in things is not being, is not the thing, but what appears, what is represented to the senses and lies on the surface of things.

Teo. Just so. Beyond this, however, I want you to grasp more heads of this most important science, this most solid foundation of the truths and secrets of nature. First then, I want you to note that here is one and the same ladder for nature descending to the production of things and intellect ascending to the cognition of them; and that one way, like the other, proceeds from unity to unity, passing through a multitude of middle-positions.

I leave aside that, in their mode of philosophising, the Peripatetics and many Platonists derive the multiplicity of things, as also the middle-position, from pure act at one extreme and from pure potency at the other—just as other philosophers, by the use of a certain metaphor, assert that darkness and light come together in the constitution of innumerable grades of forms, representations, figures, and colours. Then besides those who consider two principles and two princes, there rise up others, hostile and impatient of polyarchy, who make the duality coincide in one, which is simultaneously abyss and darkness, clarity and light, profound and impenetrable obscurity, supernal and inaccessible light.

Secondly, consider that the intellect, wanting to liberate and detach itself from the imagination to which it is joined, has not only recourse to mathematics and to symbolic figures, so that by them and by the analogies they offer it may comprehend the being and substance of things, but also comes to refer the multiplicity and diversity of species to a single and identical root.

Thus, Pythagoras, who posited numbers as the specific principles of things, understood the basis and substance of all to be unity. Plato and others, who have set the subsistent species in figures, understood the point as the same stock and root of all, as substance and universal genus; and perhaps the surfaces and figures are what in the end Plato meant by his Great, and the point and atom are what he meant by his Small, twin specific principles of things, which are then reduced to one, as every divisible is reduced to the indivisible.

Those then who say that the substantial principle is one, are declaring that substances are like numbers. Others who interpret the substantial principle as the point, are declaring that the substances of things are like figures. And all agree in positing an indivisible principle. Better and purer however is the method of Pythagoras than that of Plato, since unity is cause and reason of indivisibility and of the point, and is a principle more absolute and agreeable to universal being.

Gerv. Why has Plato, who is later than Pythagoras, not carried on along the same lines or done better?

Teo. Because he preferred to speak less well and in a less suitable and adequate way, and to be esteemed a master, than to speak better on a better doctrine and gain the name of a disciple. I mean that the aim of his philosophy was more his personal glory than the truth. For I cannot doubt that he knew very well his doctrine was more appropriate to things corporeal and corporeally considered, while that of Pythagoras was no less useful and suited for such questions than it was for those which reason, imagination, intellect, or both sensible and intelligible nature, know how to produce.

Everyone will admit that there was nothing hidden from Plato in the fact that unity and number are indispensable for examining and grasping the meaning of point and figures, though the figures and points are not indispensable for examining and grasping the meaning of unity and number—just as dimensional and corporeal substance depends on the incorporeal and indivisible—and further that unity and number are independent from figures and points, because the essence of numbers is found without that of measure, but the latter cannot be independent from the former, because the essence of measures is not found without that of numbers.

That is why arithmetical analogy and proportion are more suitable than geometric to guide us by means of multiplicity to the contemplation and apprehension of that indivisible principle, which, as the unique and radical substance of all things, cannot possess a certain and determined name or any designation that has a positive rather than a privative meaning. That is why some call it point, others unity, others infinity, and so on according to various similar concepts.

Add to what has been said, that when the intellect wants to grasp the essence of a thing, it proceeds by simplifying as much as possible. I mean that it moves away from composition and multiplicity, rejecting corruptible accidents, dimensions, signs, figures, and turning to what lies under these things. Thus, we understand a lengthy piece of writing, a prolix oration, only by contracting it to a simple design. The intellect, by so doing, demonstrates clearly how the substance of things consists in unity, which it proceeds to seek out either in fact or in analogy.

Believe that that man would be the most consummate and perfected geometrician, who could reduce to a single proposition all the propositions scattered in the principles of Euclid. The most perfected logician would be he who reduced all the propositions in logic to one.

This is how we can tell the grade of intelligences. The inferior cannot understand multiplicity except through many species, analogies, and forms; the superior understand it better with less; the highest understand perfectly with the least [such apparatus].

The first intelligence comprehends the whole with the utmost perfection in one idea. The divine mind and absolute unity, without any species, is at one and the same moment that which understands and that which is understood. And so, in ascending to perfect cognition, we proceed by bringing together [into one] multiplicity— just as, in descending to the production of things, unity proceeds by unfolding it. The descent is from a single being to infinite individuals and species; the ascent is the other way about.

To conclude then this second consideration, I say that when we aspire and strive to the principle and substance of things, we make progress towards indivisibility; and we never believe that we have arrived at the first being and universal substance unless we have attained to this indivisible one, in which all is contained; and so likewise we do not believe that we understand any more of substance and essence than we are able to understand of indivisibility.

Hence the Peripatetics and the Platonists reduce infinite individuals to a single indivisible essence shared by many species. They group countless species under determinate genera, of which Archytas first declared there were ten; and they bring back the determinate genera to a single being, a single thing: which thing and being is understood by them as a name, a mere term, a logical formula, and finally a vanity. So, when they treat of physics, they do not recognise a single principle of reality and being for all that is, as [they have recognised] a formula and common name for all which is expressed and comprehended. All that is certainly a result of their weakness of intellect.

Thirdly, you must know that substance and being are distinct and independent from quantity, and in consequence, measure, and number are not substance but are relative to it; not being, but things of being. It follows that we must define substance as essentially without number and measure, and therefore as a unity and undivided in all particular things. The latter have their particularity from number, that is from things that are relative to substance.

Anyone who apprehends Poliinnio as Poliinnio does not apprehend particular substance, but substance in the particular and in the differences that are relative to it. Substance, through their means, comes to posit this man in number and multiplicity under a species.

And just as certain human accidents cause multiplication of these that one calls individual examples of humanity, so certain animal accidents cause multiplication of the species of animality. Likewise, certain vital accidents cause multiplication of the animated and living. Not otherwise certain corporeal accidents cause multiplication of corporeal reality. In the same way certain accidents of existence cause multiplication of substance. And similarly certain accidents of being cause multiplication of entity, truth, unity, being, the true, the one.

Fourthly, take the signs and verifications through which we wish to conclude that contraries coincide in unity: from which it will not be difficult to infer that all things are one, just as all number, whether odd or even, whether finite or infinity, is reduced to unity—and unity, repeated in the finite series, posits number, and, repeated in the infinite series, negates number.

You will take the signs from mathematics and the verifications from the other moral and speculative faculties. Hence, as regards signs, tell me: What thing is more unlike the straight line than the circle? what thing is more contrary to the straight line than the curve? Yet in the principle and in the minimum they coincide; since, as the Cusan, discoverer of geometry's most beautiful secrets, has divinely observed, what difference will you find between the minimum arc and the minimum chord? Further, in the maximum, what difference will you find between the infinite circle and the straight line? Don't you see that the circle, the larger it grows, approximates with its arc more and more to straightness?

Who is so blind as not to see how the arc BB by being larger than the arc AA, and the arc CC by being larger than the arc BB, and the arc DD by being larger than the other three, turn out to be

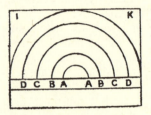

Fig. 1.

parts of ever-larger circles, and hence tend ever more closely to the straightness of the infinite line represented by IK? Therefore we must certainly assert and believe that just as the line that is greater according to the concept of greater size is also the straighter one, so the greatest line of all must be superlatively the straightest. Thus in the end the infinite straight line becomes the infinite circle. Here then we see that not only do the maximum and the minimum converge into one being, as we have several times shown, but also that in the maximum and the minimum contraries coincide as one, undifferentiated.

Further, if you like you can compare the finite species to a triangle. For all finite things are understood, by a certain analogy, to participate in finitude and limitation through that which was first finite and first limited—as in all genera the analogous predicates take their grade and order from the first and greatest of the genus. And inasmuch as the triangle is the primary figure which cannot be resolved into any other kind of simpler figure (as, on the contrary, the quadrangle can be resolved into triangles), the triangle is the primary basis of every limited and configurated thing.

You will find that the triangle, which cannot be resolved into another figure, likewise cannot proceed in triangles in which the three angles are greater or lesser [in sum], whatever may be the variety and diversity—the various and diverse figures—and whether it's a question of greater or lesser size, minimum or maximum. Thus, if you take an infinite triangle—I do not mean really and absolutely, since the infinite has no figure; I use the term infinite by supposition and insofar as a [tri]angle has relevance to what we wish to prove—this triangle will have no greater angle than the smallest finite triangle, not to mention the middle-sized ones or the next greatest.

But letting stand the comparison of figures with figures, I mean of triangles with triangles, and taking the relation of angle to angle, great or small, they are all seen to be equal: as is shown in this square. The square is divided diagonally into so many triangles; and we see that not only are the angles of the three squares A, B, and C, equal, but also all the acute angles brought about by the diagonal division which constitutes as many pairs of triangles, all of equal angles. Thus by a very definite analogy we see how the one infinite substance can be whole in all things, though in some finitely, in others infinitely: in one case with less, in the other with greater, measure.

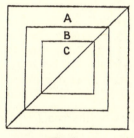

Fig. 2.

Add to this—to see further that contraries coincide in this one and infinite—that acute and obtuse angles are contraries. But don't you see how they are born from the one and same indivisible principle—that is, from an inclination which the perpendicular line, joined to the horizontal line BD, makes at the point C? At that point the line M, with a simple inclination towards the point D, after indifferently making right angle and right angle, comes to produce a much greater difference of acute and obtuse angles as it approaches the point C. When it joins that point and is united with it, the sharp and obtuse angles are merged and cancel one another, since they all become one in the potency of the same line.

The line M which has been made to unite and merge with BD can also disengage itself and become separate from BD; it then brings out the most contrary angles from the same single and indivisible principle—angles ranging from the maximum acute and the maximum obtuse to the minimum acute and the minimum obtuse, and thence to the indifference of the right angle and the

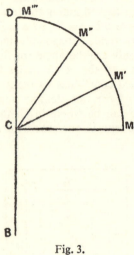

Fig. 3.

concordance constituted by the contact of the perpendicular and the horizontal.

Now for the verifications: first of all, who does not know, as regards the active primary qualities of corporeal nature, that the principle of heat is indivisible and therefore separated from all heat, because a principle must not be any of the things it governs? If this is so, who will hesitate to affirm that the principle itself is not hot or cold, but is an identity shared by both heat and cold? How then does it happen that a contrary is the principle of its opposite and that transformations are therefore circular, unless there exists a substratum, a principle, a limit, and a continuity and a union of the two opposites? Are not the minimum cold and the minimum heat wholly one? At the limit of the maximum heat do we not grasp the principle of movement towards the cold?

It is clear then that not only do the two maxima sometimes coincide in resistance and the two minima in agreement: but *etiam* [also] the maximum and the minimum coincide through the vicissitude of transmutation. Hence not without good cause are doctors apprehensive when faced with an extremely good condition of health; the foresighted are cautious at the supreme degree of felicity.

Who does not see that there is a single principle for corruption and generation? Is not the end-point of corruption the principle of the generated? Do we not say in the same breath: That was taken, this brought in—that was, this is? Certainly, if we estimate well, we see corruption to be none other than a generation, and generation none other than a corruption; love is a hate, hate is a love, in the last resort. Hate of the contrary is love of the similar; love of one thing is hate of another. In substance and root, then, love and hate, amity and discord, are one and the same thing.

Where does the physician seek the antidote more profitably than in the poison? who offers a better theriac than the viper? In the worst venoms are the best medicines. Is not one potency common to two contrary objects? Now, where do you believe this comes from if not from the fact that, as the principle of being is one, so is the principle of conceiving the two contrary objects—and that, as the contraries are relative to a single substratum, so are they apprehended by one and the same sense? I leave aside the point that the orbicular rests on the plane surface, the concave sinks down and settles into the convex, the irascible lives together with the patient, the humble most fully pleases the most arrogant, the prodigal the miser.

In conclusion, he who wants to know the greatest secrets of nature should regard and contemplate the minima and maxima of contraries and opposites. It is a profound magic to know how to draw out the contrary after having found the point of union.

To this end, poor Aristotle was tending in his thought when he posited privation, with which is united a certain disposition, as progenitor, parent, and mother of form; but he could not attain to it. He failed to arrive because he halted at the genus of opposition and remained shackled by it; he thus did not go down to the species of contrariety, did not break through and set his eyes on the goal. Instead, he strayed wholly from the way by stating that contraries cannot actually come together in the same subject.

Pol. Sublimely, rarely, extraordinarily have you reasoned on the whole, the maximum, being, principle, the one. But I'd like to see you discriminate about unity, for I find a *vae soli* [woe to him that is alone]. Besides, I feel a great anxiety because there isn't a single widowed copper in my purse and moneybag.

Teo. That unity is all that is not unfolded, not brought under distribution and distinction of number, and is of such singularity that you would perhaps understand it, if it were not comprehensive and embracing.

Pol. Exemplum [an example]? For to tell the truth, I strain to understand, but do not grasp it.

Teo. Just as the decade is a unity in the same way, but is more embracing, so the hundred is no less a unity, but yet more embracing; the thousand is a unity no less than the others, but yet more embracing. What I am setting out to you in arithmetical terms, you must understand in a higher and simpler sense of all things. The highest good, the highest object of desire, the highest perfection, the highest blessedness, consists in the unity that embraces the whole.

We delight in colour not in any single express colour, but above all in a unity that embraces all colours. We delight in sound, not in any particular one, but in a single embracing sound which results from the harmony of many. We delight in a sensible impression, but above all in that which comprehends in itself all sensible impressions. We delight in one knowable thing, which comprehends all that is knowable; in one apprehensible, which draws together all that can be apprehended; in a single being that includes all, above all in the one which is itself the all. As you, Poliinnio, would take more delight in the unity of a gem so precious as to be worth all the world's gold, than in the multitude of thousands on thousands of coppers such as the one you have in your purse.

Pol. Optime [very good].

Gerv. See how learned I've grown. The man who doesn't understand the one, understands nothing. Inversely, the man who truly understands the one, understands everything. And the more anybody advances to the intelligence of the one, the closer he comes to the apprehension of all.

Dics. I too—if I have properly understood, I go away much enriched by the thought of Teofilo, faithful reporter of the Nolan philosophy.

Teo. Praised be the gods, and may all the living magnify the infinite, most simple, most unified, highest and most absolute cause, principle, and one.

END OF THE FIVE DIALOGUES

ON CAUSE, PRINCIPLE, AND UNITY

NOTES AND APPENDICES

1. Translations of Bruno

Though England led the way in translating Bruno with W. Morehead's version of *The Expulsion of the Triumphant Beast* in 1713, not much has been done to follow up. John Toland, the Deist who doubtless drew Morehead into his work, translated the introductory letter of *On the Infinite* and gave an account of the whole book. The first part of *Gli Eroici* was done by L. Williams in 1887 as *The Heroic Enthusiasts*; the second dialogue of the *Causa* was done by I. and K. Royce in Rand's *Modern Classical Philosophy*, 1908; and D. W. Singer translated *On the Infinite Universe and Worlds* in her *Giordano Bruno, His Life and Thought*, 1950. In America Sidney Greenberg gave a version of the *Causa* in *The Infinite in Giordano Bruno* (Columbia University, 1950); but as this was not satisfactory from my point of view, I felt the need to make my own version of this key-work of Bruno's. A German version by A. Lasson appeared in 1872, and a French one by E. Namer in 1930.

2. The Impetus and the Celestial Mechanism

John Buridan, who became rector of the university of Paris in 1327 and died after 1358, gave both movement and quantity a place as independent categories, unlike Ockham. Ockham thought movement was to be attributed only to that which moves; Buridan declared that it resulted from an impulse, *impetus*, which was acquired in the original process of projection and which in the fall of heavy bodies was continuously acquired. A body in motion was thus maintained, not by the air as Aristotle held, but by the velocity of the initial impulse, which was proportionate to the body's mass. To account for the accelerated fall of heavy bodies, Buridan argued that such a body falls faster because an impetus is added to its fall; he also argued that a heavy body does not travel as far as a lighter one because it contains more matter.

To understand the importance of these contentions we must know something of the ruling Aristotelian concepts, which considered terrestrial motions and celestial motions as belonging to quite different categories and subject to quite different laws. Only the continuance of motion had to be explained in each case, the condition of rest being accepted as the natural condition of bodies everywhere. The motions

153

of the celestial bodies were perfect and circular, the bodies being whirled round by the transparent spheres; each of them was moved by a soul, which was its essential nature. But near the earth's surface heavy bodies sought the centre of the universe (inside the earth), similarly following the dictates of their own natures. Other terrestrial motion was 'violent.' It went on only as long as an operative cause persisted —a cause that often had to be found in the medium of the body's movement, in the disturbance of air or water, as the case might be, transmitting a continued motion to the moving body. (Violent motion was inconceivable in a vacuum; so it was argued that there could not be any empty space.)

As has been remarked, 'A universe constructed on the mechanics of Aristotle had the door half-open for spirits already... the modern theory of motion is the great factor which in the seventeenth century helped to drive the spirits out of the world and opened the way to a universe that ran like a piece of clockwork.'[1] But already in the 14th century, as the medieval synthesis broke down, the effort to construct a purely mechanical universe had begun, as we have noted, with Buridan.

Not that he was the first thinker to raise the subject of the impetus. The idea can be traced back to John Philopon in the Byzantine East, where various Arabs took it over.[2] Aquinas and Walter Burley mention it to reject it. What Buridan did was to expound it with a new fullness and detail.

Nominalists in France, Germany, and Italy, took over his positions. Albert of Saxony (1316–90), like Buridan, fought Nicholas of Autrecourt's atomism, and applied the theory of the impetus to the planets. Marsilius of Inghen (died 1396) took the impetus in a more metaphysical way, considering it distinct from movement, which had its own specific nature. Followers of Averroes, by their attacks, helped to spread knowledge of the doctrine. The Italian geometers of the Renascence, fighting on its behalf against the Averroism and Aristotelianism of the universities, developed their mathematical science and ultimately made possible the mechanics of Galileo. Through Nicholas of Cusa the theory affected Kepler, and through him, Newton.[3] Buridan's system was the 'paradise of mathematical sciences' of which Leonardo da Vinci dreamed and which he sought to apply to all the problems haunting him, though he went on the wrong track by accepting the idea that a projectile began by accelerating. (The growth of

---

[1] Butterfield, *The Origins of Modern Science*. See N. Feather, *Mass, Length and Time*, 1959, ch. 8. From Buridan's thesis was also developed a connected idea which became in time a law of modern mechanics: a constant force produces a uniformly accelerated movement.

[2] Philopon (converted from Alexandrian Neoplatonism to Christianity, *c.* 520) severely criticised Aristotle's mechanics and attacked his idea of empty space. For Buridan's *Q. de puncto*, Zoubov in *Med. and Ren. Stud.* v.

[3] P. Duhem, *Études sur L. de Vinci* (20 s.), 201–11; Kepler, *Mysterium Cosmographicum* (*Op.* 1858; Frisch, i, 122): *divinus mihi Cusanus*. He cites Nicholas in several of his books.

ballistics in connection with firearms played an important part in developing mechanics and dynamics.) The experiments carried on by Galileo at Pisa 1589–91 gave a new turn to his thought; and the doctrine of impetus, which had much affected his early thinking, became the principle of inertia, at least in a limited field of application.

Galileo came to the conclusion that the acceleration of different bodies down a fixed inclined plane are the same under ideal conditions; and by experiments with a ball rolled down one of two inclined planes making a shallow V and mounting up the other plane (to a point above the horizontal which was equal to the height from which it started), he deduced his second qualitative conclusion. 'The slowly dying impetus of the Parisian philosophers was seen as essentially inexhaustible, except by the action of restrictive forces. On a horizontal plane, in the ideal situation, rest, and uniform motion in a straight line with any velocity, were equally "natural" conditions for a material body. The principle of inertia took shape in this statement' (Feather). In regard to local motion near the earth's surface, Galileo went wrong and failed to universalise his conclusion. Descartes however made the universalisation on general grounds, and Newton made it part of an effective system of dynamics.

Bruno was well aware of the doctrine of the impetus and wrestled with some of the problems in works like *The Supper* and *The Infinite Worlds*. He 'had published *The Ash-Wednesday Supper* a year before Benedetti printed his *Diversae speculationes*. If one puts together what these two works added anew to John Buridan's dynamics, one gets almost all the principles that Gassendi was to adopt in 1644 in his *Epistolae tres de motu impresso a motore translato*. The year of *The Supper* is also that in which Galileo reached his twentieth year. The Pisan was arriving at the right moment. For centuries, philosophers had turned and turned in all directions the thoughts that contained in germ the science of movement. Now, those thoughts were ripe. They awaited only for a geometer of genius to bring out into the full light the truths which lived in them, and to give scope to the Mechanics of modern times. Galileo was this geometer' (P. Duhem: Summary, Charbonnel, App. viii).

3. Bruno and Christianity

There can be no doubt that Bruno had entirely rejected Christian dogma in its entirety and that he considered Christian ethics as developed by all the Churches to be generally deleterious and anti-social. He is for the most part chary of the use of the term God. In *Cause* he prefers terms like *nume* or *divinità*, Jove or gods; he tends to use God only in an uninhibited way when he is thinking of absolute substance or matter and wants to lavish all terms of praise or supremacy upon it. In his effort to accommodate himself at all to the world, he began early to work out allegorical translations of dogmatic positions, *e.g.* to see the Holy Ghost or the Trinity as the world-soul.

He makes continual attacks on the Christian creed as pessimistic and ascetic, vilifying and mortifying human nature, destroying the impulse to action and cramping the quest for knowledge by rules of obedience and humility. He says in *The Expulsion* that there has been adoration of dead men (the saints) who were 'infamous, doltish, abusive, fanatical, disgraced.' He contrasts the ancients, the Greeks and the Romans, who 'knew that God was in things and that the divinity lay hid in Nature, shining and discovering itself in different subjects, and made them partakers of itself.... Whence, with magical and divine rites, they mounted by the same ladder of nature to the very height of the divinity which descended to the meanest and lowest things by the communication of itself.' He goes on to compare these attitudes with those of the present. 'But what I think most deplorable is that I see some senseless and foolish idolaters' (the Christians), 'who no more imitate the excellency of the Egyptian worship than the shadow partakes of the nobility of the body, who look for divinity, without any manner of reason, in the excrements of dead and inanimate things.... And what is worse than all this, they triumph for joy to see their own foolish rites in so much reputation, and those of others vanquished and annulled.'

Bruno refuses to believe in a universal deluge, in the recent creation of man, or in the descent of the races of men from a single couple; if so, it must have been by a miracle like that of Jonah's voyage, 'a handsome way of transporting men by some blast of wind or some passage of whales that have swallowed persons in one country and gone to spew them alive in other parts and upon other continents.' Momus in *The Expulsion* declares that Orion (Christ) 'who can walk upon the waves of the sea without sinking or wetting his feet, and consequently can likewise do a great many other pretty tricks,' shall be sent among men, 'and let us order him to teach them everything which he pleases, making them believe black is white, and that human understanding, when it thinks it sees best, is mere blindness, and that what appears to reason good, excellent, and choice, is base, wicked, and extremely evil; that nature is a whorish baggage, that natural law is knavery, that nature and the divinity cannot concur to the same good end, that the justice of the one is not subordinate to the justice of the other, but are things as contrary to one another as light is to darkness, that the entire divinity is the Mother of the Greeks and is like a hard stepmother to all other generations, whence none can be acceptable to the gods but by becoming Greeks. For the greatest Russian or poltroon who lived in Greece, as being allied to the generation of the gods, is incomparably better than the most just and magnanimous who could come from Rome.' Bruno is using the term Greek here to mean Christian; Roman to mean pagan. He adds that the 'Roman' is condemned, 'however preferable in manners, science, valour, judgment, beauty, and authority;

because these are natural gifts, and therefore despised by the gods, and left to those who are not capable of greater privileges; that is, those supernatural ones which the divinity gives, such as dancing on the waters, making lobsters sing ballads, cripples cut capers, and moles see without spectacles, and such other fine gallantries without number' —all wonders paralleled in the *Acta Sanctorum*. 'Let them persuade also that all philosophy, all contemplation, and all magic, which may make them like us [the gods], is nothing but bagatelle; that all heroic acts are nothing but knight-errantry; that ignorance is the finest science in the world, because it is acquired without labour and pains, and keeps the mind free from melancholy.'

He attacks the idea of religion or morality based on future rewards. It is 'foolish, unworthy, profane, and injurious to imagine that the gods seek reverence, fear, love, worship, and respect from men for any other good advantage or end than that of men themselves, being most glorious in themselves, and not capable of receiving any glory from without.' 'Give a blow,' says Jupiter, 'to all prophets, diviners, fortune-tellers, and prognosticators, and all such as traverse and run about to spoil my progress.' Again Bruno expresses contempt for the saints—for 'altars and statues erected to certain persons whom I am ashamed to name, because they are worse than our satyrs, fauns, and other half-beasts, viler than even the crocodiles of Egypt.' He attacks also Judaism and Mohammedanism.

In *The Expulsion* he expresses respect for Christ himself and for the original creed which was one of love, but makes it clear that he considers the whole ecclesiastical system a perversion. Momus makes derisive remarks about the centaur Chiron (*i.e.* Christ, a person made up of two natures). Jupiter tells him that he cannot understand the matter and that Chiron was a most just man, 'healing the sick, teaching the way to climb the stars. I judge him most worthy, because in this heavenly temple, at the altar where he assists, there is no other priest but himself.'

However he satirises the eucharist. Saulino in *The Expulsion* cries, 'Our professors of a sham religion cry that we should glory in I-don't-know-what cabalistic tragedy;' and Bruno repeats the comment in *De Monade*. In the *Seal of Seals* he declares, 'They teach men not to be afraid on account of evil deeds and to have faith in I-don't-know-what most sordid fantasies; and to such credulities about Ceres and Bacchus the retributory gods pay more attention than to good deeds.' In *The Expulsion* he says that new evangelists have found out 'better bread, better flesh and wine than that of the Saone, Candy, or Nola.' In *De Immenso* he says:

> We seek divinity's splendour, not in bread
> and drink and some yet more ignoble materials.

We have already seen (in the Introduction) the sort of thing he was ready to say about the Papacy. It is little wonder that the idea got around, shared by Leibniz, that the Triumphant Beast was the Pope. But such an interpretation badly cramped Bruno's false intentions, his effort to define all the greeds, falsities, and power-lusts which preyed on life and prevented the free play of the creative and productive capacities.

The citations given above, which could be much added to, showed that he had decisively broken from Christianity, however much he might hope to find a *modus vivendi* with the all-powerful Church through the philosophic allegorising of its dogmas or through the doctrine of a total difference between the fields of faith and reason.

Bruno's criticism did not halt at a rejection of Christianity; he rejected religion altogether and an essential aspect of the freedom he offered men was the total elimination of myth, the return to nature in her fullness—man himself having become whole in making this return.[1] The matter is however complicated by his political theory, which accepts the need of religion for the government of the common folk— at least in any immediate future. For the moment the most he can hope for is the liberation of the cultured (or ruling) classes. Note the way in which he praises Elizabeth or looks to the emperor for ending religious strife. Here is a limited and tactical aspect of his thinking which is in fact in contradiction with his vision of the general Expulsion of the Triumphant Beast. That vision implies the liberation of all men through philosophy, science, and socially valuable work. (The unresolved contradiction appears further to some extent in the concepts of Contemplation and Work—to the degree that Bruno has no clear programme of scientific and social activity to unite the two concepts in full concreteness, or to link them in turn with his idea of the unity of the arts.)

4. Bruno and Donne

There is no space here to work out in any detail the influence of Bruno on Donne and the metaphysical poets, or on the line of thinkers that extends from Ralegh to the Cambridge Platonists.[2] Naturally he was not the only influence helping to bring about the positions of these poets and thinkers, but he certainly played an important part. Here I shall merely indicate some of the ways in which his impact can be detected in the young Donne.

First, here is an example of what seems direct borrowing. Bruno: 'Let us see then to what innumerable discoveries we are enabled to

[1] See further, Badaloni, 113ff, 179ff, 194-7

[2] Though the theme has not been effectively explored: see for example, F. A. Yates, *A Study of Love's Labour's Lost*, 1936; A. M. Pellegrini (Sidney, Spenser) in *Studies in Philology*, xl, 2 (April 1943), 128-44; A. Ferrulo (Astrophel and Stella) in *Convivium* 1948, v 986-99; F. B. Newman (Greville and 'a possible echo') in *Philol. Quart.*, xxix, iv (Oct. 1950), 367-74.

proceed by way of trial, experiments, comparison, observation, and abstraction. For does it not sometimes occur that, as we pursue a certain end, another nobler still arises before us, as with alchemists, who, in seeking gold, find that which is far better and more desirable.' Donne:

> No chemic yet th'Elixir got
> But glorified his pregnant pot
> If by the way befall
> Some odoriferous thing, or medicinal.

Throughout *The Expulsion* Bruno insists on the universality of change and vicissitude. He glorifies change as the basis of all life, health, beauty. 'If there were no change in bodies, no variety in matter, and no vicissitude in beings, there would be nothing agreeable, nothing good, and nothing pleasant.... We see that pleasure and satisfaction consist in nothing else but a certain passage, progress, or motion from one state to another. It is certain that the state of hunger is irksome and unpleasant, and satiety is a state of sadness and dullness, but what is pleasing in any of these is a change from one to another.' This theme runs throughout Donne's *Elegies*:

> ...Change is the nursery
> Of music, joy, life, and eternity... (iii)
> The heavens rejoice in motion... (xvii)

Donne's delight in motion and variety is extremely close in terms and in emotion to Bruno with his insistence on various aspects of relativity, 'No body is the same today as yesterday,' and so on. When Donne writes in *Elegy*, xviii:

> Whoever loves, if he do not propose
> The right true end of love...
> Perfection is in unity: prefer
> One woman first, and then one thing in her...
> Can men more injure women than to say
> They love them for that, by which they're not they?
> Must I cool my blood?...

He is making his own playful version of Bruno's stress on unity and his attack on Petrarchism in the dedication of *Gli Eroici* to Sir Philip Sidney: 'What do I hold? Am I perchance a foe to generation? Do I hate the sin? Do I regret having come into the world? Shall I keep men from the delicious fruits of our earthly paradise? Is it for me to bar the holy law of nature? Shall I try to set myself or others free from the sweet-bitter yoke which God in his providence has set on our necks? Am I to persuade myself and others that we are not born to carry on the life we have received? I think I am not cold. I doubt if the snows of Caucasus could put out my fires. What do I conclude? Eminent knight, that we should render unto Caesar the things that are Caesar's, and to God the things that are God's. That women, being women,

6*

should be honoured and loved as such.' Donne continually writes in the key of this passage and of other passages of anti-Petrarchan polemic in *Gli Eroici*—e.g.

> If we
> Make love to woman; virtue is not she...

He builds his prose paradox on virginity in the same way as Bruno's: 'In itself Virginity is neither virtue nor vice, implies no goodness, dignity, or merit, and when it resists the command of nature, it becomes a wrong, an impotence, folly, madness' (*Op. ital.*, ii, 182). His complex conceits about unity and the centrique part are exactly what we would expect to result from a witty and *libertin* application of Bruno's universal circle with its centre everywhere; his dialectic of constancy and change is similarly an application of Bruno's opposition of absolute resolution and ceaseless change-and-contradiction. His *Progress of the Soul* reads as a reaction to Bruno's treatment of metempsychosis in the *Cabala*.

One could show that other influences also went to shape Donne, who like Bruno would have known for example the writers of paradoxes such as Landi and Estienne. Donne too was learned in medieval philosophy; but the way in which such ideas as those mentioned above come together to create a unity in his poetic dialectic as they do in Bruno's philosophic dialectic is too striking to be accidental. Donne has his own original application of the positions, but that does not obscure his close relation to Bruno.

5. Bruno's Notion of the Organic

The main reason why he played about, largely as a conceit, with the theme of transmigration, lay in his sense of the unity of all life; but his understanding that the form and level of any organism determined its consciousness in fact made nonsense of any theory of metempsychosis which involved memory. In the *Cabala*, Onorio defends the doctrine of Pythagoras and the Druids:

'*Ser.* Do you hold that the soul of man is substantially the same as that of the beasts and that the only difference is one of form?

'*Onor.* That of man is the same in its specific and generic essence with that of flies, oysters, plants, and everything which lives, or has a soul; it is not matter, which it possesses in a more or less lively way —there is a thorough permeation of spirit in itself. Now, the aforesaid spirit, by fate or providence, order or chance, unites itself to this or that kind of body, and, by reason of difference in structure or of members, reaches different grades and perfections of faculty and act. Hence, that spirit or soul, which was in the spider, and possessed its industry, claws, and members of a certain number, mass, and shape, united with human seed, acquires another intelligence, instruments, postures, and deeds.'

In a further digression he stresses the key-part played by the hand in gaining man his position among animals. Man's dominance is due less to intelligence than to that 'organ of organs.' Bruno is quite sure that mental functioning is dependent on physical structure and physical operations. 'Could the form of a snake change, could its head mould itself into human form, its belly swell and grow into the shape of the human breast, its tongue enlarge, shoulders spread out and arms and hands shoot forth from it, and its tail bud into legs, it would understand, breathe, speak, work, and walk like a man, and seem to be so because it would have become no other than a man.'

He always insists on the community of intellect between men and animals. His theory of the origin of life includes three main ideas: the material basis of the origin; the dependence of the intellectual capacity of individual beings on the configuration of their bodies' material elements; and the complex constancy of the universe which implies the repetition of forms, and, in this sense, an intelligence objectively inherent in things (Badaloni, 132f). He thus presupposes, in Averroist manner, the eternality of the world and the power of matter in its movements to bring about this or that particular form. His strong sense of the unity of all organic life prevents him from working out any hierarchies except insofar as he stresses the central importance of the hand in bringing about human excellence. (Like Montaigne he says that the American natives were in many respects wiser than civilised peoples and less ignorant in religion: that is, closer to nature.)

He lays much stress on water as an active part in matter with its movements; in its vital aspect water is equivalent to *spiritus*. Indeed it is the source of *spiritus*. 'Water is that which produces union, density, thickness, and gravity.'[1]

6. Notes

Prefatory Epistle

M. de Castelnau, died 1592. He had two sons and two daughters. He composed *Mémoires de Messire Michel de Castelnau*, printed 1621. Dedicated to his son Jacques, they stop before his period in England.

[1] *Op. Ital.*, i, 278; cf. i, 357f, 360, and *Op. Lat. Consc.*, iii, 416: 'The spirit, that is the aggregating force of water, passes from body to body; the dry matter of the atoms receives it, attaining now one mode of aggregation, then another,' Badaloni, 104. See *De Monade* for B.'s idea of a formative energy within the universe, *e.g. Op. Lat. Consc.*, I, ii, 338, 346, 408. The *minimi* are the constant points of change and transformation. *Op. Ital.*, i, 321.

The woman to whom Bruno angrily alludes is not known. It has been suggested that she is the fat Englishwoman he satirises in the First Dialogue.

Argument 3rd Dialogue: for David, cf. *De vinculis*, art. 15, where Avicebron is added. Amaury taught that as God was in all things, he was no more in the eucharist than in anything else; the consecration merely affirmed his presence; David took the logical step of reducing God, Matter, Intelligence to a single substance: 'The substance of which all bodies are made is called matter; the substance of which all souls are made is called spirit. ... God is simultaneously the principle of all souls and the matter of all bodies:' Albert the Great, *Summa Creat.*, ii, 5, 2.

First Latin poem: for opening imagery cf. *160 Articles, dedicatio*, 'in the free field of philosophy I shall shelter myself from the ever-moving flood and seek the society of those who open their eyelids.'

First Sonnet: inserted in pt. 1, dial. 1, *Eroici*. For end of *Second:* cf. Petrarca, ii, 57.

First Dialogue

Speakers: Filoteo (Teofilo)=Bruno. Eliotropio=Heliotrope, that is, a sun-follower, an adherent of the Nolan philosophy. He seems here to be meant for a fair-minded Englishman. In *De Umbris*, written before the English visit, he also appears. Armesso (Harmesso, Hermesso) is an English friend.

Opening: cf. *De Immenso*, 1, 2. It is a Platonic reminiscence: cf. *Repub.*, vii, 514–5.

Merlin: the Merlino of Ariosto, *Orl. fur.*, iii, 10–6 and xxxiii, 9. The same speech has refs. to Virg., *Aen.*, ii, 246f and 122–4; *Numbers*, xxii, 21–30. Triphonius suggests Erasmus, *Moriae Enc.* (1648) 21f; *Adagia* (Choset, 1593) 325. There is a reminiscence of *Candelaio*, antiprol.

St Paragorio: probably a ref. to the church of S Paragorion at Noli (where B. stayed five months in 1577). Both here and in *Candelaio* the text has Sparagorio. The picture of the fat Englishwoman inspired Berni in *Alla sua innamorata* and Aretino (*Mogliazzo* and *Ragionamenti*).

Smith, etc.: speakers in *Cena*.

Oxford: see Introduction for the great tradition of thinkers such as Grosseteste and Roger Bacon. Add Robert Kilwardby and Duns Scotus. See Rashdall, *Medieval Universities*, 'The place of Oxford in Medieval Thought.' For a briefer account, G. Leff, *Medieval Thought*.

Doctors with rings: cf. *Cena* on Nundinio and Torquato. Sir Philip Sidney wrote to H. Languet in 1574, 'Of Greek literature I wish to learn only so much as shall suffice for the perfect understanding of Aristotle.' However he later remarked that the four faculties were reducible to one, that of the grammarians—and 'while they chase words, they neglect things.' Bartholmèss, *J. Bruno*, i, 128f n. Perhaps he was influenced by Bruno: cf. *Cena*, 'Seek as much as you like: you will find only doctors in grammar.'

Tobie Matthew, Archbishop of York (1606), born at Bristol 1546; in 1579, vice-chancellor, then chancellor of Oxford. Famous as orator. When Campion published his *Decem Rationes*, M. was the first to reply from Oxford; in October 1581 in a Latin sermon he defended the Reformation, asking that the doctrine of Jesus and primitive Christianity be taught. In 1583 he was sent north to preach the new religion. Died 1628. In Bruno's time he was dean of Christ Church. Culpepper, rector of New College 1573–99, had been dean of Chichester since 1577.

Salmoneus: Virg., *Aen.*, vi, 585–6.

Alexander Dicson published *De umbra rationis et judicii, sive de memoriae virtute prosopopoeia*, London 1583; *Thamus, sive de memoria virtute*, Lugduni Batavorum, 1597.

Filoteo's speech against the grammarians has reminiscences of *Candelaio*; Poliinnio is throughout linked with the pedant Bartolomeo in the play, whose anti-feminism is brought out by his ambiguous relation to his pet pupil. *Spicelegium:* work of Napoletan grammarian L. G. Scoppa, which dominated in the 16th century schools and on into the 17th century. Ambrogio Calepino, 1435–1511, Augustinian, author of the first Latin vocabulary for the schools. *Cornucopiae sive commentaria linguae latinae,* work of Nicola Perotti 1430–80, published 1489. Mario Nizzoli, published *Observationes in M. Tullium Ciceronem* 1535, or *Thesaurus ciceronianus*; reprinted more than thirty times when Bruno cites it. In general, cf. *De Min.,* iii, 1.

Perissology etc.: Donato in his *Ars Grammatica* (Gramm. Lat., Keil, iv, 394f) enumerates the barbarisms and solecisms. Cf. *Candel.,* ii, 1. *Escrilogie* =obscenities (Gr. *aischrologiai*); *cacoefati, cacenphata. Candel.,* ii, 1. 'This *cacoephaton idest* bad elocution.'

For possible inspiration here of G. Florio (*Secondi frutti*): Gentile, ed. 1925, i, 171 n.

Fil. ends with praise of Elizabeth because under her England has not been riven by religious wars like the rest of Europe.

Second Dialogue

For some reason here Bruno gives Dicson the name of Arelio. As Gervasio is obviously an Englishman I call him Gervase; but I keep to the Italian name of the pedant, which Bruno spells both Poliinnio and Poliimnio.

Art of Arts: ref. to Lull's work.

Divine Substance: cf. Nicholas of Cusa, *Docta Ign.,* i, 3: *quidditas ergo rerum...in sua puritate inattingibilis est.* Cabalists: *Book of Zohar* (ed. Leroux, 1, 19b).

Timaeus: 41b; Bruno, *De Imm.,* 11, 5 (commentary).

Matter and form in a composite body: Aristotle, *Phys.,* ii, 2, 194, A12 (matter as correlative of a specific form in a compound). Aristotle uses the terms *arche* and *aitia* for principle and cause: synonyms, *Metaph.,* v, 1, 1013a, 16, and different, iv, 2, 1013b, 18e, 24; see also xii, 4, 1079b, 22. And Bruno, *Summa term. metaphys.*

Empedocles: was in fact a hylozoist, but Bruno as in so many matters dealing with the Greek philosophers draws on medieval traditions which Neoplatonised them. To attempt to sort out all these details would take much space. See Namur, *Cause,* 89n.

Plato distinguishes demiurge and world-soul, *Tim.* 28E. In *De Triplici,* B. compares the Soul to a spider weaving its web. 'Birth is an expansion of the centre...death is a contraction into the centre.' Same idea in *Spaccio* and *Lampas.* Tocco, *Opp. inedite,* 57–61.

Lampas also has 'All particular intellects are formed from one intellect.' For *idea ante rem* etc., *Theses de Magia* (*Op. lat. consc.,* 462, 13).

Empedocles (2nd ref.): B. may refer to fr. 35 (Diels). *Perfection:* cf. *Tim.,* 29e–30a: Namer, *Cause,* 94n. and *Aspects,* 58ff, for Bruno's inability to explain differences; also, *Cause,* 95n. on Aristotle, *De Anima,* iii, 3, on the potential intellect. See also *De Anima,* ii, 1, 413a, 8f; iii, 5, 430a, 17–25. For Pythagoreanism as implying a ground of equalisation: all beings born from a common nature: *Op. Ital.,* ii, 301.

Aristotle: writer or lutanist: *Phys.,* ii, 8, 199b, 26. Plato in Teo.'s following speech: *Tim.,* vi, 29E; x, 37C–D (Gentile, 184 for Ficino's translation); 30C. *Beauty: Eroici,* 'Reason then seizes the more real beauty by assimilating itself to what puts beauty into the body...and it is the soul which thus constructs and figures.' Cf. Plotinus, *Enn.,* i, 6, 2. As we would expect, Bruno claimed that there is a unity of all the acts, which in turn are closely related to philosophy: *De Imag. Comp.* For Aristotle and general animation: *De part. anim.*, i, 1 and i, 5; *De caelo*, i, 2 and i, 9; *Eth. Nic.*, vi, 7; elements, *De gen. anim.*, iii, 11; earth, *Meteor.*, i, 14; nature proceeding from the lifeless to the living, *De part. anim.*, iv, v. For Plotinus, *Enn.*, iv, 4, 36. All movement for Aristotle is brought about by a final cause: *Metaph.*, xii, 7, 1072a, 25.

Anaxagoras does say all is in all, fr. 6; but adds, fr. 11 that the Intelligence stands outside this—outside the primitive mixture (fr. 12 etc).

For end of Teo.'s following speech: cf. Plotinus, vi, 4, 2; iv, 3, 20–3. For the stress on necromancy: *Sig. sigill.*, ii, 4; *De Magia, de magia math.* Our guides are Love, the producer of all things; Art, which is highest when nearest nature (since in nature the world-soul operates); Mathematics and True Magic, which reveals the inner nature of things: *Sig. sigill.*, P. ii, 2–5. Other occasions: it has been argued that *De Imm.* was in part written in England. Fiorentino, pref. to *Opera*, i, 1, p. xxxi.

Intrinsic formal principle: cf. *Lampas trig.* in *Opera*, iii, 253, 256; *Spaccio* (G. 8f); *De Min.*, i, 3.

Plotinus, *Enn.*, iv, 7, 9: 'There is then a nature primarily alive, necessarily incorruptible and immortal, since it is the principle of life for all the rest.' Also, 'All things would fade out without return if ever the being that conserves the individuals and the universe came to perish.' Bruno develops this to say that if the least fragment of being perished, all would end.

Aristotle (after the Ovid quotation): Namer remarks well: 'Bruno's manner consists in a slow graduation of the boldnesses of his philosophy and at times in the adoption of a viewpoint which will not be his own. At the same time, at places, he throws out hints as to his conclusions. The knowledge of this procedure seems to us capital for resolving difficulties and contradictions that are solely on the surface.' *Cause*, 107.

Immortality: B. believes only in the eternality of the underlying principle of unity: Namer. *Aspects*, 41. Tocco and Charbonnel go wrong on this point.

Empedocles again: fr. 1 (Diels); Aristotle, *Phys.*, i, 4, 187a, 26. B. follows the medievally Neoplatonised idea of E. (who in fact held that particulars came from the Sphere, which is not conceived as Intelligence).

Grandazzo: Randazzo in province of Catania, famous in the Cinquecento. See *Commedie of G.B. della Porta* (ed. Spampanato, i, 326). The statue was Byzantine, in wood, by Mattinatai of Messina, made for a village church, according to the tale; a downpour of rain prevented it being carried beyond Randazzo, where it was bought. Cf. the crucifix of Monreale, miraculous bringer of good weather: Pitre, *Bibl. trad. popol. sic.*, xviii, 262; xii, 326f, 367. Milazzo, in prov. of Messina; Nicosia, in prov. of Catania. The voice-analogy occurs in Plotinus, *Enn.*, iv, 4, 12.

Third Dialogue

Calicut: for the district, Malabar, or the area of English India. *Man as Microcosm:* cf. Aristotle, *Phys.*, viii, 2, and *De Anima.* iii, 8.

Those plants that Diogenes, etc.: bawdy allusion to anecdote about Diogenes of Sinope: 'plant a man.'

Paracelsus: B. drew much on him for his notions about magic. In the preface to *De Lamp. comb.* Paracelsus appears as *ille medicorum princeps*; cf. *Sig. sigill.*

Idolatry of Aristotle: Albert the Great said that Aristotle had been put by nature as the norm of Truth: *De Anima*, iii, 2, 3. *Pre-socratics:* B. seems to have known well only the texts of Plato (ed. M. Ficino) and Aristotle (many editions at Venice, Lyon, Frankfurt in 15th–16th centuries), but he put his ideas about the pre-Socratics together from various scraps.

Pierre de la Ramée caused a scandal by upholding an anti-Aristotelian thesis; published *Scholae dialecticae* 1543 and *Animadversiones in dialecticam Aristotilis*; was condemned as 'impudent' and interdicted from teaching philosophy. Francisco Patrizzi, 1529–97, published *Discussiones peripateticae* 1571–81; also later *Nova de universis philosophia*, his main work; in *Aristoteles exotericus* he tried to prove A. was not in agreement with the faith. Bacon jeered at him: *De Aug.*, iii, 4. See Fiorentino, *B. Telesio*, i, 370–6, and Tocco, *Fronti*, 35–7. For Telesio and Bruno, Fiorentino, ii, 67; Tocco, 72–5; Charbonnel, *Pensée*, 453–9. Bruno attacks Ramus in *Eroici*.

Sterility: see Pliny, *N.H.*, xvi, 26 on the *salix*.

Avicebron: Latin version of *Fons* (Baeumker, 1895): see Gentile, *Causa*, 203n.

For Soul as organising force: De Min., i, 2.

Nature and art: Plato, *Tim.*, 50 ab; Aristotle, *Phys.*, ii, 1, 193a; Plotinus, *Enn.*, ii, 4, 12.

Timaeus the Pythagorean: the pseudo-Tim. of Locri, *De anima mundi et natura* 94a (v. Mullach, *Fragm.*, ii, 38). See also Plato, *Tim.*, 50e and Aristotle, *Phys.*, i, 5, 188a, 28.

Teo.'s long speech, 'Hence we may conclude . . .': In *Acrotismus*, art. viii, B. says that Aristotle considered matter as a pure logical and abstract possibility, not as a reality. He says that for Aristotle, *non aliud esse praeterquam historiam* of individuals. He continues with a polemic against Gilbert de la Porée and the Scotists. *Entelechy* etc: Aristotelian definition of the soul: *De Anima*, ii, 1, 412a, 27. (Already in *De Umbris* Bruno had attacked the idea of nature as a man *universale logicum*: *Op. lat. consc.*, ii, 1, 60.)

Heraclitus: the living fire of H. is assimilated to the world-soul as conceived by Plotinus.

Hermes Trismegistus: name set to some writings of late 3rd century A.D. which mixed a form of Platonic-Pythagoreanism with Egyptian Gnosticism, etc.: held in high esteem in medieval days, esp. among alchemists. Bruno mentions H.T. in *De Imm.*, iii, 8 and *Cand.*, i, 9. It was with the help of the *Book of the 24 Philosophers* ascribed to H.T. that Alan of Lille (1125–1203) reached the formula on the Trinity that became famous: 'The monad only engenders the monad and only reflects its own love for itself.' Nicholas of Cusa cites H.T. (*Poimandres*, v, 10) on the *universitas* of things: Betts, 115.

Aristotle on void: but see *Ifinito* (G. 302f).

Humours: the four humours of Hippocratic and Galenian medicine, combatted by Paracelsus.

Absolute elements: allusion to indivisible atoms. In *De Min.*, i, 5, he makes a distinction between the relative minimum, related to our perception, and the absolute minimum, irreducible in itself.

Theo.'s speech: 'Certainly, this principle . . .': Plotinus, *Enn.*, ii, 4 (theory of two matters): Chalcidius, *Timaeus*, ch. 320 (refusal to consider matter as corp. or incorp. since it is pure possibility: so, no reason why it should not belong to the soul as to the body: ed. Wrobel, 1876, 344). Various links with N. of Cusa: *Docta Ign.*, ii, 7; ii, 1, and *De possest* (ed Bâle), i, 250: Tocco, *Fonti*, 42f, and *Avicebron* (Munck, v, 43, *Fons*). The *Cena* also sets out the doctrine that each part comes (*i.e.* successively) to have all the aspects that all the other parts have. See also *Anaxagoras*, fr. 6.

Theo.'s speech: 'These things are not act. . . .' See again N. of Cusa,

Opera, i, 250f. The comparison with the sun, 252. Again 254: Tocco, *Fonti*, 42f. Absolute quantity, *Docta Ign.*, i, 4, and *De Possest* (Bâle), 254. Bruno, *Lampas trig.* (*Op. Lat. Consc.*, iii, 44).

   Dicson: 'This absolute act....' Cf. *Docta Ign.*, i, 3. Cf. *Eroici* (G. 443), and in general for theory of knowledge *Sig. sigill.*, *De umbris idearum*.

   Theo.: 'The coincidence of this act....' *Timaeus:* B. seems thinking of Chalcidius, *Tim.* (Wrobel, ch. 320, p. 344). Aristotle: *Gen.*, i, 4, 319b, 14. 'The terms of the latter': cf. Plotinus, *Enn.*, ii, 4, 4: 'There is below an intelligible world, and the sensible world is an imitation of it; this latter is composed of matter and form; then there is necessarily matter in the former.' Cf. Chalcidius, ch. 320. Parmenides, Aristotle, *Phys.*, i, 3, 186d, 22; *Metaph.*, 986b, 36; and Bruno, *Acrotismus*, art. iii, and *Sig. sigill.* (*Opera*, 11, ii, 180).

Fourth Dialogue

Poliinnio alone: Manfurio in *Cand.*, ii, 1, repeats the remark on the vulva. Aristotle compares matter to form as woman to man, *De gen. anim.*, i, 2; matter is passive, inert (*De gen. et corr.*, ii, 9), so woman is without activity (*De gen. anim.*, iv, 1). Matter is the defective element, *kakopoion*, disturbing, which obstructs the ends of nature and causes monstrosities and mutilations if form does not dominate (*Phys.*, i, 9; *De gen. anim.*, iv, 4). Hence woman is something incomplete, a sort of castrated man (*De gen. anim.*, ii, 3, and iv, 1)—cf. Freud's theory of women's penis-envy! (But Plato also compares matter to woman: *Tim.*, 50D; and Plotinus, *Enn.*, iii, 6, 19: *Tocco, Op. Lat. Consc.*, 343f, n3.)

   Complexio: figura rhetorum, quae repetitionem et conversionem amplectitur: Cicero, *Ad Herenn.*, iv, 14. Chalcidius seems the first to translate Greek *hyle*, matter, as *silva*: ch. 123.

   Philosopher (against women): see Orelli, *Opuscula Graec. vet. sententiosa et moralia*, 1819, i, 220f; known from L. Guicciardini's *Ore di ricreazione*, 1567. Biscayans did much of the carrying trade of the Neapolitan kingdom. Cicala: cf. *Spaccio* (G. 67, 71) and *Eroici*: acquaintance, if not friend, of L. Tansillo and B.'s father, if, as seems correct, he is Odoardo-Cicala, to whom in 1598 G. Cesare Capaccio dedicated his fishing eclogues *Mergellina*: Cicala served King Philip with his galleys and held the barony of Angri; same tale in *Facezie* by Domenichi, 1593, and T. Folengo's *Baldo* (xii, 570–80 and xiii, 117–21).

   Marie Bochetel, daughter of Jacques Bochetel, seigneur of Brouillamenon, maître d'hotel of the king, and Marie de Morogues, was married at Bourges, June 26th 1575, to Castelnau.

   Avicebron: 'The first matter that carries all is one; for it unites the matters of sensible things and those of intelligible things, so that they become all a single matter,' *Fons*, iv, 15.

   Pure verbal distinction: In *Lampas*, iii, 29, B. says that Matter is separable from Intelligence only by abstraction, in *Acrotismus* (art. ii) he holds that the matter of Aristotle is a mere logical abstraction.

   Plotinus on Matter: Enn., ii, 4, 4. Bruno is rather thinking of Cusa, *Docta Ign.*, i, 5, 'Take away number, the distinction of things (*discretio*), the order, proportion, harmony, and the very plurality of beings cease.' The order and harmony suppose parts, and so matter, says Plotinus, ii, 4, 11, since 'division into parts and separation-out are affections of matter.' 'But if, although multiple, it is indivisible, this multiplicity in unity is in unity as in matter,' ii, 4, 4. 'Multiplicity is posterior to unity,' ix, 8, 23.

   The light-metaphysic plays its part in developing the monistic idea of matter. Thus Grosseteste holds that corporeal reality is both matter and form. The first action of corporeality is to extend itself in three-dimensional space: its volume is measured by the force of expansion. If this extension is not explainable by the single metaphysical matter or by a light that would be pure form, it can be understood only in terms of the fundamental energy of physical matter or concrete corporeality. This energy is of luminous essence since it is light which by its diffusion creates the spherical space of the world. Light or luminous energy is thus at the base of all material expansion in space, consequently of all possible action and all visibility: luminous energy then does not result from pre-existing corporeality; it constitutes it in its physical being by its natural and fundamental union with primary matter: *De luce*, 51—E. de Bruyne, *Études d'esthet. med.*, iii, 1946, 20ff. In the body, light constitutes the essence and source of all perfection: S Bonaventura, ii, *Sent.*, 12, 2, 1a, 4.

Such ideas show how Bruno could feel a certain affinity with the anti-Aristotelians of the 13th century (but we cannot link him otherwise with medieval positions, as Yates tries to). Light seemed at once both material and immaterial, and provided a basis for moving towards a monistic outlook without admitting it, while at the same time encouraging mathematical science. For Bruno on light as a spiritual substance in all things: *De Rerum Principiis* (*Op. Lat. Consc.*, 513). For the light-aesthetic and N. of Cusa: Santinello. The use of the art-analogy for the formative process of nature (treated theologically) is also found in medieval times: see J. M. Parent, *La doctrine de la création dans l'école de Chartres*, 1931, 127—with relation to maths. and physics: Garin (c), 86. For N. of Cusa: Santinello, 179ff.

Table-manners: Other English usages are dealt with in *Cena*. Trans-alpine=Italian.

Matter in incorp. things: Plotinus, *Enn.*, ii, 4, 5, 'Those who assert that matter is substance would be right if they were speaking of intelligible matter.' Bruno sees the two matters as expressions of a single substance. David of Dinant said, 'By God's grace, man and ass are one, but they appear different.' Albert the Great, *Comm. Phys.*, i, 2, 10.

Theo.: 'Not in absolute power...': cf. *Infinito*: 'Since the first principle is very simple, if it was finite according to one attribute, it would be finite according to all attributes.' For Dicson's answer: cf. *Eroici*, G. 357.

Averroes: the commentator supreme. In *Eroici* (G. 382) B. calls him 'the subtlest Peripatetic,' and in *De Imm.*, i, 6, *subtilis Averroes*: Tocco, *Fonti*, 27–9. For Averroes, there exists a single subject which can receive all determinations, but an agent is needed to make them pass from potency into act; this agent is not interior to matter, the Intellect is separated: *Metaph.*, ii, 12, fo. 334v. Plotinus in this speech by Theo., *Enn.*, ii, 4, 3. For Dicson's answer: cf. *Lampas trig.* (*Op.*, iii, 25): 'The shadow (matter) is not to be regarded as being invented and as if purely logical, but as something most stable (*constantissimum*), indeed most constant nature....'

Supernatural light: cf. *Summa term. metaph.* (*Opera*, i, iv, 100). For Teo.'s reply: cf. *Lampas* (*Op. Lat. Consc.*, iii, 49) for the claim that the *intellectus agens*, the *spiritus vivificans* always work from within, *ab intrinsico.* 'It is the artificer, who works not in connection with matter but within matter and nature.' For B. on inner illumination ('wherein object and sensitive subject are one'): *De Compositione*, I, i, 1.

Dicson: 'Very well. I think....' Vulgar philosophy is the Aristotelian. Certain monks: ref. to the *haeccitas* of Duns Scotus and his disciples as the principle of individuation. He makes afresh his critique of so much of medieval thought as being concerned with words or logical principles, not with realities. Aristotle in *Phys.*, ii, 192b says, 'Each natural being has in itself a principle of movement and fixity.' And in *De Gen.*, i, 3, 4, he says that if anything is produced, it must have a certain substance, 'which is at least in potency even if it is not in reality and in entelechy, out of which comes the production of the thing and into which it must change back when destroyed.' Poliinnio's comment is correct. For Aristotle, the act, the reality, is in a determined being; for Bruno it is in the source from which it emerges.

Dicson: 'And I say...': Anaxagoras, etc.: Bruno refers to Aristotle, *Phys.*, i, 4, 187a.

Peripatetics and art: Aristotle, *Phys.*, i, 7, 190b, 7. Note also Theophrastus' *Metaphysics*, 8a, 19, 20.

Ideal Signs: Platonic ideas. Bruno uses *signum* in his mnemonic systems, but in a different sense: *De imaginum...compositione*, i, 3 (*Op.*, 11, ii, 98). Note that he despised the sort of Neoplatonism expounded by a Pico della Mirandola: L. Auvray, *Mém. de la Soc. de l'hist. de Paris*, xxiv, 288–99, sub December 7th. Note that in the latter half of the 16th century Platonism in Italy had definitely become an expression of the seigniorial reaction, *e.g.* Scipione Ammirato, *Discorsi sopra Cornelio Tacito*, 1598, 71.

Statue: Bruno inverts Aristotle's position by finding reality in matter, not in the determination of it.

Poliinnio: '*Quaeso*...': Aristotle, *Phys.*, i, 2, 199a. 25.

David of Dinant: his book was *De tomis idest de divisionibus* (influenced by John the Scot): refs. in Albert the Great, *Summa Theol.*, i, 4, 9, 20 and ii, 1, 4; Aquinas, *S.T.*, 1, iii, art. 8; Charbonnel, *Pensée*, p. xlix. See also Bruno, *De vinculis* (*Opera*, iii, 696). For a difficulty in the text of this speech of Teo.'s (*in sé*), see Namer, *Cause*, 188n. The need of Christian thinkers to unify the Trinity kept a monistic and dialectical line of thought in existence. Thus John the Scot identifies, as Father, Son, and Spirit, *ousia, dynamis, energeia—essentia, virtus, operatio*—which are present in all things. Nicholas of Cusa uses this triad several times (Betts 147), with slight variations: *essentia, potentia, operatio*. But generally his triads are different and he varies them considerably. His favourite is unity, equality, connexion. Once he has *unitas, species, utilitas*: *Excit.*, ii (*Fides autem Catholica haec est*) 385: a variation on Hilary. Unity is identified with Being. Eckhardt has many triads: Pfeiffer, 124; Jostes, *Meister Eckhardt und seine Jünger*, 16.

Albert the Great had many triads; he finds in each a supreme term synthesising the two preceding ones and subordinating the triads themselves in a rhythm of forward movement: E. de Bruyne, *Études d'esthetique medivale*, 1946, iii, 154. See p. 15 for the scheme of Albert's dialectic of the Beautiful.

Fifth Dialogue

Teo.'s opening speech: Many passages from N. of Cusa could be cited as showing the link here between the two thinkers; also some Plotinus, *e.g. Enn.*, iii, 8, 8; and David of Dinant, in Albert, *Summa Creat.*, ii, 5, 2. The idea of the sphere with centre everywhere, etc., goes back to the hermetic writings (*Hermetica*, ed. Scott): see note in G. 250, citing S Bonaventura, etc. (also Pascal, who may have got the idea from De Gournay's intro. to Montaigne's *Essays*, 1595). Bruno repeats the idea, *e.g. De Min.*, i, 4, 31. Again for the primal undifferentiated matter, Avicebron, *Fons*, i, 7; David of Dinant, 'What makes plurality is not true being but that which appears' (Albert, *Comm. Phys.*, i, 2, 10).

Natural philosophers: these are such as the pre-Socratics, as opposed to the Aristotelians who establish categories in the real. 'Vulgarly called': that is, by the Aristotelians.

Dicson's first speech: In *Acrotismus* (art. 28) B. rejects the Aristotelian definition of space as the limit of a containing body. Parmenides: in *De Min.*, i, 4, 31, he attributes the theory of the infinite sphere to Xenophanes; P.'s sphere was finite. The 'commentator' is Aristotle, *Metaph.*, i, 5. See *Acrotismus* for B.'s mature ideas on space, movement, and time, *e.g.* movement in space is the measure of time, not time the measure of motion; we know duration through change.

Equi-vocal, uni-vocal: M. Capella, *Artes liberales*, iv, 355f: '*Aequivocum* is where there is one name for many things, but not the same definition. *Univocum* is where there is one name and definition for two or more things.' Bruno is translating the Aristotelian terms *homōnymon* and *synōnymon*: *Categs.*, i, 1a, 1; *Metaph.*, 1070a, 4.

Theo. 'Just so. Beyond this...': Plato in the *Tim.* sees the world as composed of matter and act; the world-soul is an intermediary substance, comprising both the nature of the Same and the Other, 35a. For Aristotle, *Phys.*, 193a, 28, nature is both matter and form. Bruno is still close to N. of Cusa, *e.g. Docta Ign.*, i, 11 and 24. For Plato's Great and Small: Aristotle, *Phys.*, iii, 4; Bruno sees here his dialectic of minimum and maximum. Archytas: the pseudo-Archytas. The later Pythagoreans wanted to prove that Archytas discovered the categories before Aristotle. Teo.'s 'thirdly': N. of Cusa, *Docta Ign.*, i, 5; and *Lampas trig.* (*Op. Lat. Consc.*, iii, 42). 'Fourthly': N. of Cusa, *De math. perfectione* (*Op.*, iii, 1120f) and *De berillo*, xxv (i, 276); also *Docta Ign.*, i, 18ff. Cf. *De Min.*, i, 4, 64. Nicholas and Bruno were near the discovery of the infinitesimal calculus invented by Leibniz in *Nova Methodus pro maximis et minimis*. Heat: Bruno thinks of Telesio. Physicians: cf. *De Rerum Principiis* (*Op.*, iii, 549f). Poor Aristotle: *Metaph.*, ix, 4, 1055b, 11. He is throughout polemising against Aristotle's mechanical logical outlook: *Phys.*, i, 189a, 24—a contrary is not born from another contrary: 'friendship does not combine hate, nor draw anything from hate ... but the action of both is produced in a third term.' And *Phys.*, i, 6: 'It is impossible for contraries to be one, for the contrary is not one.' Cf. the attack by Nicholas in *De Berillo*, xxv (i, 276). The demonstration of the third figure is repeated in *De Min.*, i, 4, 34ff. The middles are the universals. The *actio mediorum* lies 'between the doer and the sufferer, so between ... the lover and the beloved is loving or love; whence *amans*, *amabile*, and *amor* make up an indivisible *amabilitas*': *Op. Lat. Consc.*, 11, ii, 274. See Badaloni 47ff.

In these notes I have drawn in places on Lasson, Namer, and Gentile. The reader can further turn to the forthcoming edition of the *Causa* by G. Aquilecchia, which will clarify many points. I had finished the translation and introduction before reading Badaloni's book, which seems to me by far the best general book on Bruno; and from it I have added various points of clarification or amplification in my exposition.

7. Citations

First Dialogue

Penitus etc.: Virgil, *Ecl.*, i, 67. *Umbras vocat* etc.: *Aen.*, vi, 432 f. *Natura non può* etc.: Ariosto, *Orl. Fur.*, xxvii, 120.

Second Dialogue

Totamque infusa etc.: *Aen.*, vi, 726f (cf. *Georg.*, iv, 219). Bruno cited these lines from the *Aeneid* in the examination at Venice June 2nd 1592. Plotinus: 'The world-soul...' *Enn.*, ii, 9, 7: Bruno retranslates from Ficino: Tocco, *Opp. lat.*, 340 n2. Cf. also *Enn.*, iv, 4, 36. *Cuium pecus: Virg., Ecl.*, iii, 1.— followed by *Genesis*, vliii, 23; *Isaiah*, lxvi, 1; *Tobias*, viii, 9. *Principio caelum,* etc. *Aen.*, vi, 724. *O gelidus*, etc.: *Ovid, Met.*, xv, 153–9, making one verse of 158–9: cf. *De Min.*, 1, iii, 1–50; and ded. to *Candelaio.* Solomon: *Ecclesiastes,* i, 9–10: Bruno liked this motto: see Gentile, *Causa*, 1925, 191n. Poliinnio at end: ref. to Terence, *Eun.*, iv, 7, 46.

Third Dialogue

Nolite vocari Rabi: Matthew, xxiii, 8. *Cedant*, etc.: *Cicero de meo consulatu.* *Quae Caesaris: Matthew*, xxii, 21 (cf. *Eroici*, Gentile, 390). *Vox faucibus: Aen.*, ii, 774 (cf. *Candelaio*, ii, 1).

Revealer: *Exodus*, iii, 14; then *Revel.*, i, 17 (*Isaiah*, xli, 4; xliv, 6; xlviii, 12); *Psalms*, cxxxviii, 12. *Bonis avibus:* cf. Ovid, *Fasti*, i, 513 (used by Manfurio in *Cand.*, i, 5).

Fourth Dialogue

Proverbs of Solomon, xxx, 15f; *Psalms*, 1, 6; *Genesis*, iii, 12–14. Couplet on woman: Ariosto, *Orl. Fur.*, xxvii, 119.

Credite Pisones: Horace, *Epist.*, i, 1, 88, and ii, 3, 6. Jacob, *Revel.*, xix, 10, and xx, 9, where the angel speaks to St John, not Jacob; but B. had perhaps a vague memory of *Genesis*, xxxi, 30. Spirit covering waters, etc.: *Genesis*, i, 24, 30, also i, 2, and i, 6f and 9f. *Parcius*, etc.: Virg., *Ecl.*, iii, 7.

Fifth Dialogue

Vae soli: Ecclesiastes, iv, 10.

8.   List of Terms

The following is a list of the main philosophical terms used by Bruno in *Causa*, and the way in which each is translated. Where the Italian words are translated otherwise in the text, the variation is given in the following textual notes. *Soggetto* is translated sometimes as subject, sometimes as substratum; whenever subject or substratum occur in the text, the Italian is always *soggetto*. And so on.

The word which causes the most difficulty in the effort to represent the Italian terms with uniformity is *raggione*, reason. Where however it is not translated as reason, the variation is given in the notes. Bruno's rationalism appears in the way in which reason—the reason for a thing—can be used to express a thing's nature or essence, and so on. Thus, 'the term *raggione* is regulator of sense, which does come from the subject, but which is objectively present in the reality and hence is already itself nature' (Badaloni, 144).

Act, action: *atto* (occasionally *azione*).
Actuality: *attualità*.

Being: *Essere*, sometimes translated 'existence.' In the last dialogue, where 'being' becomes abstracted, B. uses *ente* (also in the introduction, presumably written last).

Cause: *causa* (material, efficient, formal, final).

Change: *mutazione, cangiamento.* Note also *alterazione*, translated 'alteration.' There are a few alchemist terms such as 'transmutation.'

Cognition: *cognizione.*

Concept: *concetto.*

Contradiction: *contradizione, contrarietadi.*

Contrary: *contrario.*

Deity: *numo.*

Divinity: *divinità*—where he uses *Dio*, God is given.

Elements: *elementi.*

Essence: *essenza*, but see *raggione.*

Explicit: *explicato*—also translated as 'unfolded.' This is one example of a set of terms (explication, implication, complication) which are important for B.'s imagery of form-and-matter, and which go back to neoplatonic ideas.

Form: *forma.*

Formation: *formazione.*

Indivisible: *indivisibile* and *individuo*, also *impartible.* 'Divisible' is *divisibile* or *dividuo. Individuo* is at times translated 'individual.'

Instinct: *instinto.*

Intellect: *intelletto.*

Intelligence: *intelligenza.*

Matter: *materia*, a few times translated as 'materials.'

Nature: *natura.*

Notion: *notizia.*

Object: *oggetto.*

Possibility: *possibilità.*

Potency: *potenza*, also a few times as 'power.'

Principle: *principio.*

Reality: *realità.*

Reason: *raggione*, at times translated as 'nature, essence, viewpoint, etc.,' as recorded in notes.

Science: *scienza.* The term must be understood as applying to the whole of knowledge. Science in the modern sense is Natural Philosophy.

Sensible: *sensibile*; sense, *senso*; sensibility: *sensibilità*; sensitive: *sensitiva.*

Subject: *soggetto*, also given as 'substratum.'

Species: *specie*, at times translated as 'sort' when there is no particular colour to it.

Thing: *cosa.*

Unity: *Unità*, at times *l'uno* as mentioned in notes.

World-soul: *anima del mondo.*

9. Some Textual Notes

Besides recording variations in the use of *raggione*, etc., I have cited various words or phrases which may be of interest to students of Bruno. The order is that in which they appear in the various dialogues.

INTRODUCTION

Lines of thought: *raggioni*. Subject and principle: *soggetto principio*. External activity: *atto di supposito*. Manners and degrees: *raggioni e ordini*. Its aspect: *di volto*. Ogre: *l'Orco* (Orcus). Basis: *raggion*. (Substantial) nature: *raggione*. Degrees: *gradi*. Nature (of cause): *raggion*. Views, viewpoints: *raggioni*. Nature (of matter): *raggion*. Scale: *scala* (ladder). Basis (shared): *raggion*. Concordance: *imitazione*. (Opposing) arguments: *raggioni*. (Diversities of) nature: *raggione*. Actual existence: *attualità*. Explicit: *esplicato*. Explication: *esplicazione*. States: *suppositi*. Concept: *proposito*. Principle and principled: *principio e principiato* (a phrase that recurs). Unfolded universe: *l'universo esplicamente*. Natural science: *scienza naturale*. Mind: *animo*. Titan: *Titone* (but the sense is Sun and Apollo): cf. Titan in 1st Dialogue, and Apollo, *De Imm.*, 1, 2. ('The sun, true Apollo, as Bruno used to call it,' Kepler: Badaloni, 291.)

FIRST DIALOGUE

Gone out of fashion: *con disusato applauso*. Discourse together: *raggionaranno*. Element: *campo* (cf. first Latin poem). Thought: *sentimento*. Discourse: *raggionarò*. Meninges: membrane enveloping brain and spinal cord (*dura mater, arachnoid, pia mater*). Clarification: *splendor*. States of body: *affetti*. Develops: *succede*. Analogy: *conseguenza*. Contradictions and oppositions: *contrarietade e diversitadi*. Symbolic: *tipico*. Sciences: *scienze*. Opposing visions: *contrarii sogni*. Sting and impede: *opprimere* (note *urtiche* metaphor). Science: *scienza*. Enthusiastic: *affetto*. Nation: *generazione*. Fundamentals: *principii*. Coincide: *hanno coincidenza*. Related subjects: *prossimi suggetti*. Wits: *ingegni*. Human beings: *vomini*. Gentlemen: *signori* (civil persons). Sense of power: *autorità*. Traditions: *abiti*. Fineness: *gentlezza*. Leader: *principe*. Theories: *teoremi*. Sixpence: *carlino* (Neapolitan coin of low value). Fields: *professioni*. Ale: *cervosa* (*cervogia*, Latin *cervisia*). Faculties: *studii*. Deep learning: *dottrina*. Learned: *dotti*, contrasted with *dottori*. Breed: *semenza*. Knowledge: *scienza*. Most profound way: *esquisitissimo camino*. Rustic: *rustici* (boorish). Masquerade: again *prosopopeia*. System: *via*. Responsible, etc.: *causa che questa materia sia stata messa in campo*. Sensual: *fisico*. Sentence: *orazione*. Senses: *animo*. Soul: *anime*. Acrilogies, etc.: vices of grammar. Antithesis: *contrarietà*. Grasp, etc.: *per la notizie de le scienze ed enti*.

SECOND DIALOGUE

Vestiges: *vestigio*. So far as, etc.: *secondo la raggione della cause efficiente*. Method-makers, etc.: *meteodici e analitici*. Natural philosophy: *filosofo naturale*. System: *disciplina*. Cognition which apprehends: *cognitione apprensiva*. Which are the furthest bounds, etc.: *che sono l'ultimo termine del corso della nostra discorsiva facultade*. Master: *il principale*. Less ground: *con minor raggione*. Reformed philosophies: *riformate*: correctly developed; no reference to Reformed Churches: see 'systematise' below. Expression: *cosa*. Struggle towards: *si forzano alla*. Well-regulated minds: *regolati sentimenti*. Being out of themselves: *l'essere da per sé*. Expanse and bosom: *ambito e grembo*. Different points of view: *con diverse raggione*. Of before and after: *da priore e posteriore*. Value: *dignità*. Valuable: *più degna*. As far as natural things, etc.: *in proposito naturale*. Activity: *operazione*. Position-whence: *il termine onde*. Exact: *proprie*. Systematise: *parlano piaù riformatamente*. Motive power: *motrice*. Trustworthy: *sicuro*. Precise: *distinto*. Essential (faculty): *propria*. Efficacious: *potenziale*. In the right way:

come si conviene. Parallel production, etc.: *congrua produzione di specie razionali.* Agitator: *esagitator.* Artificer, builder: *fabro.* Harmony: *amicizia.* Breaking-up: *per la distanza de le parti.* Type: *raggione.* Shaping: *figurari.* Systems: *ordine.* Differentiator: *distintore.* Craftsman: *artefice.* Sap: *umori.* Original: *prima.* Unfolded faculties: *l'esplicate facultadi.* Forethought: *discorso.* Shape: *fengere.* Imitative effort: *imitazione.* Image: *effigie.* Creative intellect: *intelletto artefice.* Middle: *mezzo.* Artificer: *artifece.* Ideal basis: *raggione ideale.* Construction: *architettura.* Certain principles of form: *secondo certa raggion formale.* Actually: *gia.* Omnipresent: *universale.* Purpose: *fine.* Nature (of intrinsic part): *raggione.* Does not rank: *non ha raggione di.* Relation (to the body): *raggione verso.* According to its existence: *secondo la sua subsistenza.* 'Existence' in the next sentence is *essere.* Soul: *anima.* Value: *raggione.* Arrangement, etc.: *la distribuzione degli ordini de l'universo.* Reasoning: *discorso.* Harmonious: *condecente.* Reason and reflect: *discorse e ripenza.* Image: *imagine.* Creation: *opificio.* Complete organism: *l'animale intiero.* According to the substance, etc.: *secondo la sustanza e non secondo l'atto ed operazione conoscibile da peripatetici tutti, e quelli che la vita e anima definiscono secondo certe raggioni troppo grosse.* Living creatures: *animali.* Organisms: *animate.* Perceptible, etc.: *secondo l'atto sensibili d'animalità.* Primordial: *certo atto primo.* Irregular pieces: *pezzi disordinati.* Symbolic principle, etc.: *principio simbolico vitale e animale.* Mind: *mente.* Outlook: *senso.* Position: *sentenza.* Commerce: *commercio.* Degrees: *gradi.* Power (of material principles): *facultà.* Condition (of matter): *raggione.* Place and circumstance: *sedie e vicissitudine.* (No less) real: *subsistente.* Part of substance: *de la sustanza . . . quelcha cosa.* Absolutely constant: *constantissimi.* For its existence: *a fin che subsista.* Definitely: *sicuramente.* Defined in abstractly logical way: *compresa logicamente.* Sensitive: *sensitiva.* Possessing intelligence: *che intenda.* Common terms: *il modo commune.* Grades: *gradi.* Vulgar sense: *intenzione volgare.* Ground: *raggione.* Determination: *distinzione.* In the sense of: *secondo.* Ground: *raggione.* Capacity: *facilità.* Finds its delimitation: *viene a terminarsi.* Opinion: *senso.* Intelligence: *intelligenza.* Creator: *formatore.*

THIRD DIALOGUE

Discussion: *raggionar.* Smattering: *un tratto di scatto.* Fads and fancies: *grilli.* Occupation: *linea* (ref. to Pliny's adage). Science: *scienza.* Meanings: *sensi.* Knowledge: *cognizion, connizione.* Schools: *ludo.* Dexterity: *prattica.* Meaning: *senso.* Natural science: *le cose naturali.* Ideas: *sensi.* School: *setta.* Are profound thinkers: *profondano ne' sentimenti.* Knowledge: *cognizione.* Opinions: *sentimenti.* Learning: *Letteratura.* Performance: *atti.* Gentleman: *signor.* Science: *scienza.* Drawn into the systems: *avuto participazione con.* Presumptuous, etc.: *presunzion del vostro naturale.* On the same stage: *nel medesmo teatro* (note *scena,* above). Ideas: *sentimenti.* Honoured men and rare wits: *galantuomini e pelegrini ingegni.* Their feet, etc.: *il piè dentro* (*i.e.* have some competence). Character: *abito.* This view: *questo parere.* Power, potency: both *potenza.* Reasons correctly: *ben misura.* Totality of forms: *ogni forma.* Shaper: *figuratrice.* Shaped: *figurata.* Term: *nome.* Meanings: *significazioni.* Mechanist: *mecanico.* Work of dividing: *divisione.* Extension: *ambito.* Adapted sense: *appropriato modo.* Analogy: *similitudine* (several times later again). Material: *materia.* Images: *ritratti* (portraits). Endowed: *formato.* (No natural form) in itself: *in sua natura.* Perceptible: *sensibile.* Eyes of sense: *ochi sensitivi.* Develop, etc.: *formar questa raggione.* Reference: *riguardo.* Allowing for the due differences: *secondo la debita proporzione.* As a subject: *soggetivamente.* Idea: *pensiero.* In certain analogical

terms: *con certa analogia.* Disposition: *Abito.* Invented: *trovato.* To take
the place of: *per.* Substance of plurality: *la sustanza numerale.* Starting,
etc.: *per ordine.* That in which principle, etc.: *principiato.* Recognised, etc.:
conosciuta, nominata, considerata. Individuation: *individuazione.* Not one
that exists in nature, etc.: *ma non naturale, ma logica.* Concept: *intenzione.*
In reality: *per realmente.* Value: *riputazione.* In relation to matter: *circa la
materia.* Problem: *proposito.* Bare: *pura.* Nature (of matter): *raggion.* Void
and plenum: *vacuo e pieno.* Science: *scienza.* In oneself alone: *a se medesimo.*
Mere natural philosophy: *come puro naturale.* Get the hang of: *aver raggione.* Physicist: *fisico.* Chemist: *chimico.* Laws governing: *raggione.* Change:
vicissitudine. Regulated system of thought: *regolato sentimento.* Philosophic
grounding: *termine di filosofia.* Uncultured: *plebeii.* Fantasies: *imaginazioni.*
Mysteries: *arcani.* (Experimental) knowledge: *raggione.* Unfold (forms):
esplicare from *un implicato.* Source: *fonte.* State of possibility: *possibilità.*
Our specific nature: *la propria raggione.* (Explicit) sense: *raggione.* Aspect:
modo. Unity: *uno.* Aspires: *se pur guarda.* Enfolded: *complicato.* Unfolded:
esplicato. Image: *imagine.* Sole-begotten: *unigenita.* Contents: *continenza.*
Entire and single: *tutta e unica.* Differentiations . . . particulars: *differente,
individui.* Sharing: *occupazion.* Specific kind: *specie.* Globe: *convessitudine.*
Ability: *attitudine.* Apt: *atto.* Contrary and opposed: *contrario e opposito.*
Essence (of matter): *raggione.* Opinions: *sentenze.* Their opponents: *gli altri*
(Bruno writes as if he is coupling others with Plato). Definition: *signifi-
cazione.* Terms, ideas: *linguaggi, sentimenti.* Concept: *raggione.* Their own
particular application: *differenti poi nella propria.* Line of argument: *nostro
proposito.* In the permitted measure: *secondo tal proporzione quale è lecito.*
Particularising: *numerale.* Separable from: *absoluta da* (separated or independent from: thus used later). Limits: *termini.* From angle of, viewed as:
secondo la raggione de.

FOURTH DIALOGUE

Alone: I add the stage-direction. Topless: *altigrado.* Nature of this
thing: *questa natura.* Cause: *caggione.* On an equal footing: *nel medesimo
equilibrio.* Flat inflexibility: *rigore.* Flourish: *color.* (Divine) spirit: *ingegno.*
Equation: *proporzione.* Thoughts: *sentimento.* Liberal arts: *buone lettere.*
Concepts: *concetti.* Gerv. Then you don't, etc.: Given to Dicson in text.
Truffle: *tartufo* (= hypocrite). Cause: *caggione.* Harmony: *formazion.*
Essence: *essenza.* Suffering: *passione.* Insofar as it is possible for it: *al suo
possibile.* Identical potency: *potenza di medisemo geno.* System of dependencies: *una dependenza.* Proportional, etc.: *per mezzi proporzionali e copu-
lativi e partecipazioni.* While separating, etc.: *e, secondo la raggione propria,
neutri.* Union: *colligazione.* Line of reasoning: *raggione.* Verbal and logical:
vocale e nominale. (Common) essence: *raggione.* Every essence: *ogni essenzia.*
Appeal: *mendicar raggioni.* Our domain: *nostra messe.* Whatever may be the
direction, etc.: *quantunque discorrono.* Function: *luogo.* Aspects: *conditioni.*
Are united: *si uniscono.* Concept: *concetto.* No less: *non con minor raggione.* Essence: *raggione.* Specific: *propria.* Taken in that specific meaning:
per la raggione propria. As a result of: *per mezzi de.* Sense: *raggione.* Specific
aspects: *la raggion propria.* (Common) nature: *raggione.* Contrary: *ripugna.*
Particular (species): *certa.* Unity: *unità.* Indivisible (genus): *individua.*
(Formal) essence: *raggione.* Dimensional existence: *dimensionalità.* Essence:
raggione. Quite freed: *absoluta.* Nature (of the form): *raggioni.* Potentially:
in facultà. Sense: *senso.* Change: *Mutarsi,* then *cangiar,* then *certa vicissitudine.* In a temporal succession: *a tempi e tempi si fa cosa e cosa.* Enfolding,
unfolding: *complicamente, esplicamente* (Bruno inverts the last three pairs).

Deprived: *privata.* Has the power: *è potente.* Individual existences: *individui.* Purpose: *scopo.* Term: *termine.* Limits: *termini.* Idea: *raggione.* Determination: *termino.* Act of entity: *atto entitativo.* Insist on answer: *dimandareste raggione.* Explication, etc.: *esplicazione, implicazione.* Expressed: *espresso.* Unfolded: *esplicato.* Essence: *raggione.* Living beings: *anime viventi.* Unfold, etc.: *esplica lo che tiene implicato.* Lasting qualities: *durazione.* Essence of higher actuality: *raggione di meglior attualità.* Ideas: *idee.* Contrary: *nemechi.* Embody a principle: *principiate* (opposed to *principio*). Expressed form: *forma espressa.* A less degree: *minor raggione.* Superficies: *superficie.* Composition: *composto.* State of potency: *la quale* (referring back to in *potenza*). In relation to: *circa.* Rest: *stato.* Undifferentiated: *indistinta.* Surface: *dorso.* Individual (form): *numerale.*

FIFTH DIALOGUE

Contradictions: *contrarietadi.* Unity: *unità.* Harmony: *convenienza.* Determined, determinable: *terminato, terminabile.* Analogy: *similitudine.* Limit: *termino.* The immensity: *l'immenso.* Foot, etc.: *palmo, stadio, para-sanga.* Unity that is motionless: *uno immobile.* Multiple beings: *altro e altro essere.* Change, etc.: *seco né in sé mutazione alcuna.* Surface: *superficie.* Beyond all limits: *oltre e oltre.* Basis: *supposito* (support). In a totality: *totalmente.* In all modes, in the one mode: *omnimodamente, unimodamente.* Nature of a principle, etc.: *raggione di principio né di principiato.* Unity: *unità.* (Absolute) essence: *raggione.* Multiplicity: *multiformità.* Specific things: *cosa per cosa.* But that it appears: *ma* (*sia* understood). Many-moded, etc.: *moltimodo e moltiforma e moltifigurato.* Transformation: *mutazione.* Changes, etc.: *la alterazione.* Oneness: *uno.* Aspect: *volto.* Beloved Wisdom: *amica Sofia.* Lack of differentiation: *indifferenza.* Statements: *sentenze.* Area: *luogo.* Gap: *intervallo.* A single... whole: *uno* (moving here is transitive). Mass: *mole.* Relationships: *communitadi.* Conglomerated *agglomerati.* Separation-out: *sglomeramento.* Fulfilment: *compimento.* Level: *grado.* Universality: *università* (unitary universe). Being and existence: *ente ed essere.* And so on: *e di altri raggioni.* Conditions: *raggioni.* Relation, etc.: *relazione, azione, passione.* Involvedly one: *complicamente uno.* Unfoldedly: *esplicamente.* A unity: *uno.* Contradictory propositions: *contradittorie enunciazioni.* Science: *scienza.* Proceeding from unity to unity: *da l'unità procede all' unità.* Middle-positions: *mezzi* (more than intermediaries; the points-of-union). Intermediary: *mezzo.* Metaphor: *metafora.* Representations: *effigie.* Duality: *doi.* Detach itself: *disciorse.* Symbolic: *imaginabili.* Method: *modo.* And of the point: *e puntualità.* His doctrine: *suo modo.* Both sensible and intelligible nature: *l'una e l'altra natura.* Meaning: *raggione.* Independent: *absoluta.* By means of: *per mezzo.* Designation: *dizione.* Concepts: *raggioni.* Design: *intenzione.* In fact or analogy: *in verità e in similitudine.* Proposition: *intenzione.* Bringing together: *complicando.* Unfolding it: *esplicando.* (Indivisible) essence: *raggione.* Shared by: *di.* A mere term: *dizione.* Formula: *intenzione.* Is expressed: *si dice.* Independent: *assoluto.* Relative to it: *circa la sustanza.* (Accidents of) existence: *sussistenza.* Contraries, etc.: *gli contrarii concorre in uno.* Is reduced to unity: *si riduce all'unità.* Repeated in the finite series: *iterata con il finito.* They coincide: *concordano.* Concept: *raggione.* Undifferentiated: *indifferente.* Analogy: *analogia.* Limitation: *terminazione.* Limited: *terminato.* Analogous predicates: *predicati analogi.* Horizontal: *iacente* (BD). Principle... governs: *principio, principiato.* An identity: *uno medesimo.* Its opposite: *l'altro.* Limit: *termine.* Continuity: *continuazione.* Union of the two opposites: *concorso de l'uno e l'altro.* Agreement: *concordanza.* Condition of health: *ottima dispozione.* End-point: *ultimo.* He who wants to know, etc.: *chi vuol sapere massimi secreti di natura, riguardi e contemple gli minimi e massimi di gli contrarii e oppositi. Profonda magia è sapere trar il contrario dopo aver trovato il punto de l'unione.* Embracing: *complicante* (same verb in all the following sentences where "embracing" comes). Sound: *voce.* Thought: *contemplatione.* Most unified: *unissima.* Figures: in the third, B and D are inverted, to make Bruno's points clearer.

10. Brief list of Books on, or connected with, Bruno

For a full list up to recent times, see V. Salvestrini, *Bibliografia di G.B.*, 1958. The following gives only a short list of works showing the main trends in dealing with Bruno or his background. In England, since Frith and Boulting, there has only been the book by D. W. Singer and the various studies by F. A. Yates connected with Bruno in England.

Badaloni, N. (a) *La Filosofia di G.B.* (1955); (b) *Appunti Intorno alla Fama del Bruno nei sec. xvii e xviii in Società*, 1958, xiv, no. 3, 487–519; (c) *I Fratelli Della Porta e la cultura magica e astrologica a Napoli nel '500* in *Studi Storici*, 1959–60, a.I, n.4.
Caramella, S. *Raggion di Stato in G.B.* in *Atti del II Cong. Internaz. di Studi Umanistici*, 1952.
Carradori, C., *G.B.*, 1947.
Cassirer, E. (etc. ed.) *The Renaissance Philosophy of Man*, 1948.
Charbonnel, R. (a) *La Pensée Italienne au xvie s. et le courant libertin*, 1919, and (b) *L'éthique de G.B. et la deuxième dialogue du Spaccio*, 1919.
Cicuttini, L., *G.B.*, 1950.
Corsano, A., *Il pensiero di G.B. nel suo svolgimento storico*, 1940.
D'Amato, F., in *Giorn. Crit. d. Filos. Ital.*, 1950, xi.
Fenu, E., *G.B.*, 1938.
Firpo, L. (a) *Il processo di G.B.*, 1949, and (b) *Scritti scelti di G.B. e di T. Campanella*, 1949.
Fraccari, G., *G.B.*, 1951.
Gandillac, M. de (a) *La philosophie de N. de C.*, 1942; (b) amplified in the German *N.v.C.*, 1953.
Garin, E. (a) *Rescensione ad A. Mercati*, in *Ann. d. Scuola Norm. Sup. A.*, 1953, fasc. iv; (b) *l'Umanesimo Italiano*, 1952; (c) *Studi sul platonismo medievale*, 1958; *Rinascita* ii (1939) 641–71.
Gentile, G., *Il Pensiero Italiano del Rinascimento*, 1940.
Gilbert, N. W., *Renaissance Concepts of Method*, 1940.
Giusso, L., *Magia, Barocco e Metempsicosi in G.B.*, *Nuova Antologia*, Nov. 1948, fascicolo 1775.
Greenberg, S., *The Infinite in G.B.*, 1950.
Guzzo, A. (a) *G.B. nel quarto centenario della nascita*, 1948; (b) *Opere di G.B.* (selected, with Campanella), 1956; (c) *I Dialoghi del B.*, 1932.
Horowitz, I. L., *The Renaissance Philosophy of G.B.*, 1952.
Labriola, A. (a) *Lettere a Engels*, 1949, and (b) *Scritti varii*, 1906.
Licitra, O., edition of *De la Causa*, 1948.
Limentani, L. (a) in *Civiltà Moderna*, Lug.-Ott., 1937; (b) in *Sophia* (Palermo), 1933, 1, 3–4.

Mercati, A., *Il Sommario del Processo di G.B.*
Michel. P.-H., *G.B. Des Fureurs héroiques*, 1954.
Mondolfo, R., *La filosofia di G.B. e l'interpretazione di F. Tocco*, 1911.
Namer, E. (a) *Les Aspects de Dieu dans la Philosophie de G.B.*, 1926, and (b) *Cause, Principe et Unité*, 1930).
Olgiati, F., *L'anima dell' Umanesimo e del Rinascimento*, 1924.
Olschki, L., *G.B.*, 1927.
Robb, N. A., *Neoplatonism of the Italian Renaissance*, 1935.
Rossi, (a) *Niccolo di Cusa e la Direzione Monistica della Filosofia nel Rinascimento*. (b) on Lull in *Med. and Renaissance Studies* v.
Saitta, G. (a) *Il Pensiero Italiano nell' Umanesimo e nel Rinascimento*, 1951, iii; (b) *N.C. el l'umanisimo italiano*, 1957.
Santinello, G., *Il Pensiero de N. Cusano nella sua prospettiva estetica*, 1958.
Sarno, A. (a) 'Le genesi degli Eroici Furori,' in *Giorn. Crit. d. fil. ital.*, 1920, i; (b) *Lo Spaccio*, the same.
Singer, D.W., *G.B. His Life and Thought*, 1950.
Spaventa, B. (a) *Rinascimento, Riforma, Controriforma*, 1928; (b) *La filosofia italiana nelle sue relazione con la filosofia europea*, 1936; (c) *De Socrate a Hegel*, 1908.
Spini, G., *Ricerca dei libertini*, 1950.
Springarn, *Lit. Criticism of the Renaissance* (esp. pp. 163–7).
Toland, J., *A Collection of Several Pieces*, 1726.
Togliatti, P., *G.B. e noi*, 1950.
Troilo, E. (a) *La filosofia di G.B.*, 1907; (b) *G.B.*, 2nd ed., 1940; (c) *Prospetto, sintesi, e commentario della filosofia di G.B.*, 1951.
Yates, F.A. (a) *J. of Warburg and Cortauld Inst.*, 1939, ii, 227–42; (b) the same, April–July 1939–40, iii, 181–207; (c) *French Academies of 16c*, 1947; (d) *A Study of Love's Labour's Lost*; (e) *John Florio*, 1934; (f) *J. of Warburg Inst.*, 1937–8, i, 103–16.